ELEMENTS OF SELF-DESTRUCTION

ELEMENTS OF
SELF-DESTRUCTION

Brent Potter

The style used throughout this book is in accordance
with the *Publication Manual of the American Psychological
Association* (Fifth Edition, 2001) and *Pacifica Graduate Institute's
Handbook* (2004–2005)

First published in 2013 by
Karnac Books Ltd
118 Finchley Road
London NW3 5HT

British Library Cataloguing in Publication Data

A C.I.P. for this book is available from the British Library

ISBN-13: 978-1-78049-059-5

Typeset by V Publishing Solutions Pvt Ltd., Chennai, India

www.karnacbooks.com

Aunque sepa los caminos
yo nunca llegaré a Córdoba

—Frederico Garcia Lorca

CONTENTS

ACKNOWLEDGEMENTS   ix

FOREWORD   xi

ABSTRACT   xv

CHAPTER ONE
Introduction to the phenomenon of self-destructiveness   1

CHAPTER TWO
Pursuing that which withdraws from us   29

CHAPTER THREE
The emerging consciousness of self-destructiveness
     in history and psychology   41

CHAPTER FOUR
Bion: the ghosts of abandoned meaning and formless
     destructiveness   83

CHAPTER FIVE
Heidegger: the eclipse of the sacred and the darkening
    of the world   101

CHAPTER SIX
Contemporary manifestations of self-destructiveness   117

CHAPTER SEVEN
Conclusion and discussion   139

CHAPTER EIGHT
Limitations and suggestions for future research   165

REFERENCES   169

INDEX   179

ACKNOWLEDGEMENTS

This book is a re-visioning of my dissertation and I want to thank the members of my dissertation committee: Michael Eigen, Robert Romanyshyn, and Lisa Sloan. I am grateful for Michael's genius insight into psychoanalysis, concretely situated in human experience, spanning the breadth and depths of the psyche, from formless destructiveness to the spiritual. I value his continued support, advice, and conversation. I am grateful to Robert, for the passion he brings and his pioneering work linking analytic psychology, archetypal psychology, and phenomenology. I am indebted to him for his generosity of time for the dissertation and ongoing support. I am grateful to Lisa for her angelic timing and practical steering of the project. Their work and my continued dialogue with these distinguished people are blessings.

The word 'gratitude' hardly expresses my indebtedness to Ronald Shaffer, who introduced me to the field of phenomenology and then promptly gave me guidance and free reign over exploring the field for two years as an undergraduate. I am also indebted to Michael Sipiora for his brilliant instruction and anchoring of my thought in Heideggerian phenomenology.

In addition to these remarkable people, I also want to express my heartfelt gratitude, respect, and admiration towards the teachers, friends, and colleagues who were kind enough to offer their opinions on the manuscript and/or the topics contained therein. These people include, but are not limited to, James Hillman, Robert Stolorow, Allen Bishop, James Grotstein, Avedis Panajian, Kathy Rives, Daniel Burston, Dennis Slattery, Theodor Itten, Andrew Feldmar, Corwin Fergus, and Russell Lockhart. I would like to thank Constance Kellogg for her loving-kindness and moral support as I completed the project. The metamorphosis from dissertation to book has taken time and I apologize if I have neglected mentioning anyone who was helpful. I am humbled and honoured that such remarkable men and women would give me their time and consideration.

FOREWORD

This book began as my doctoral dissertation at the Pacifica Graduate Institute. The stated purpose of this phenomenological psychoanalytic study was to make the phenomenon of self-destruction and its vicissitudes intelligible. The unstated purpose of the study was to present self-destruction itself, as it shows itself from itself. Phenomenological psychoanalysis, as I practice it in research and clinical work, is the art and science of engaging myself with the other in such a fashion as to see the world through the other's perspective. There is a hermeneutic intimacy inherent in this relationship that differentiates itself from the cold, objective, linear perspective vision of natural scientific inquiry with its guiding agenda of explanation, prediction, and control.

This is not a self-help book. In its pages I do not offer quick and practical ways to end bad habits. There will never be a workbook to accompany this text. This is a book for those interested in understanding the phenomenon of self-destruction, which is one fundamental feature of all psychopathology, individual and collective. It is a phenomenon that psychology, philosophy, and religion have contended with since their inceptions. In giving thought to the phenomenon of self-destruction, I give thought to something essential. Remember, phenomenological psychoanalysis asks us to become intimate with the 'object' of our interest. Phenomenologists are not afforded the 'objective' distance and neutrality that defines the natural scientific, calculative disclosure of the world. So engaging this phenomenon, writing about this phenomenon and reading about this phenomenon *phenomenologically* is to become close to that which, by definition, is pathological.

This book is for those who are resolute and unwavering in their desire to understand and give thought to the elements of themselves and others that oppose life. The benefits of such an endeavour, I believe, outweigh the risks. Let us bravely stand nose-to-nose with the phenomenon and look it straight in the eye. I suspect that the phenomenon may not be as terrifying as suspected when granted the opportunity to be sincerely heard and understood. We can comport ourselves with an evenly hovering attention, being steady yet engaged, to paraphrase Freud. Doing so does not endorse, promote, nor invite more self-destructiveness. Rather, we are able to further our own understanding and thus enable ourselves to maneuver into relationship. It is testimony to the fact that we are not in relationship with it that self-destructiveness (and its projection, outward destructiveness) runs unabated, with growing ferocity and autonomy.

As I sit and write this, the news is abuzz with the three so-called "cannibal killings", where people ingested the highly toxic street drug "bath salts" and acted out their own destructiveness in the most primitive fashion. There is the recent attack in Florida where a naked man stripped a homeless man and proceeded to rip 80% of his face off with his teeth. He reportedly snarled at a police officer, mouth dripping with flesh, who ordered him to stop before shooting him to death. This coincides with another killing where a Morgan State University student killed a man and ate his brains and another where a woman killed her baby and ate parts of the child's head. Astonishing.

Knowledge of the essence of self-destruction is what allows us to differentiate ourselves from it yet keep it in safe sight. It is not a matter of seeking to subdue it, even if that were possible. It is not a matter of explanation, prediction, and control but propriety. It is a matter of finding the most fitting way or ways in which to live with our own destructiveness, both individually and collectively. By establishing the most fitting relationship with destructiveness, we are more able to align with the kind of destruction inherent in acts of creativity. The alternative is (unconscious) destruction for the sake of destruction, which

FOREWORD

acts of its own accord, out of relationship, continuing its course after existence, time, and space are obliterated, often gruesomely. If we are brave and have faith and humility in the process, we may survive and even grow from our own self-destructiveness individually and collectively. Our disease will set us free.

Elements of self-destruction

By Brent Potter

Why are humans, who are motivated by self-preservation, motivated to engage in behaviours that threaten and even extinguish their existence? The present work has given thought to this question and examined the phenomenon of self-destruction through the perspectives of empirical psychology, psychoanalysis, analytical psychology as well as existential-phenomenological psychology.

A thematic hermeneutic method was employed to explore the phenomenon of self-destruction, as the subject matter asks for a method in which reflection and dialectic can increase awareness and understanding. Regarding the hermeneutic aspect of this study, I first presented the predominant themes of the study. Each theme was a chapter revolving around the central theme of self-destructiveness. These themes included (1) the emerging understanding of self-destructiveness in culture, religion, philosophy and psychology, (2) Bion's investigation into the self-destructive capacity of the mind, (3) Heidegger's ontology of Being and the Enframing of technology, (4) identifying and delineating the 'who' who most experiences the impact of human-to-human destructiveness in our contemporary culture. The phenomenon of 'disposable' children was delineated as well as other ways children suffer from contemporary self-destructiveness, such as child trafficking. A case vignette presented a case of one such 'disposable' child to offer a more salient understanding of what such children often have to endure to survive.

This book then presented the nature of the relationship between the essence of technology and the essence of self-destructiveness. The book outlined the ways Heidegger and Bion may benefit from each other's perspectives on this score. It also delineated the shadow of Being and the seduction of self-destructiveness. The study presented three examples of this: pornography, manifest destiny and the holocaust. The notation "X" was suggested as another way to give thought to the phenomenon of self-destruction and as an organizing sign for the many elements explored in the study. This book concluded by discussing the necessity of having a relationship to the phenomenon of self-destructiveness without it holding sway.

CHAPTER ONE

Introduction to the phenomenon of self-destructiveness

Introduction

That a species seeks to further its own existence is common sense. What is more complex is gaining a salient understanding of why humans, who are also motivated by self-preservation, engage in behaviours that threaten and extinguish their survival. Theorists and mental health professionals from numerous and often conflicting perspectives have given thought to this paradox, from the inception of psychology and into the present. While this has produced countless theories, Walters (1999) notes that little has been written providing an integrated and cohesive narrative of this antilogy.

Self-destruction refers to the act or process of destroying oneself physically or psychologically. Not surprisingly, *self* in its most ancient form means *left to oneself* and it refers both to the sense of *I* that I am as well as to the overall personality. *Destruction* in its essential meaning means a pulling down, to pull down, to destroy (*Webster's*, 1956) and metaphors associated with self-destruction are of depth, going down, or, more accurately, being *taken down*. In today's contemporary technological culture people are being taken down in a variety of ways such as smoking, injecting, drinking, and snorting toxic substances. While

1

some turn to substances others cut, burn, hit, and even amputate parts of themselves. Like substance abuse and self-mutilation, suicide has reached epidemic proportions in the United States and abroad. On a larger scale people are beginning to see the self-destructiveness of taxing the earth's resources and polluting the planet. Along with this is the increasing technology available for military purposes. Laing said:

> We have achieved, in the last two or three generations the capacity to kill ourselves. We are the only species that can do that ... This is a *crisis* for the human species. We have biological weapons, nuclear weapons, and chemical weapons that can wipe us out—and other life forms—at the snap of a finger ... Now we have the *capacity* to do that, and the capacity is sweet. Oppenheimer, when asked why he went for the hydrogen bomb, said, "Well, it was so *sweet*, the capacity to do it was so sweet it was *irresistible*." Can we resist species suicide? (Laing, 1988)

This text is an attempt to give thought to the phenomenon of self-destructiveness. It attempts to provide an integrative, cohesive account of self-destruction as it appears in early history and in depth psychology. It also focuses specifically on its treatment in psychoanalysis (Bion) and phenomenology (Heidegger) as well as its contemporary manifestations.

Review of the literature

The phenomenon of self-destructiveness is examined from the perspectives of descriptive statistics, psychoanalysis, Jungian psychology, and existential-phenomenological psychology. In addition the literature review includes current theories about the psyche's capacity for self-destruction. When discussing depth psychological perspectives I do not mean to be polemical. It is often the case that a thinker's views of things change, sometimes radically, over the course of his or her career. It is for the purposes of clarity and organization that I have chosen specific themes and contributions of specific professionals in depth psychology.

Empirical psychology. It has been suggested that two million Americans suffer from the psychological disorder of self-mutilation (Levenkron, 1999). Major self-mutilation involves eye enucleation and limb or genital amputation. Such behaviours tend to be associated with psychosis or marked gender identity disturbances (Favazza, 1989a; Pies & Popli, 1995). Skin cutting is the most common form of self-mutilation. Moreover, seventy-five per cent of people who engage in self-mutilation utilize other techniques in addition to self-cutting (Favazza, 1989b; Favazza & Conterio, 1988b; Herpertz, 1995; Suyemoto, 1998). Researchers Favazza and Rosenthal (1993) have specifically studied the alternate behaviours of self-hitting and self-burning. Despite theoretical orientations, researchers tend to agree that a significant number of individuals who self-mutilate were sexually abused as children (e.g. Alao, Yolles & Huslander, 1999; Crowe & Bunclark, 2000; Romans, Martin, Anderson & Herbinson, 1995; Turell & Armsworth, 2000). For the most part, self-injurious behaviour is understood as a way to manage painful affect or to relieve painful feelings. This may lead to an addictive, self-destructive cycle as self-injurers become increasingly distressed about their lack of control over the very behaviour that serves to manage powerful affects (Favazza & Conterio, 1988a). Self-injurious behaviour does not necessarily represent suicide attempts, although these behaviours may result in more harm than intended, leading to medical complications or death.

Nearly 30,000 people commit suicide every year in the United States and it is the eleventh leading cause of death. Homicide is the fourteenth leading cause of death, which means that more people kill themselves than other people. The rate of suicide in the American population is 10.7 per every million and a person every eighteen minutes dies by suicide. An estimated 5 million Americans have attempted suicide. Males complete suicide 4.1 times more often than females and females attempt suicide 3.0 times more often than males. Most people with suicidal ideation communicate their intent to kill themselves before following through with the act. Each suicide emotionally impacts at least six other people and since 1970, the number of suicide survivors in the United States is estimated at 4.4 million and grows by 175,000 each year. Suicide among adolescents has tripled since the 1950s and today it is the third leading cause of death among teens, behind accidents and homicide. While it is not generally believed that suicidal behaviours are inherited, the risk may be higher for family members who have lost a close relative or loved one to suicide. Throughout all age groups, white males have the highest incidents of suicide and minority females have the lowest rate. It is interesting to note that the average number of suicides per day increases during the summer, not during the December holidays (Hoyert, Arias, Smith, Murphy & Kochanek, 2001). The Institute of Medicine (2002) cites an incidence of ninety-four suicide cases (health care services, autopsies, funerals, and police investigations) costing $535,158. For the year of 1998 the value of lost productivity alone is calculated to be $11.8 billion. At the rate of 30,000 suicides per year, the cumulative cost per year is estimated at $25 billion.

According to a report by the Substance Abuse and Mental Health Services Administration (2001), the social cost of substance abuse in 1995 was $276 billion. Alcohol abuse expenditures were $6.4 billion and drug abuse expenditures were $5.5 for the year of 1995. For both alcohol and drug abuse, spending on treatment is roughly only five percent of the total costs to society for these disorders. Men tend to have a higher rate of current illicit drug use than women (7.7% vs. 5.0%). Approximately 2.1 million youths age twelve to seventeen used inhalants at some time in their lives as of the year 2000 and 3.9 per cent used glue, shoe polish, or Toluene, and 3.3 used gasoline or lighter fluid during the same year. Among youths who were considered 'heavy drinkers' in the year 2000, 65.5 per cent were also currently using illicit drugs. Of the 11.8 million adult illicit drug users in the year 2000, 9.1 million (77%) were employed full or part time. An estimated seven million people reported driving under the influence of drugs and/or alcohol at some time in the past year. In the aforementioned study, almost half of Americans aged twelve and older reported current use of alcohol, which translates to roughly 104 million people. There were an estimated 6.6 million binge drinkers and 2.1 million heavy drinkers among the population of ages twelve to twenty in the year 2000. An estimated 65.5 million Americans aged twelve and older reported use of tobacco in 2000.

According to the Schneider Institute for Health Policy (2001), it is difficult to estimate the total cost of substance abuse due to hidden costs such as costs of medical care for related illnesses (e.g. cirrhosis, cancer, heart disease, traffic accidents), productivity losses caused by premature death, and impaired ability to perform typical activities at the workplace. Other hidden costs include crime and destruction of property. The total cost to America for alcohol abuse is estimated to have been $99 billion in 1990. Productivity losses as well as premature deaths constitute 34 per cent of total costs and productivity losses related to illness resulting in inability to work accounted for thirty-seven per cent of this total. Eleven per cent represents direct costs to the health care system with another two per cent related to the custodial care of those with foetal alcohol syndrome. The cost of drug abuse was $67 billion in 1990 and over two-thirds of the total costs of drug abuse are accounted for by other costs, mostly related to losses from crime and incarceration. The costs associated with AIDS represent almost ten per cent of the total and this is anticipated to increase, as drug abuse exacerbates the AIDS epidemic. Deaths and illness account for seventeen per cent and medical costs less than five per cent. The costs for tobacco smoking were $72 billion for the year 1990 and premature deaths represented the largest component (63%). Direct medical costs to the health care system constituted twenty-eight per cent for the same year.

In review, while researchers struggle with precise ways to measure the impact of substance abuse on society, they agree that the impact is substantial and grows unabated, with increasing levels of hidden costs for the criminal justice system, healthcare system, families, and the workplace. For the most part, the major impact of alcohol abuse relates to productivity losses associated with illness, death, and crime, which plays the major role in drug-related costs. Premature deaths constitute the most significant losses for nicotine abuse. Researchers also agree that all substance abuse problems and their vicissitudes are preventable.

Psychoanalytic perspectives. The body of psychoanalytic literature is replete with research examining the phenomenon of self-destructiveness. Much of this is owed to Freud's seminal notion of the repetition compulsion, also called fate neurosis. The repetition compulsion is the compulsion of individuals to repeat self-destructive situations throughout the course of their lives, without realizing their participation in creating such situations. Freud (1920) was so struck by the power of the repetition compulsion that he published *Beyond the Pleasure Principle* to emphasize that it is the most biologically primitive dynamic of the psyche. The repetition compulsion is linked to the death instinct, the anti-life inertia of an organism to return to the inorganic state of death. Freud asserted that the repetition compulsion is more fundamental than masochism, as it is uninfluenced by the pleasure-unpleasure principle.

Freud understood masochism as the active pursuit of physical or mental suffering to achieve erotic gratification. In 1924 Freud differentiated between three kinds of masochism: erotogenic, feminine, and moral. Erotogenic masochism is simply sexual gratification gained through physical or psychological pain, such as beatings and humiliation. Feminine masochism, or more specifically the feminine form, is not limited to women. Freud noted that both men and women could suffer from feminine masochism. He named it feminine because the fantasies typically associated with this masochism are that of being castrated, childbirth, or being penetrated. The third kind of masochism is perhaps the most destructive, since it involves the unconscious need for punishment, which in turn leads to various neuroses and overt self-inflicted suffering such as job loss, accidents, and failed relationships. Unlike the other two forms of masochism, the moral variety is disconnected from both the sexual impulse as well as an object. Instead, the sadistic superego takes the place of the sadistic object and becomes like a father beating a child. Thus, Freud deduced, the unconscious fantasy is that of being passive before the father and having the secret wish to have a feminine sexual relationship with him. Freud noted that moral masochism explains much of analysand's resistance to giving up neurotic patterns and explains negative therapeutic reactions, including suicide.

Freud explained the psychogenesis of masochism in terms of disturbed Oedipal development, which leaves an individual with latent homoeroticism and the tendency to sexualize, unconsciously and regressively, feelings of guilt. Sexualization, or instinctualization as it was sometimes called, represented an unconscious attempt to convert terror, pain, or any overwhelming affect into excitement. Thus a child's fears of death, abandonment, abuse or other catastrophe could be turned into a life-affirming sensation (McWilliams, 1994). Stated differently, moral masochism was a compromise formation allowing for the undoing of early developmental fears of abandonment, castration, and parental rejection. Freud further theorized that even with healthy Oedipal development, a primary masochism remains in the psyche, remnants of fused life and death instincts after a portion of one's self-destructiveness were projected outward, which was sadism (Fine & Moore, 1990). Therefore destructiveness was essentially self-destruction since it was the destructive impulse being projected outwards.

Klein adopted Freud's notion of a punitive, attacking superego and took this topic further than Freud intended. Not only did Klein emphasize the drives, she placed primary importance upon the death drive, which tended to be experienced as a fear of annihilation. It manifested as persecutory fear and the fear of impending death. The death instinct, for Klein, reflected innate ambivalence and the destructive aspect of the ambivalence was interpreted as a defensive projection outwards of the innate instinct to self-destruction (Rycroft, 1995).

Klein introduced the clinically invaluable notion of projective identification. Projective identification is the process whereby parts of the personality and internal objects are split and then projected into an external object. This object becomes identified with the split-off aspect as well as possessed and manipulated by it. Projective identification serves several purposes, which enable survival of the individual's mind, but tend to contribute to further fragmentation. Excessive projective identification promotes neurotic and even psychotic states of mind. Specifically, projective identification allows one to (1) manage powerful affects, (2) identify with the external object to preclude separation, (3) to manipulate the destructive, persecutory bad objects (Fine & Moore, 1990).

Klein conceives of libido as working against the internal destructive drive haunting the psyche. In Kleinian psychology:

> Love circulates in the psyche in the form of good feelings/good objects, which try to offset bad feelings/bad objects. The psyche develops a kind of fantasy pump, attempting to use fantasies of good objects ... to counteract bad ones ... Bad affects/objects are expelled; good objects/affects are taken in. But things are never so simple, and the reverse happens (e.g. bad in—good out). (Eigen, 1996)

Klein demonstrated how ways of managing powerful affects may, in themselves, be pathogenic agents. An excess of splitting and projecting bad objects can fragment the personality and, conversely, introjecting good objects and feelings can numb spontaneous affective life. Klein saw the destructive, self-deadening moments of psychological development as by-products, outcomes of the mind's struggles with annihilative anxieties.

Bion adopted many classical psychoanalytic tenets and also incorporated Klein's clinical findings about psychosis, especially splitting and projective identification. Following Freud's belief that psychotics hate reality, Bion found that such hatred may result in innate aggression being turned inwards, thus destroying perceptual functions and rendering one increasingly incapable of contending with reality. In considering psychotic processes, Klein accented and expanded Freud's notion of a tyrannical superego. Bion took this idea further by suggesting that the ego is not the only aspect of the mind under attack in psychotic processes. Rather, Bion asserted that the sadistic superego attacks all linking processes between thoughts, emotions, and external reality (Fine & Moore, 1990). He utilized the concept of the "psychotic part of the personality" to discuss "the destructive attacks which the patient makes on anything which is felt to have the function of linking one object with another" (Bion, 1959, p. 308). Fueling the destructive aspect of the mind is hatred of emotional reality and the need to avoid awareness of it at all costs, including one's own sanity.

Bion (1959) traced the beginnings of psychopathology back to the infant-mother dyad. The infant was born in complete helplessness, dependent upon the breast. Inherent in this situation was the infant's innate aggressiveness, mortality salience, and envy. Given these innate factors, the infant naturally attacked all that links it to the breast. These attacks were tempered, not extinguished, by the mother's ability to be receptive to the infant's mind; to accept, digest, and re-introject projections in a more palatable form. However, if the mother was unreceptive, the infant would become overwhelmed with its envious hatred of the mother's ability to be calm and its dependence upon her. Over time, this envy and hate became a self-destructive "greed devouring the … psyche" and "similarly, peace of mind becomes hostile indifference" (ibid., p. 312). Bion posited that the breast and penis are linking symbols and central objects of the infant's internal world; hence attacks upon them were attacks upon what they symbolize, that is, (1) connections to external objects and (2) cohesion and integration among internal objects. The resultant "ego-destructive superego" destroyed the mind's capacity for thought, arrested development, and facilitated an experience of the internal world as both chaotic, dead, and deadening (p. 313). The self-destructing psychotic mind became steeped in its own unmanageable hatred and envy, internal and external experience stripped of all meaning. Reality was experienced as a mocking reminder of one's limitations and inability to relate to others and one's own emotional life.

Jungian perspectives

Jung understood the self-destructing capacity of the mind primarily in terms of trauma. Following Jung, Kalshed writes:

> The psyche's normal reaction to a traumatic experience is to withdraw from the scene of injury. If withdrawal is not possible, then a part of the self must be withdrawn, and for this to happen the otherwise integrated ego must split into fragments and *dissociate* … This means that the normally unified elements of consciousness … are not allowed to integrate. Experience itself becomes discontinuous. Mental imagery may be split from affect, or both affect and image may be dissociated from conscious knowledge. (Kalshed, 1996, p. 13)

Kalshed goes on to point out that such dissociation requires large amounts of aggression and violence. The self-attacking dissociative process becomes personified in dreams as tyrannical figures that violently behead, shoot, or in some way mutilate other more innocent dream figures. The continued fragmentation serves to disburse emerging traumatic pain. Jung noted that fantasies in themselves might be as traumatic as literal traumatic events. Concerning the destructive inner figure, Kalshed notes, "In effect, the diabolical inner figure traumatizes the inner world in order to prevent re-traumatization in the outer one" (ibid., p. 14). This diabolical figure operates in the internal world as a kind of 'supervisor', ensuring dissociative episodes and doing anything necessary to attack emerging consciousness of the trauma.

Jungian analyst and one of the leading thinkers of archetypal psychology, Hillman summarily dismisses developmental theory: "Working through the parental fallacy is more like a religious conversion—out of our secularism, out of our personalism, out of monotheism, developmentalism, and belief in causality" (Hillman, 1996, p. 91). Hillman offers the acorn theory as an alternative to explaining human life in terms of genetic determinism or as a sheer accident. The idea for the acorn theory came from Plato's Myth of Er in the *Republic*. Hillman (1996) asserts that every soul is granted a unique daimon before birth, and this daimon has chosen a pattern that individuals must live while on earth. The daimon leads the soul into the world but the daimon is forgotten at birth. Despite being forgotten, the daimon remembers the destiny of the soul and guides the person through life, "therefore the daimon is the carrier of your destiny" (ibid., p. 8). Going further, Hillman states that prior to birth, people chose the body, parents, place, and circumstances most suited to the soul. We are summoned into the world with a calling. From this Hillman concludes three things: (1) The daimonic call is a fundamental fact of human existence; (2) People should strive to align life with the call and (3) come to understand that accidents, illnesses, and all maladies are in the service of fulfilling the call.

The daimonic call becomes demonic when one becomes possessed, mistaking the timeless, immortal qualities of the daimon as one's own. Examining the biographies of multiple serial killers, Hillman demonstrates how the daimonic call becomes the demonic call. In each instance he shows that from an early age there are certain characteristics:

> the cold eyes and icy heart; the humourlessness; the certitude, arrogance, inflexibility, purity; the fanatical projection of shadow; the being out of step with time; the mystical sense of luck; rage at being blocked, crossed, or dissed; the paranoid demand for trust and loyalty; the attraction to myths and symbols of "evil" (world, fire apocalypse); raptures, seizures, and moments of estrangement and/or call to transcendence; the fear of powerlessness as ordinariness, ignorance, impotence. (Hillman, 1996, p. 239)

Hillman stresses that all that is destructive to others and ultimately destructive to the self, arises from an unwillingness to recognize human limitations. Feeling as though one must literally live up to all the daimon's expectations, one becomes absorbed in the daimon's "boundless vision and manic impulsion" (ibid., p. 241).

Along with developmental theory, Hillman (1998) summarily dismisses the notion of there being a death drive. In considering suicide, Hillman sees the suicidal impulse in relationship to the daimon. Does the daimon want to depart, to go elsewhere, or is the person the most urgent cause? Only the daimon knows. Hillman suggests people do not need to commit suicide to rid themselves of the idea. He suggests that we can see the idea through to our end or its end. Moreover, Hillman sees the question of suicide as a portal to deeper societal, religious, and existential questions that may enrich the soul.

Hillman (1996) sees the person obsessed with suicidal fantasies as being stuck in the literal, unable to experience psychological death. Conversely, when one is able to deliteralize such fantasies, psychic reality may take on a numinous and non-destructive quality. Hillman does not only accuse the suicidal patient of being stuck in literalism, but also the medically minded psychology that treats such patients. Steeped in the medical perspective psychologists understand suicide as pathology that is in need of a cure, rather than as a reality to be lived and explored. Seeing through suicidal fantasies, the therapist welcomes the soul and presents its desires in psychological form. Not only is the therapist hospitable to soul, but also he or she does not ignore or reduce any of its intentions. This therapeutic discourse is more shamanic than medical, more concerned with experience than silencing symptoms. The therapist welcomes the arrival of the suicidal urge as a sign of transformation and helps the patient see through such experience. By focusing on experience and by confirming psychic death, the patient may be freed from organic fixation.

Kunnap (2000) understands self-destructive behaviour as a function of an *internal critic*. Surveying the inner critic theme historically, through psychoanalysis, analytical psychology, and contemporary perspectives, Kunnap asserts that it is less of an inner tyrant, than an imaginary landscape. She writes, "the inner critic is not a psychical bogeyman but a vast panorama filled with inhabitants, each with its own agenda. A single entity could not account for the broad spectrum of feelings one experiences when caught up in this critical landscape" (Kunnap, 2000, p. 51). Especially concerning contemporary self-help literature on the inner critic, Kunnap notes that most approaches to contend with it are based upon attacking and eliminating it. Like Hillman's approach to suicide, Kunnap sees the critical landscape as a potentially rich area of exploration and self-discovery:

> The essence of this work is respect and honouring of each individual's experience. There are countless ways that people can encounter the aspects of their own unique inner critical landscape. Image, duration of interaction, and physical characteristics of the terrain all have significance for the unique individual. (ibid., p. 52)

Based upon her clinical experience, Kunnap suggests that manifestations of the critical landscape tend to be self-destructive, such as feelings of worthlessness, deadened creativity, and lack of connection to aspects of the personality. Associated with these underlying beliefs tend to be maladaptive cognitive distortions and addiction. Despite these things, Kunnap maintains that the critical landscape is paradoxically the place where self-honouring can be reclaimed.

Self-destruction in existential-phenomenological psychology

Existential-phenomenological therapists tend to focus on the individual's experience and ways of being-in-the-world. Interestingly, some existential-phenomenological therapists do not necessarily view self-destructive behaviours as being immoral or wrong. Binswanger a father of existential-phenomenological psychology, states:

> Existential aging had hurried ahead of biological aging, just as existential death, the "being-corpse among people," had hurried ahead of the biological end of life. The suicide is the necessary-voluntary consequence of this existential state of things. And just as we can only speak of the gladness of old age as the "most intimate and sweetest anticipatory relish of death" when the existence is ripened towards its death, so too in the face of self-induced death only gladness and a festive mood can reign when death falls like a ripe fruit into the lap of the existence. (Binswanger, 1958, p. 295)

In a similar vein, May (1961) asserts that humans can experience existential as well as physical death. In our contemporary society with its glorification of production and consumption, people constantly experience the threat of non-being or complete conformity. These threats produce ontological anxiety, the fear of losing one's existential meaningfulness and uniqueness. In this situation, it is easy to see how people could consider self-destructive behaviours (e.g. addiction, cutting) and even suicide as ways of managing ontological anxiety. Self-destructiveness may be seen by some as the final means to feel valued and potent. According to Meerloo (1962), many people are capable of feeling alive only when they are suffering from anxiety and pain. For these people, life is experienced as a constant struggle with death and so they want to become close to it and feel it, so they can come to know their last friend; fate.

Farber notes that suicide is more than a means to resolve conflict, but is one's assertion of power: "It is as if the victim cries: 'At least I am competent to do this'" (Farber, 1968, p. 42). Where other self-destructive behaviors tend to reflect hopelessness with the difficulties of life, suicide represents an act of choice, in which life is not a viable option. Existentially, this is the ultimate choice one can make about one's being. "The right to live one's own life is part of the right to die one's own death" (Meerloo, 1968, p. 83). For Frankl (1955) and Binswanger (1958) people are free to choose the nature of their being, and this decision extends even to the possibility of choosing non-being. As decision-making beings we may choose possibilities towards life or death and, according to Rank (1936), May (1961), Hillman (1998), and Menninger (1969), those who kill themselves tend to have developed an unwavering will.

The human meaning-making capacity and ability to choose are central areas of interest to existential-phenomenological therapists. Frankl (1955) stresses that *logos*, one's life meaning, is of paramount importance and his research reveals that there is a positive correspondence between one's meaning orientation and psychological health. Further, the meaning orientation may promote and serve to save one's life. Frankl's logotherapy is based on the idea that humans have freedom to will, will meaningfulness, and will meaning to life. Similarly, Hutschnecker (1951) conceives of the will to live as being psychologically and physiologically rooted. He hypothesized that the presence of a will to live bespeaks a sense of purpose in one's life. One who continually strives to find meaning in life will reinforce the will to live, which will further fulfill one's sense of purpose. Frankl (1959), a World War II concentration camp survivor, concludes that the will to live and the meaning-making capacities of the psyche are of the greatest significance. He noticed that a prisoner's ability to make sense of his or her experience corresponded to an ability to continue living. An inability to hold onto one's moral centre and inner strength leaves one vulnerable to destructive elements in the environment.

In a similar vein, Shay discusses the vicissitudes of the ongoing self-trauma system as well as the specific destructive environmental elements in war. In *Achilles in Vietnam: Combat Trauma and the Undoing of Character* (1995) Shay presents common themes that have emerged from his psychotherapeutic work with Vietnam veterans suffering from post-traumatic stress disorder (PTSD). These environmental elements are: (1) the betrayal of *themis*, a normative sense of what's right, (2) the shrinkage of social and moral horizons—the destruction of ideals, ambitions, and affiliations, (3) not having the opportunity to grieve the death of companions, which may lead to (4) beserking—a loss of all restraint, a lack of trust in others, and a sense of being impervious. Shay notes the similarities between these conditions and the battle conditions in Homer's *Iliad*. He also notes some things specific to the soldiers of the Vietnam War: deprivation, friendly fire, fragging, civilian suffering, and the inability to see the enemy as a worthy opponent. One has to listen to the narratives of the veterans themselves to get a sense of the destructiveness evoked to survive under such unimaginable conditions:

> Once I came on a guy raping a hooker. She was screaming and screaming, and it was easy to tell he was hurting her bad. I yelled at him, and he turned around and started reaching behind his back. He was carrying. I ran on him so fast and had his elbow before he could pull his piece [gun], and I pounded the shit out of him. That felt so-o go-o-d. (p. xvi)

> Well, at first, I mean when I just come there, I couldn't believe what I was seeing. I couldn't believe Americans could do things like that to another human being ... but then I *became* that. We went through villages and killed everything, I mean *everything*, and that was all right with me. (p. 31)

> And it wasn't that I couldn't be killed. I didn't *care* if I was killed ... I just didn't care if I lived or died. I just wanted blood. (p. 52)

> I pulled the trigger on my M-16 and nothing happened. He fired and I felt this burning on my cheek. I don't know what I did with the bolt of the 16, but I got it to fire and I emptied everything I had into him. Then I saw blood dripping on the back of my hand and I just went crazy. I pulled him out into the paddy and carved him up with my knife. When I was done with him, he looked like a rag doll that a dog had been playing with. Even then I wasn't satisfied. I was fighting with the [medical] corpsmen trying to take care of me. I was trying to get at him for more ... I really loved fucking killing, couldn't get enough. For every one I killed I felt better. (p. 78)

> All I wanted was to fucking hurt people. All I wanted to do was rain
> fucking destruction on that fucking country. If it fucking burned,
> I burnt it ... To see what napalm does—napalm was for *revenge*.
> Napalm would suck the air right out of your breath. Take it right
> out of your lungs. (p. 96)

Once these conditions, these possibilities, are actualized it is nearly
impossible to cover them over again. As one veteran put it:

> I became a fucking animal. I started putting fucking heads on poles.
> Leaving fucking notes for the motherfuckers. Digging up fucking
> graves ... They wanted fucking body count, so I gave it to them.
> I hope they're fucking happy. But they don't have to live with
> it. (p. 83)

Sadly, the possibility of complete recovery is very remote for such
individuals. Shay notes that most Vietnam veterans remain highly
symptomatic. For a thorough account of the horrors that soldiers were
exposed to during the Vietnam War I recommend Shay's book. I briefly
mention these narratives here because they are gripping accounts of the
human psyche's propensity for human-to-human destructiveness and
the irrevocable damage that continues relationally and psychologically
long after the events occur. The human capacity for destruction and the
not infrequent delight in such destruction calls to be thought about.

Understanding the will to death is equally, if not more, complex than
understanding the will to life. The will to death has an unwavering
quality for the person determined to end his or her existence. How do
we understand this fixation? Farber (1969) reports that the reason can
be found in the extensive examination of someone considering suicide.
An individual who has made the decision to die has questioned his or
her entire existence. For the truly suicidal individual, suicide becomes
increasingly fascinating as it becomes the answer to all one's troubles
and doubts. Also, suicide becomes interpreted as confirmation of one's
bravery and competence.

Existentialism took Freud's notion of Thanatos out of drive theory
and placed it in context of the individually existing subject. Moreover,
existential-phenomenological therapists do not necessarily consider suicide a pathological option because they tend to understand the human

being as being self-determining. It is interesting to note that Hillman supports the existential-phenomenological stance on suicide. He too supports the notion that death should be the centrepiece of one's existence and sees self-destructiveness as entering death by choice. Since all death is essentially suicide, the suicidal individual is simply choosing the method. Paradoxically, a suicidal individual may be seeking a more meaningful life through the death experience. In short, self-destructiveness is an option open to the human psyche.

Menninger (1938) understands suicide in existential terms, but differs from Hillman and others in his belief that suicide should be researched and treated. Though he acknowledges the unconscious vicissitudes of suicide, he understands it as being essentially a voluntary conscious decision. Suicide is a dynamic, complex phenomenon that an individual struggles with over time, not a single impulsive act. Menninger notes the chronic character of suicide, that an individual may take years killing him or her self through asceticism, drug use, and alcoholism. What's worse is that society tends to promote self-destructive behaviors: "Every culture contains many elements which tend to encourage ... the individual's self-destructive trends" (Menninger, 1938, p. 104).

Adopting a phenomenological perspective, Menninger (1938) asserts that suicide has three essential components: (1) the wish to kill, (2) the wish to be killed, and (3) the wish to die. The wish to be killed represents an extreme form of submissiveness. Like the enjoyment of pain and defeat, the wish to be killed is essentially masochistic. Menninger describes the wish to kill as an attacking, annihilating will that, if not satisfied, may turn back against the self. Of course, this wish tends to be turned against the self, due to the measures society takes to inhibit it. Menninger also differentiates the unconscious suicide wish from the conscious. The conscious death wish is a complex co-mingling of cooperating and conflicting dynamics. The unconscious suicide wish manifests in psychosomatic illnesses, accident proneness, and other similar behaviors. Such people are those who neglect to take medication for physical illness as well as those who keep the same breakneck schedule after having a heart attack. The chronically suicidal person has a fundamental conflict between the wish to live and the wish to die. Menninger's research shows that chronically suicidal people tend to not kill themselves when they are young. Alcoholism, for example, is considered "as a kind of lesser self-destruction serving to avert a greater self-destruction" (ibid., p. 158). Menninger takes organic disease as often reflecting a part of the personality's destruction of itself. An existence becoming devoid of meaning may increasingly experience suicide as an option, consciously or unconsciously. Frankl provides an example from his experience in a concentration camp:

> One day a prisoner told his fellows he had a strange dream. He dreamed that a voice spoke to him and asked whether he wanted to know anything at all—if he could foretell the future. He answered: "I should like to know when the Second World War will end for me." Whereupon the dream voice replied: "On March 30, 1945." It was the beginning of March when the prisoner narrated this dream. At the time he was very hopeful and in good spirits. But as the thirtieth of March came closer and closer, it began to seem less and less probable that the "voice" would be right. In the last days before the prophesized deadline the man gave way to more and more discouragement. On March 29 he was taken to the infirmary with a high fever and in a state of delirium. On the crucial thirtieth of March—the day when the Second World War was to end for him—he lost consciousness. Next day he was dead of typhus. (Frankl, 1955, p. 81)

Paradoxically, the decision to end one's life is often a necessary condition of living. The majority of existential-phenomenological therapists attempt to help patients become aware of their unique existence and to take responsibility for it. Humans, as self-determining beings, necessarily have free will, which includes the possibility of harming or ending life. For some people, suicide is a viable option to a life devoid of meaning or ridden with ontological anxiety. With few exceptions, existential-phenomenological therapists do not necessarily see suicide as something immoral or even irresponsible. A few things remain unclear in the existential-phenomenological account of self-destructiveness. What about the instances where such decisions negatively influence or limit other people's existential freedom? What about the instances where an individual's ability to make free and responsible decisions about his or her existence are impaired by situational factors, medication, or drug and alcohol use? Despite these largely unanswered questions, existential-phenomenological psychology has done much to tend to the patient's experience itself rather than viewing it through preconceived notions and diagnoses. Also, it is difficult to argue with their assertion that without the option of self-destruction humans would not truly be free.

Summary of the literature

The literature suggests that self-destructiveness is prevalent in the consulting room as well as in our everyday lives. Theorists and therapists view self-destruction in different and often conflicting ways; however, most writing on the subject views self-destruction and even suicide as attempts to preserve one's self. Many psychoanalytic thinkers look at self-destructiveness developmentally, taking into consideration the individual's early relationships to primary objects, the environment, and drives such as Thanatos. Most clinicians utilizing a Jungian perspective focus on trauma, resultant dissociative defenses, and the archetypal drama of the psyche. Existential-phenomenologists abandon the notions of development, drive, and archetype in favour of understanding the individual's subjective experience. From this perspective, self-destruction is a function of societal alienation, corresponding anxiety, and loss of meaning in life. These thinkers also distinguish themselves in that most of them do not consider suicidal and para-suicidal behaviours to be necessarily immoral. Some existential-phenomenological thinkers suggest that the decision to kill oneself might be the first existentially free and responsible decision a person makes. It is clear from the literature that there is not a universal definition or understanding of self-destructiveness.

Depth psychology and phenomenology have a wide range of positions concerning the human psyche's capacity and even enjoyment of destructiveness. I have chosen specific examples and thinkers to highlight elements inherent in destructiveness. I would like to again note that in choosing some things, others are necessarily set aside. Moreover, a thinker's views of things change, sometimes radically, over the course of his or her career. For example, it is not just the Jungians who speak about trauma. Bion's work emphasizes catastrophe and traumatic impact in its way too. Winnicott says there is an environmental factor in psychosis. Kohut emphasizes trauma in narcissistic injury associated with self-destructive acts and, in reverse fashion, Jung's later work emphasized what he thought was a chemical or toxic factor in psychosis (Eigen, personal communication, October 4, 2002).

Statement of the problem

This book explores the theme of self-destructiveness in the work of Bion and Heidegger. This study attempts to answer the following questions:

1. How has self-destructiveness been understood in the traditions of depth psychology and existential-phenomenological psychology?
2. How has self-destruction been understood specifically by Bion and Heidegger?
3. How does the phenomenon of self-destructiveness manifest in our contemporary culture?

Self-destructiveness is an important topic to explore. In 1920 Freud noted that psychological illnesses have three essential characteristics: they are repetitive, compulsive, and are linked to the death instinct. There is a possible reason that Freud did not conceive of the repetition compulsion without the death instinct. Behaviours can be both repetitive and compulsive without necessarily being pathological. The death-seeking, self-destructive aspect is critical since there are behaviours that are both repetitive and/or compulsive and yet do not constitute psychological illness. Most people, for example, are compelled to wake up and go to the same place of employment day after day, year after year. The homeowner has to have just the right pattern on the lawn he is mowing. The artist, the chef, the researcher, the writer, the business-man, the politician; all need to have their work exactly so and yet none of this is considered mental illness.

Although there is no shortage of studies about self-destructiveness, there are no thematic hermeneutic examinations. Further, there has been no research exploring the ontological dimensions of self-destructiveness, since most researchers and clinicians focus on ontic manifestations such as statistics, cognitions, and behaviours. Such a thematic hermeneutic investigation may uniquely contribute to the literature on this topic and assist those mental health professionals who work with self-destructive patients.

Organization of the text

This theoretical study gives thought to the phenomenon of self-destructiveness. Self-destructiveness has been a central theme in the history of psychology and this work presents some of the major ways it has emerged in the field of psychology. In Chapter one I note that during the inception of psychology, Freud noted that all mental illness has repetitive and compulsive features. I acknowledge this as a seminal idea and accent his notion that destruction is of equal, if not greater importance. Further, I suggest that there are behaviours that are both repetitive and compulsive, which are considered normal, or even praiseworthy, in our culture. Such behaviours are only deemed signs of mental disturbance when the element of destruction is evident. Moreover, I explore the notion that human-to-human destructiveness is essentially the self-destructive impulse projected outward.

The paradoxical nature of human self-destructiveness is discussed and then a number of theoretical perspectives are explicated. Empirical psychology examines self-destructiveness in terms of specific maladaptive behaviors and through descriptive statistics. Specific self-destructive behaviours are presented and I discuss the impact such behaviours have on society as a whole. Psychoanalytic views tend to take their direction from Freud's seminal notion of the death instinct, Thanatos. I turn to Klein who amplifies this theme and even places it as the centrepiece of her psychology. Following this I follow Bion who took Klein's research and made further discoveries concerning the role it played in primitive mental states. Next, I present the work of Jung who understood the self-destructive capacity of the psyche primarily in terms of trauma and its subsequent dissociative pathology. Hillman, offering a post-Jungian perspective, argues that self-destructiveness emerges when one becomes identified with the daimon. Kunnap understands self-destructiveness as a function of the *inner critic*, which can hold sway in the psyche causing addiction and feelings of worthlessness. Existential-phenomenologists understand Thanatos less psychodynamically and more in terms of the individually existing subject. Binswanger, a pioneer of existential psychiatry, asserted that self-destructiveness is a fundamental aspect of human freedom, for we would not truly be free if we could not choose otherwise. Farber, unlike Binswanger, noted that self-destructive acts often represent desperate attempts at self-empowerment.

The literature suggests that self-destructiveness is rampant in society and in the consulting room. Though theorists and therapists often have conflicting views, they tend to see self-destructiveness in light of some larger struggle to survive. Psychoanalytic thinkers tend to examine self-destructiveness from a developmental perspective, taking into account such factors as drives and early object relations. Jungians tend to focus on trauma, associated dissociative defenses, and the archetypal unfolding of the psyche. Existential-phenomenologists focus more on the individual subject and the larger socio-cultural forces at work. For them alienation, anxiety, and one's personal freedom are paramount in understanding self-destructive behaviour. They do not always agree on whether self-destruction should be reduced, or if it is a genuine expression of one's existential freedom.

I provide a thematic hermeneutic disclosure of self-destructiveness and, to this end, choose certain themes among the more prominent thinkers in depth psychology and existential-phenomenology. Admittedly, theorists and therapists often change their stance on clinical matters throughout their careers as they gain more experience and insight. Heidegger is largely responsible for the development of contemporary hermeneutics. For him meaning is always hermeneutic in the sense that the structure of meaning already has the art of interpretation. Each chapter gives thought to self-destructiveness and provides an interpretive narrative.

In Chapter Two I explicate the design and the interpretive process utilized in this work. I describe its method as a thematic hermeneutics and I go on to discuss the origins of hermeneutic theory. Hermeneutics refers both to the art of interpretation as well as the philosophy concerned with the phenomenon of interpretation. In its origins hermeneutics referred primarily to the interpretation of legal and sacred texts. In contemporary academia, hermeneutic theory is not limited to law and scriptural interpretation but to other fields such as history, cultural studies, and psychology.

In reviewing the history of hermeneutics I point out that it has always been concerned with meaning and the explanation of meaning. The art of explaining concerned itself not only with interpretive processes, but also with the application of interpretation. Over time hermeneutics developed different schools. One such school could be called intuitivism. Intuitivism asserted that the text is the holy site for spiritual union with God or another person. Rules and procedures are regarded as secondary to the sacred connection and the interpreter's spirituality. The guiding logic of intuitivism is that the written word often does not represent a literal entity. There is some variance between the written word and its transcendent spiritual meaning. Therefore, from this perspective, the most fitting way to access the transcendent meaning of the word is through spiritual communion. The text becomes the sacred ground for such a union. In contrast to intuitivism was positivism, which was concerned primarily with legal hermeneutics. Positivism, standing in sharp contrast to intuitivism, asserted that if the rules of interpretation are perfected, then problems of interpretation would essentially become problems of operational procedures. While the intuitivism interpreter noted the variance between the word and its meaning, the positivism accented the congruity between the two. A third school to take into account is perspectivism, which takes into account the various ways the same object can appear depending upon one's perspective. The perspectivist interpreter does not believe in the existence of a singular from the text. Rather, the meaning of a text is largely dependent upon the perspective of the interpreter.

From this point I go on to discuss the threefold movement of hermeneutics into modernity. Specifically, I delineate the work of Schleiermacher, Dilthey, and Heidegger. Among their many contributions to hermeneutics were the beliefs that (1) hermeneutics was the art of understanding, as opposed to explicating, applying and translating, (2) hermeneutics should be applied universally to all subject domains, and (3) that interpretation should include all aspects of the phenomenon including the interpreter's psychological makeup, the language of the text, its historical context and so forth. Dilthey, Scheiermacher's biographer, extended Kantian philosophy to the social sciences. He believed that hermeneutics could address all texts whether it was the written word or human behaviour. In his later work, he asserted that studying the corpus of an author's material would yield certain themes that, in turn, would yield further meaning. The third movement I explore is Heideggerian hermeneutics. Heidegger, who openly acknowledged his debt to Dilthey, gave thought to the nature of the relationship between hermeneutics and thinking. Heidegger went so far as to posit that the human being is essentially hermeneutic in that humans are always already engaged in the interpretive act of deciphering meaning. Heidegger maintained that even inaccurate interpretation was a kind of interpretation nonetheless. For Heidegger hermeneutics was of primary philosophical importance since the structure of meaning always references the *as* of interpretation.

Following this section I discuss the praxis of this text's method. I describe the thematic hermeneutic image as being like a wheel. The spokes are to the wheel as the chapters are to the dissertation. Each spoke (chapter) takes on and releases some of the energy as the wheel moves. Stated differently, each chapter both reveals and simultaneously conceals some aspect of the phenomenon in question. This process is guided largely by my intuition and reverie. While it is impossible to view the phenomenon of self-destructiveness, or any other phenomenon, in its entirety a thematic hermeneutic may shed light on its constituent parts and proffer greater salience.

Chapter Four of this study focuses on the understanding of self-destructive behaviour throughout history. I presented early historical attitudes towards self-destructiveness before moving on to consider depth psychological and existential-phenomenological perspectives.

Greeks living during the Homeric period tended to view suicide as a natural and logical solution to a meaningless life. Noteworthy opponents to this position were the philosophers Pythagoras and Plato. Both considered suicide to be an unnatural and cowardly act that violated the sanctity of the soul. Aristotle carried the idea further, suggesting that suicide should be punishable by the State. The ancient Stoics were more tolerant about suicide, believing 'Where we are, death is not, when death has come, we are not.' The Stoics viewed suicide as reasonable and a part of an individual's freedom. Interestingly, as early as the first century a Stoic philosopher named Seneca conceptualized the notion of *libido moriendi* (death instinct). As the city-state emerged, suicide continued to be tolerated. Between 200 and 400 AD Romans introduced a system whereby suicide would be permitted if the individual provided a logical rationale to the Senate. By 400 AD individual rights were of high concern and the decision of suicide was left largely to the individual.

The earliest attitudes about suicide in Hebrew societies can be found in the Torah and these views influenced early Christian societies. There are only four suicides in the Old Testament and the rare suicides that were documented largely represented acts of bravery, such as dying in war. From its earliest beginnings Judaism has deemed suicide an act that demeans the holiness of life. Early Christian cultures adopted the Roman's disinterest in suicide and added to it that corporeal existence was essentially meaningless. To commit suicide was not only to follow in Christ's example, but also to expedite the process of entering heaven. Realizing it was losing its best members the Church pronounced suicide a sin. Over time suicide was considered to be a crime against the Church and those who had failed suicide attempts were excommunicated. The bodies of those who committed suicide were not given religious burials. Christianity's view of suicide influenced civil law and so it became a punishable offense. Punishments included loss of possessions, institutionalization and even (ironically) death. Suicide remains taboo and considered a crime to our day.

Following this section, I explore historical depth psychological views of self-destruction. I look to the some of the philosophers who unknowingly came to influence depth psychology. First I describe Hegel's rationalism and historicism. Hegel (1817) understood reason (*Geist*) and history as mutually unfolding, transcending the various contradictions in different cultures and time periods towards transcendent reason (the Absolute). Humans participate in this unfolding and the two are essentially bound to each other. Authentic self-consciousness can only be gained by acknowledging one's fundamental attachment to the larger humanity. Hegel noted that people tend to deny their dependence on the other and that two fundamental forms of consciousness emerge, the Independent and the Dependent.

Hegel (1817) characterized the Independent consciousness in terms of the Lord and the Dependent in terms of the Bondsman. The Lord, in his love of freedom, flees from his dependence upon the Bondsman. The Lord leads a duplicitous existence. On the one hand he enjoys more privilege in society and is freer to enjoy things since he has more time. On the other hand, the Lord lives off the fruit of the Bondsman's labour. Despite the seemingly lower status of the Bondsman, Hegel sees him as having a more authentic existence, since he does not deny his dependence.

In contrast to Hegel's (1817) rationalism and historicism I offer Nietzsche's contention that any collectivism is self-destructive. In contrast to Hegel, Nietzsche (1886, 1886, 1887) believed that every collective, especially organized religion, ultimately undermines individual responsibility. Nietzsche contrasted two elements of human existence: the Apollonian and Dionysian. Apollo represents self-restraint, thoughtfulness, and reason. Dionysius, in contrast, represents the will to reverie, intoxication, and the passions. Nietzsche believed that struggling to balance the two may lead to a more balance life and would proffer a more genuine existence. Nietzsche asserted that philosophies such as Hegel's deify reason at the expense of the passions.

Also in contrast to Hegel, Nietzsche valued the individual above all else. Collectives, he argued, lead to a bland humanity of self-sameness. Moreover, he believed that since the dawn of Christianity humanity began devolving. This is owed, in part, to Christianity's spreading of *ressentiment*, a complex synthesis of envy and impotence, which is compensated for with fantasies of moral superiority. Nietzsche's conception of humanity was a leveling down to herd-consciousness, not the global unfolding of *Geist* towards transcendence.

Freud, who was particularly suspicious of philosophy, had an affinity for Neitzsche's writings. Nietzsche actually preceded Freud by referring to the Dionysian drives as *das es* (*the id* or *the it*) and in exploring the role sublimation played in the production of art, cultural achievement, and even dreams (Kaufmann, 1992). Nietzsche's predominantly anti-religious attitude is also echoed in Freud's theorizing. During the early days of psychoanalysis, all religious sentiment was regarded as an infantile wish for father. Freud, like Nietzsche, was fascinated by the human capacity for self-destruction and self-deception. Many of the psyche's defense mechanisms can be seen as ways of maintaining self-worth by deception. Further, many of the mechanisms, themselves self-destructive, were defending against the self-destructive force within the psyche.

Unlike Nietzsche, Freud did not rely primarily on collectivism to explain self-destructiveness. Freud noted the sadistic elements of the superego and by 1920 introduced the idea of Thanatos, the death drive. Thanatos was offered as the opposite to Eros, the love principle. Left unmitigated, Thanatos could join with the sadistic aspect of the superego thus gain pleasure from pain. Once this occurs, the masochistic ego both provokes and gains pleasure from self-torment, which establishes the repetition compulsion. At the heart of this system lies the most basic impulse of all organic life, the wish to return to an inorganic state. This is the essence of Freud's dictum that the aim of all life is death.

Freud lent increasing importance to the death drive and his follower, Klein, went so far as to place it as the centrepiece of her psychology. Klein postulated that an infant's internal world is beset with vivid phantasies of destruction and violence (Eigen, 1996). It can be thought of as an internal galactic battle between objects experienced as good and those experienced as evil. The infantile ambivalence that Klein discusses is linked to an innate force within the psyche bent on destroying itself. For her it is not a question of whether it is there or not, but how it is managed primarily through projective identification. The infant must work through its ambivalence towards the good breast and bad breast to the realization that what it hates and loves is the same object.

Perhaps no psychoanalyst went as far as Bion in exploring the most primitive self-destructive forces of the mind. Bion (1964) used the notation K to refer to the healthy element of the mind that is curious about internal and external reality. In contrast to this he posited the notion of minus K (-K) to refer to the part of the mind that works against life by destroying internal and external links with relationships and reality. Like Klein, Bion looks to the earliest relationship between mother and infant. In Bion's psychology, the infant, flooded with unmanageable affects, relies on mother to take notice, internalize, and return the affect in a softer and more palatable form. As the infant's mind develops it becomes decreasingly reliant upon projective identification and more able to internally contend with distressing states. Minus K can result from powerfully negative affects or objects accruing in the infant's mind, the infant's over-reliance upon projective identification, or some combination of the two. The more menacing internal/external reality is, the more desperately the infant turns to evacuation and schizoid withdrawal. The more this takes place, the less able the infant is able to digest experience. This is discussed in greater length in Chapter Four.

In Chapter Five I discuss Heidegger's (1927) phenomenological conception of Dasein. I outline Heidegger's point of departure and go on to explore some critical elements of his philosophy: existence, existentials, existentiell, world, worldliness of the world, circumspection, taking care, Dasein, thematic, pre-thematic, handiness, objective presence, ontic and ontological. I go on to outline how, proximately and predominately, Dasein is in the world that is, as a they-self or ownmost-self. I examine the role death plays into these ways of being and the ways Dasein can respond to the call of conscience.

Having unpacked the critical elements of Heidegger's thought, I discuss his later work that gives thought to technology and Dasein's relationship to it. For Heidegger the essence of technology is nothing technological. Moreover, Dasein tends to mistake itself as the originator and master of technology and, unwittingly, falls into the reserve of useful things to be used. This leads to the denial of the world and of the mystery of Being.

I explore more contemporary phenomenological views. Boss (1971) continues the themes delineated in Heidegger's work and adds a psychological perspective. For Boss mental illness and addiction should be viewed in larger meaninglessness, alienation, and numbness associated with the business of everydayness. Van den Berg (1983), in turn, proposes that the word sociosis should replace the word neurosis, since mental disturbance bespeaks sociological factors and not the activity going on inside one's head. He notes that people in our contemporary technological age are forced to have a plurality of selves. This multitude of functional contexts cannot possibly be ordered and people live a divided existence in an increasingly complex society. Romanyshyn (1989) continues this theme, noting that we have a shared cultural vision that takes the self as spectator, the world as spectacle, and the body as specimen. Understanding the body as anatomy, while revealing critical medical information, perpetuated the fantasy of the body as machine. Romanyshyn also notes that the two fundamental features of our age are the ability to depart and destroy the earth. In essence, humanity fosters the fantasy of the body and earth being disposable and incidental to our being. I conclude the chapter by asserting that the contemporary ways of being in the world, influenced very much by technology, delimit our possibilities of relatedness to each other.

In Chapter Six I look specifically at the population who suffers the most from human-to-human destructiveness; the children of the world. I provide descriptive statistics to support this and argue that the suffering of children is rampant both domestically and abroad. I introduce Golden's (1997) concept of disposable children who suffer abuse at home, are removed from the home, and then are placed in a welfare system that often re-traumatizes the very population it is supposed to protect. When the child rebels against the system, that behaviour is often taken as further evidence of mental disturbance and need for deeper integration into the system. I concluded the chapter with a case vignette of one such 'disposable' child.

In Chapter Seven I review the material presented in this study and offer my reflections. These reflections explore the essence of destructiveness and its link with the essential character of technology. I add remarks about how Heideggerian phenomenology and Bionian psychoanalysis may benefit from each other's perspectives and further their thinking. I then discuss the dynamics symbolized by what I call X. After elaborating on X I offer my concluding remarks.

In Chapter Eight I offer suggestions for further research. These include both ontic and ontological ways of contending with the problematic ways in which self-destruction reveals itself.

CHAPTER TWO

Pursuing that which withdraws from us

This chapter explores the research design, the kind of data being sought, and the interpretive process involved in generating information. This chapter is fundamentally important to the study in that it delineates the mode of inquiry, the method, its application, and the information generated by these elements. First I will present a description of the method utilized in this dissertation and then situate this within the origins of hermeneutic theory. Next, I will review the praxis of the method used in this dissertation in order to give a salient account of the specific kind of hermeneutics employed in this particular study.

Hermeneutic engagement

This dissertation is phenomenological and utilizes a thematic hermeneutic approach. Hermeneutics, simply defined, is the art of interpretation as well as the philosophy that raises questions concerning interpretation. While hermeneutics has been used almost exclusively in regards to translating ancient scriptural text, in contemporary academia it is applied more broadly to culture, history, and psychological as well as philosophical themes. Thematic hermeneutics is the art of interpreting a theme inherent in the phenomenon or phenomena of interest.

The origins of hermeneutic theory

Historically hermeneutics was a term used only by biblical interpreters. The word's origins tend to be associated with Hermes, the messenger of the gods. This is not completely accurate, as the Greek work *Ermenia* comes from a root that predates both the messenger god and the practice of interpreting (Hirsch, 1976). In any event, Hermes mediated between the gods and men, translating godly information for the world of men and bringing the finite into the realm of the gods. The sacred association can also be found in the Latin *interpretatio* and *interpres*, interpreter or mediator, which is a soubriquet for the Roman version of Hermes, Mercury.

Since ancient times the notion of interpretation has grappled with two areas, meaning and the explanation of meaning. These two functions were known as *ars intelligendi*, the art of understanding, and *ars explicandi*, the art of explaining. *Ars explicandi* included not only the *interpretatio*, but *applicatio* (significance) as well. Interpretation contends with both the meaning and the value of the object of interest. The primary value of interpretation was *applicatio*, not *interpretatio* alone. Of course *interpretatio* was a necessary for the various functions of *applicatio*, since understanding proceeded explanation.

Hermeneutics was confined to two fields where life and death, salvation or damnation, were literally involved; the study of law and the study of scripture. It is here that Hirsch found a paradox: "The more important the issue at stake, the less we find philosophical and theological scaffolding being deployed to support interpretive decisions" (Hirsch, 1976, p. 20). Moreover, in both these domains it is the concreteness of the interpretation that made legal and scriptural hermeneutics different traditions. For all their differences, the history of hermeneutics has yielded a few fundamental philosophical presuppositions and these can be associated with the two aforementioned schools, biblical and legal.

The first position Hirsch (1976) dubbed intuitionism. From this perspective text is taken as the holy site, the ground, for a spiritual encounter with a god or another mortal. From this perspective meaning was not in words as nuts are in shells. The words of the text did not enclose the meaning to be discovered; rather, they were the occasions for spiritual communion. Rules and procedure regarding interpretation are secondary to the sacred connection and the interpreter's spiritual conviction. While words facilitate this process, the interpreter is not constrained by them or any other philological procedure. Often, certain chosen spiritual officials (e.g. priests) were chosen to make such interpretations. However, some argued that the holy interpretation belonged to the individual's unique experience with the text. Therefore, intuitionism can lead to collective homogeny or individualism. "It sanctions Catholicism and Protestantism alike. In the secular domain of literary criticism it encourages oracular, priest-like pronouncements on the one side, and rebellious subjective individualism on the other hand" (Hirsch, 1976, p. 21). Despite this, intuitionism rests upon sound principles. It is a fact that there is often an incongruity between text and spirit. If the letter perfectly reflected spiritual content, then there would be no difficulty interpreting text. The fact that a single text can be interpreted countless different ways means that there must be some variance between the letter and its spiritual meaning. Therefore the intuitive interpreter is correct in believing that the letter must be transcended and that the letter cannot be transcended except through spiritual communion.

The second position Hirsch (1976) delineates is positivism. In contrast to intuitivism, positivism tended to be associated with legal hermeneutics. An example of this was judges who made interpretations based upon evidence and the belief that the law's meaning is exactly as it is written. Positivism sharply rejected any notion of spiritual communion between interpreter and the meaning of the text. "If the rules and canons of construction are made precise, and if the tools of linguistic analysis are sharpened and refined, the problems of interpretation will be resolved into operations procedures" (ibid., p. 22). For the positivist meaning is an epiphenomenon, a secondary quality of the text itself. A philosophical presupposition of positivism is that there is congruity between the signified and the signifier. While there were clearly some strengths to positivism, such as the assertion that there is a correspondence between meaning and the letter, there are some weaknesses. Positivism had a difficult time accounting for literary phenomena such as irony. Clearly, while there was some correspondence between signified and signifier, it was a logical error to assume one linguistic form or style was directly revealed in the text. Where intuitionism paid too little attention to the persuasive quality of the text, positivism asserted the persuasive quality of the text too boldly.

A third perspective delineated by Hirsch (1976) was perspectivism. The perspectivist interpreter asserted that one must take into account how different an object can appear depending upon one's perspective. Perspectivism was highly skeptical about the possibility of the existence of the one true meaning of a text. Two major forms of perspectivism were psychological and historical. The psychological form asserted that two people could not glean the exact same meaning of the text, since no two subjective perspectives were alike. The historical perspective made a similar argument, asserting that one's interpretive stance was always located from a unique cultural-historical moment. Both of these forms of perspectivism maintain that the interpretation was largely reliant upon the interpreter. A great strength to this perspective was that it could not be refuted logically. To say otherwise would assume that two subjective perspectives could experience meaning in precisely the same fashion and that interpretation is in no way culturally-historically informed. While the arguments for perspectivism were strong, it perhaps went too far in accenting the variance inherent in interpretations without giving thought to the surprisingly large amount of consistency in interpretation. It is noteworthy that we have the same text, the same modes of communication, and the same basic meanings cross-culturally. For example, cross-culturally people tend to have words for mother, father, happy, sad, and so forth.

Despite their differences, the various schools of hermeneutics tended to agree that the process of interpretation was itself a process of validation. Hermeneutics, while utilized mostly for the interpretation of ancient text, has continued into the present. Honderich (1995) has noted a threefold movement of hermeneutics into modernity. Friedrich Schleiermacher, a prominent nineteenth century philosopher and theologian, led and gave form to the first movement.

Schleiermacher's conception of hermeneutics rested squarely on three of the doctrines developed by Herder specifically, that (1) thought and language were largely identical, (2) that meaning was word usage and (3) there were significant linguistic and intellectual differences between people. As the third principle posed the potentially greatest barrier to both interpretation and translation, Schleiermacher took that as his primary challenge. Schleiermacher's most original doctrine in the philosophy of language, known as semantic holism, was also relevant in this connection since, as Schleiermacher perceives, semantic holism greatly exacerbated the challenge to interpretation and translation. Semantic holism was the doctrine that the identity of the meaning of a sentence was determined by its place in the web of beliefs or sentences comprising a whole theory or group of theories (Honderich, 1995).

Schleiermacher lectured on hermeneutics from roughly 1805 through 1833. During the course of these lectures he delineated his main principles. First he asserted that hermeneutics was the art of understanding verbal communication, as opposed to explicating, applying, or translating it. Second, he maintained that hermeneutics should be a universal discipline that is, one that applied equally to all subject domains, oral or written language, ancient or modern texts and so forth. He believed this should apply to the interpretation of scripture such as the Bible, and that special principles like divine inspiration should not be relied upon. Schleiermacher believed that the art of interpretation was exceedingly difficult, due to the deep linguistic and intellectual variance already mentioned. He believed that a good interpreter should first gain extensive knowledge of the text's historical context prior to attempting any interpretation. Schleiermacher further maintained that interpretation always had two facets, the linguistic and the psychological. Linguistic hermeneutics consisted of inferring from the evidence constituting the particular uses of words to the rules that were governing them. Psychological hermeneutics instead examined the author's psychological makeup. Whereas linguistic interpretation focused on what was common and shared in a language, psychological interpretation examined what was unique to the particular author. Schleiermacher gave several reasons for why an interpreter needed to harmonize linguistic interpretation with the psychological. To begin, he saw the necessity as arising from the variance and distinctiveness inherent with each individual. Second, the authorial psychology was intended to help reduce variance and ambiguities at the level of linguistic meanings and the specific contexts in which they appear (Honderich, 1995).

Schleiermacher believed that interpretation required two methods. He postulated a comparative method, which coincided with linguistic interpretation. In this method the interpreter goes from the particular uses of a word towards the governing rules for using them. Second he conceived of a divinatory method, a method of tentative and fallible hypothesis based on, but also going beyond, empirical evidence. This is associated with the psychological aspect of interpretation. In addition to this Schleiermacher believed that it was optimal for the interpreter to have psychological commonality with the text.

Another facet of Schleiermacher's hermeneutics was his belief that interpretation was a holistic venture. According to him every portion of the text should be interpreted as a function of the overall text. This should be interpreted according to its language, which should be interpreted in light of history, the genre, and any other texts by the author; as well as the author's psychological makeup. Interestingly Schleiermacher did not state that all these things could be accomplished. Rather, he argued that knowledge from interpretation comes in degrees (Forster, 2002).

Honderich (1995) asserted that the second phase of hermeneutics could be found with the work of Dilthey, Schleiermacher's biographer. Dilthey extended Kant's ideas to the social sciences and many other areas, believing that hermeneutics should address all texts whether they are ancient texts or human behaviour. He added the notion of the interpreter's own lived experience and the expression of the interpreter's spirit, which was too involved in the interpretive process. Dilthey believed his method of interpreting history and the human sciences could produce objective and valid knowledge without the reductionist, mechanistic approach of the natural sciences. Furthermore he believed his approach would yield knowledge that would incorporate the contexts, historical or otherwise, inherent in the phenomena under investigation. He maintained that texts, communications, behaviours, and art held psychological intentions that should be understood. In this sense, hermeneutics was the appropriate approach to understanding human interactions. Interpreting human discourse and behaviour was more akin to translating literature or a poem than conducting natural scientific experiments. He contrasted the desired comprehension of events and expressions with the sort of explanatory knowledge produced by the reductive method of natural sciences.

In his later work, Dilthey began to accent that the objects of interpretation were products firmly embedded in history as expressions of individuals; therefore their meanings were situated in their unique cultural-historical index, as well as in the matrix of their author's intentions and experiences. From this stance, meanings were seen in light of the authors' views of the world that, in turn, reflected their unique historical timeframe and culture. Hermeneutic work involved following a circle from the text to the author's experience and psychology, to the historical context and back again. The interpretive process reconstructed the world in which the text was brought into being and understood the text within that framework. Dilthey was clear that the validity of interpretive work increased as a greater understanding of the author's psychology, rather than the values of the interpreter. Taking an author's body of literature and analyzing one or more of its parts yielded themes inherent in the work.

Dilthey was included in the third phase of hermeneutics, which Honderich found primarily in the work of Heidegger. Heidegger openly and repeatedly acknowledged the influence of Dilthey on his own work and hailed him for his achievements in the field. While Heidegger acknowledged Dilthey's influence, he pondered the relationship between hermeneutics and thinking. Heidegger (1954) maintained that thinking is response on our part to a call that issues from the nature of things. True thinking, in contrast to everyday data gathering and information processing, was therefore not willed but evoked one to be attentive to things and people as they were, and to ponder our relatedness to them. Moreover, Heidegger believed that thinking defines 'Dasein' (i.e. humanity or the human kind of being) and, as such, the more thoughtful we were, the more our Dasein was enriched. Heidegger wrote, "phenomenology means: *apophainesthai ta phainomena*—to let that which shows itself be seen from itself, just as it shows itself from itself. That is the formal meaning of the type of research that calls itself 'phenomenology'" (Heidegger, 1927, p. 30). Phenomenology gave thought to that which became latent in the everyday. Specifically, phenomenology allowed us to see something that for the most part did not show itself at all:

> [I]t is something that lies hidden, in contrast to that which proximally and for the most part does show itself; but at the same time it is something that belongs to what thus shows itself, and it belongs to it so essentially as to constitute its meaning and ground. (ibid., p. 31)

For Heidegger, meaning was always hermeneutic; the structure of meaning always already involved the hermeneutic 'as' of interpretation that is, the methodological meaning of phenomenological description was interpretive in nature. "Phenomenology of Dasein is *hermeneutics* in the original signification of the word, which designates the work of interpretation" (ibid., p. 33). Heidegger considered hermeneutics to be of primary philosophical importance, since Dasein was an essentially an interpretive being.

> And finally, to the extent that Dasein, as an ontological entity with the possibility of existence, has ontological priority over every other entity, 'hermeneutic', as an interpretation of Dasein's Being, has the ... specific sense of an analytic of the existentiality of existence; and this is the sense which is philosophically *primary*. (Heidegger, 1927, p. 62)

Heidegger gave hermeneutics ontological importance. He contended that such phenomenological hermeneutics could yield knowledge about the meaning of the human being's kind of being. Such hermeneutics sought to describe the data of immediate experience without abstraction or interpretation. From a phenomenological perspective, humanity and the world co-constituted one another in an a-causal fashion. This position stood in sharp contrast to the Cartesian notion that humans are individual thinking subjects among other thinking subjects occupying a world devoid of life. For Heidegger world did not equal earth.

> It is possible that ultimately we cannot address ourselves to 'the world' as determining the nature of the entity we have mentioned? Yet we call this entity one which is 'within-the-world'. Is 'world' perhaps a characteristic of Dasein's Being? And in that case, does every Dasein 'proximately' have its world? Does not 'world' thus become something 'subjective'? How, then, can there be a 'common' world 'in' which nevertheless, we *are*? And if we raise the question of 'world', *what* world do we have in view? Neither the common world nor the subjective world, *but the worldhood of the world as such*. By what avenue do we meet this phenomenon? (ibid., p. 92)

Heidegger went on to add:

> 'worldhood' is an ontological concept, and stands for the structure of one of the constitutive items of Being-in-the-world. But we know Being in the world as a way in which Dasein's character is defined existentially. Thus worldhood is itself an *existentiale*. If we inquire ontologically about the 'world', we by no means abandon the analytic of Dasein as a field for thematic study. Ontologically,

'world' is not a way of characterizing those entities which Dasein essentially is *not*; it is rather a characteristic of Dasein itself. This does not rule out the possibility that when we investigate the phenomenon of the 'world' we must do so by the avenue of entities within-the-world and the Being which they possess. The task of 'describing' the world phenomenologically is so far from obvious that even if we do no more than determine adequately what form it shall take, essential ontological clarifications will be needed. (ibid., p. 92)

Dasein was a human encountering of the world, which always already had a certain mood or value placed upon things and situations. Heidegger used care to describe Dasein's prevailing attitude. Dasein finds itself thrown into the world that was, of course, already in existence. Therefore Dasein's concern defines its prevailing interactions of taking care of things and tarrying alongside others. Heidegger's ongoing emphasis upon the interdependence between Dasein and world bespeaks his rejection of the Cartesian worldview. Specifically, Heidegger dispensed with the notion that humans are subjective thinking beings set against an objective world that is somehow 'out there'. Once the physical world 'out there' and one's subjective experience 'in here' were separated it was impossible to bridge the gap. Rather, Heidegger contended with the problem by stating that that separation between subject and world was erroneous. Moreover he asserted that humans could not determine the nature of the world 'out there' because they were intrinsically a part of the world they were attempting to investigate.

Heidegger brought hermeneutics out of a theory of interpretation to a theory of existential awareness. He removed the psychological element of hermeneutics by differentiating it from the empathetic consciousness of other beings. Dasein was always already rooted in the context of experiences and expectations with finite logical resources. Therefore, interpretation that depends on such existential understanding was not the logical method found in philology and the natural sciences, but referred to an engagement and interactions with the world. Dilthey's methodological hermeneutic circle was consequently replaced by the fundamental ontological hermeneutic circle, which led from existential understanding situated in the world to a self-aware interpretive stance. Heidegger insisted that this self-knowledge could not escape its own limitations to achieve a transcendental understanding.

Praxis of method

Clearly, there are many different schools in the tradition of hermeneutics. While a number of different qualitative and quantitative approaches can be used to investigate the phenomenon of self-destruction, the present study employs a thematic hermeneutic method. Shields used the image of a wheel to describe the thematic hermeneutic method:

> Each spoke connects the centre of the wheel with its circumference. As the study moves from chapter to chapter, the spoke on the wheel rotates around the central idea in such a way that each poke holds a certain tension between the centre and circumference of the hermeneutic circle. As such, each spoke plays a certain role in the *going-on-being* of the wheel-as-*Gestalt*. In this way, each chapter discloses certain aspects of the central theme, analogous to the way in which each spoke distributes a certain proportion of tension radiating between the hub and the rim of the wheel. And at the very same time, each subsequent chapter necessarily leaves untouched, or repressed to some large degree, certain other dimensions of the central theme, similar to the way in which each spoke ignores much of the tension held by the other spokes ... For the totality of energy, created as the spoke of each chapter gains and releases tension, sustains the wheel's motility. The process of holding certain qualities of tension in some areas while distributing certain qualities of tension in other is what gives the wheel the force needed to turn, overturn, and return hermeneutically while traveling down the road of thought. (Shields, 2002, p. 90)

Since this is a phenomenological analysis, I am more interested in pursuing the phenomenon and unconcealment of meanings rather than interrogating it to produce quantitative data. Moreover the path of my thinking is guided by reverie and intuition, rather than calculative thinking.

As I worked on this book, I thought from a place of reverie and tended to imagery that came to mind when I was in such a meditative space. As I thought about my approach to the subject matter one particular image came to mind: I find myself in a completely dark place holding a flashlight. I am searching for something not as a hunter, but as a curious observer who wants to catch sight of something in its natural environment. What my light illuminates affords me a brief sight of what I am seeking. The darkness that moves with and endures around the circumference of the light beam is the phenomenon itself or, in psychological work, psyche. Every little space that becomes illuminated adds to my growing understanding of the space under investigation. Of course, I cannot illuminate the entire room with my flashlight and while I shed light on one area, all other space becomes enshrouded in its inherent darkness.

It is impossible to view a phenomenon in its entirety. Rather, the importance lies in giving thought to the elements of the phenomenon that emerge. It is true that the method of this text is hermeneutic, yet it is also true that my approach is intuitive. Stated differently, I did not use a pre-formulated systematic framework when examining the material and writing this book. I was largely guided by intuition as I give thought to the phenomenon of self-destructiveness.

It became apparent as I was reviewing the literature on self-destructiveness that it would be impossible to present all the material. There are simply too many articles addressing one or more of the many elements of self-destructiveness. Therefore, I chose to discuss the thinkers or researchers whom I felt had the most influential contributions on this score. During the course of reviewing the literature I also attempted to identify less influential thinkers, who still had original ideas regarding self-destruction. This was the hermeneutic key in developing this work. Otherwise, the literature review alone would reflect articles too numerous to understand in any meaningful fashion.

Regarding the hermeneutic aspect, I first presented the predominant themes of the book. Each theme was a chapter revolving around the central theme of self-destructiveness. These themes included (1) the emerging understanding of self-destructiveness in culture, religion, philosophy, and psychology, (2) Bion's investigations into the self-destructive capacity of the mind, (3) Heidegger's ontology of Being and the Enframing of technology, (4) identifying and delineating the 'who' who most experiences the impact of human-to-human destructiveness in our contemporary culture. I also included some clinical material to offer a more personal account of the impact of self-destructiveness.

It is at this point that I would like to discuss my personal interest in and philosophical presuppositions about the subject matter. I offer my perspective because it is a part of the hermeneutic aspect of the work. Based upon my years of clinical experience I am convinced that self-destruction is an essential aspect of all psychopathology. As I have already stated, many behaviours/cognitions are not considered pathological until they represent some harm to oneself or, when projected outwards, harm to others. Moreover, self-destruction is not a phenomenon I believe to occur solely in the individual psyche. Self-destructiveness can occur in familial, organizational, national, and cultural psyches as well. I believe that the phenomenon of self-destruction has both ontic and ontological dimensions. These dimensions are not mutually exclusive; they reference and reflect each other.

The ontic dimension of a phenomenon represents the elements constituting what it is. Ontology, on the other hand, refers to a phenomenon's is-ness the meaning of its being. The ontic and ontological dimensions of a phenomenon can be seen as polar points on a spectrum that, while being in some ways polarized, remain on the same continuum. As I gave thought to the phenomenon, I realized that it would be fitting to review the work of two thinkers who represented either side of the continuum. Many thinkers and researchers could have been chosen to represent either side, but I chose two whom in my estimation gave thought to the darkest, most penetrating, elements of self-destructiveness. Specifically, I reviewed the psychoanalytic work of Bion to represent the ontic and the existential-phenomenology of Heidegger to represent the ontological. Since Bion remains largely unconsidered in Heideggerian existential-phenomnology, and vice versa, I followed the path of their literature and noted the places where it shared common ground. I hoped that this would produce what Gadamer calls a "fusion of horizons," a broad framework in which the vision of each party participates (Sipiora, 1997, p. 2). My hope is that this fusion of perspectives would co-mingle in such a way that Bionian psychoanalysis and existential-phenomenology will mutually benefit from each other's orientation. Moreover, I felt it necessary to look beyond their perspectives and examine some of the ways the phenomenon of self-destructiveness manifests in our contemporary culture.

CHAPTER THREE

The emerging consciousness of self-destructiveness in history and psychology

Early historical attitudes about self-destruction

This chapter provides a historical perspective on societal views of self-destruction. The first section follows closely the historical findings of Glick (1974) on this score and the following section delineates the theme of self-destruction as it appears specifically in depth psychology and existential-phenomenological psychology.

Greco-Roman views of self-destruction

Glick (1974) describes the origins of societal attitudes about self-destruction chronologically and into two prevalent belief patterns, the Greco-Roman and the Judaeo-Christian. He notes that the word 'suicide' is a relatively new word, derived from Latin, and first appearing in the English language during the middle of the seventeenth century. Despite its Latin origins ancient Romans did not use that word. Instead they used the phrases *sibi morten consciscere* (to procure one's own death), *vim sibi inferre* (to cause violence to oneself) and *sua manu cadere* (to fall by one's own hand). The earliest document giving thought to the phenomenon of self-destruction is the ancient Egyptian text, *The Dialogue of a Misanthrope with his Own Soul*. This story describes a man who is weary of living due to a series of unfortunate events and he contemplates suicide as an alternative. The man attempts to convince his soul to enter death with him, but the soul refuses, fearing that he would be deprived a proper funeral for killing himself. This would essentially preclude the possibility of the soul having a blissful afterlife.

The phenomenon of suicide has been documented since earliest recorded history, since everything associated with death held special importance. The consciousness of death sparked curiosity about one's ability to end one's life and death itself was considered a terrifying and taboo topic. This feeling was stronger for those humans who died before their time, the *Bianthanatoi*. The ghosts of the *Bianthanatoi* were believed to be vengeful and dangerous, since they were greatly wronged in life. The belief being that if the person had not been greatly wronged, he or she would not have suffered premature death (Glick, 1974).

In contrast to this, the Greeks of the Homeric period (800 BC) thought of suicide as a natural and appropriate solution to a number of difficult situations. Suicide was the logical outcome of a life that was devoid of meaning. Little is known of the Pre-Socratics' (470–399 BC) views on self-destruction, because little of their writing has survived. One noteworthy exception to this was the philosophy of Pythagoras (580–500 BC). According to Plato (427–347 BC), Pythagoras was against suicide despite his belief that ultimately humans were strangers in this world and that the soul's possession of the body is finite. It has been suggested that Pythagoras' opposition to suicide evolved from the notion of transmigration of souls, a belief of ancient Orphic cults. Moreover, both Pythagoras and Plato understood men as being God's soldiers and so harming oneself constitutes an act against God. Plato took this a step further, stating that suicide is an unnatural act. If man is his closest friend, it is unnatural for him to harm himself. Self-destruction behaviours were viewed as cowardly and an offense against the State.

For Plato the soul was both imprisoned and immortal. He described the death of Socrates (470–399 BC), who was condemned to drink hemlock and die for his convictions, among other things. Plato came to view suicide as being one amongst other methods judges use for capital punishment. Aristotle (384–322 BC), Plato's most influential student, came to reject much of Plato's metaphysics yet maintained the belief that suicide was cowardly. Suicide was cowardly since the State lost a citizen and it was a crime on par with a soldier abandoning his post. According to Aristotle, suicide like all other immoral acts should be punished by the State.

The ancient Stoics (about 300 BC) considered preparation for death of paramount importance in their philosophy. Suicide was considered a reasonable solution to harsh conditions in life. The Stoics possessed unwavering indifference to anything lying beyond the individual personality and they believed that the individual was largely self-sufficient. The personality, in their view, was essentially nothing more than an instrument of universal reason. The personality is the vehicle whereby universal reason is realized. The Stoics living around 200 BC had similar beliefs to contemporary existentialists concerning freedom and the importance of one taking responsibility for one's own life. Moving away from the superstitions associated with death, the Stoics were more tolerant of suicide. They believed in living each day as it came and followed the following maxim: "While we are, death is not, when death has come, we are not" (Glick, 1974, p. 17). By detaching oneself from everything external, one is free to live through his or herself. This belief is discontinued when life has no reason and one is free to commit suicide. Essentially, the Stoics understood suicide as a right given to the individual. It is also interesting to note that as early as the first century AD a Stoic philosopher known as Seneca discussed the notion of *libido moriendi* (death instinct).

As the city-state, or polis, emerged during the first century the community did not view self-destruction with disgrace. Without disgrace families would not have to suffer guilt and social stigma. Both Greek and Roman philosophers and politicians largely discontinued discussing the subject by 200 AD. The Romans viewed self-destruction somewhat indifferently, yet considered it as a chosen validation of the way the individual lived and the principles he or she lived by. Marcus Aurelius ruled from 161–180 AD and vacillated between Platonic condemnation and the Stoic belief that man is ultimately responsible for his life. Between 200 and 400 AD the Romans introduced the custom that the suicidal individual had to submit his reason to the Senate. The Senate could either accept or reject the proposal and even determine the kind of death the person should suffer. By 400 AD individual rights were taken quite seriously, as the complex decision of whether or not to kill oneself was a choice left largely to the person.

Judaeo-christian views of self-destruction

The earliest attitudes towards suicide in Hebrew societies can be found in the Torah and it is largely the early Hebrew teaching that influenced early Christian societies. In both traditions suicide is considered taboo and life is considered sacred. In the Old Testament there are only four instances of suicide and the only prevalent occurrences of suicide recorded in Jewish history are acts of bravery, such as in war. A possible reason for the condemnation of self-destruction may be found in the fact that Hebrews had been persecuted throughout time. Given this, it is easy to understand that they held the sanctity of life as the highest goal. In the rare incident that someone would commit suicide, the family was not stigmatized however, but respect was not paid to the memory of the deceased. Comforting attention was given largely to the surviving family members. Many of these beliefs hold true to this day.

Jesus was considered by early Christians to have died for humanity's sins. Through his death on the cross, he was able to cleanse himself of earthly sin and enter into a spiritual rebirth. Self-destruction was considered to be a reasonable sacrifice to achieve a greater afterlife and self-destruction gained popularity among early Christians. To Romans of all classes, how one died, not death itself, was of paramount importance. Early Christians adopted the Roman indifference to death and added that life lacked importance. A richer life meant only that one had greater temptation to sin. Corporeal existence was seen as a sin-ridden weigh station on the way to heaven. To kill oneself was not only to follow Christ's example, but also to release oneself from earthly shackles.

This sentiment is embodied in a statement from an Augustinian priest to the King of Poland:

> Follow our Lord's example, and hate your body; if you love it, strive to lose it, says Holy Scripture, in order to save it; if you wish to make peace with it, always go armed, always wage war against it; treat it like a slave, or soon you yourself shall be its unhappy slave. (Delumeau, 1991, p. 448)

During the era of Augustus and the century following self-destruction was not taken as the alternative to facing a difficult life, as with the Romans, but was a shortcut to heavenly afterlife. Early Christians often allowed others to kill them, frequently in grisly ways.

The change in Christianity's stance on suicide seems to have instilled in leaders a fear that self-destruction would deplete the Church of its best followers. In 452 the Council of Arles renounced suicide as a crime that could only be inspired by evil. During the following century, at the

536 AD Council of Prague, it was determined that victims of suicide would be denied mass and a proper Christian burial. There was no name given to the four suicides found in the Bible. Over time the term *meabed azmo ladaat* was used when describing a victim of suicide. Christians utilized the term destroys rather than kills to emphasize the eternal damnation following suicide. The word *ladaat* implied that the person committed the act intentionally and was of sound mind and could therefore be punished. In the Council of Orleans in 533 AD suicide became understood as a crime against the Church, and the Council of Toledo in 693 AD determined that attempting suicide would result in excommunication. Civil legislation followed Canon Law, adding civil punishment to religious punishment. The body of the suicide victim was tried before civil authorities and his or her possessions were directed from the heir to the baron. The taboo upon suicide in Christianity lingers to this day (Glick, 1974).

The Judaeo-Christian views of suicide were an expression of the religious and political leaders, rather than explicitly from material in the Old and New Testament. The sanctity of life was the rationale given for condemnation by the Church. Religious systems were solidified into civic laws and punishment was imposed upon those with failed suicide attempts. Punishments included material loss, institutionalization and (ironically) death. In our times, suicide remains a taboo topic and a crime in some areas (Glick, 1974).

Historical depth psychological views of self-destruction

Hegel's rationalism and historicism. Nietzsche, arguably the first great depth psychologist (Kaufmann, 1992), addressed the phenomenon of self-destruction through the themes of self-deception, self-knowledge, and spirituality. Nietzsche's thinking can be understood, in part, as a reaction to the Hegelian tradition. I will begin by briefly delineating Hegel's rationalism and historicism, Nietzsche's response, and then its impact upon Freud's thinking and therapy.

For Hegel, reason and history were not mutually exclusive. Rather, Hegel asserted that reason, what he called *Geist*, and the slow unilinear unfolding of history, were virtually identical. Truth, though, was shrouded by the various contradictions found in the mind of the individual, different societies, and varying epochs of history. Reaching past the world of appearances meant overcoming these various contradictions. This process was a constituent part of the progression of history toward ultimate transcendence in the form of authentic self-consciousness known as the Absolute. Hegel equated the Absolute with God: "On its highest plane philosophy contemplates the concept of all concepts, the eternal absolute—the God who is worshipped in religion" (Hegel, 1817, sec. 17).

Congruent with his notion of the absolute, Hegel asserted that the whole always takes precedence over its particular individual parts. Human beings were instruments of *Geist*, the ordering force operating in nature and history. In this interconnectedness, Hegel viewed self-consciousness as existing only in so far as it was perceived through the other. Necessarily, then, an isolated self-consciousness was impossible. Nevertheless, Hegel implied that people do not settle for being self-conscious in an interdependent fashion, but attempt to minimize or ignore their dependence upon the other. They attempt to close the circle and become completely a self-contained entity, but in doing so, they ignore their facticity. This striving for one's sense of self-being can be thought of as egoism. Egoism sought, albeit unsuccessfully, the negation of the other in whom one's self-consciousness is grounded. Tension results from this struggle between being-for-another and being-for-oneself. Two polarizing modes of consciousness result from this tension, the Independent and the Dependent.

Hegel characterized Independent consciousness in terms of the Lord. The Lord cares only for only thing, freedom, and he world pay the price for this self-freedom, even his very life. Conversely, Hegel characterized the Dependent consciousness in terms of the Bondsman, whose fear of death ruled his life. The Lord sought to negate his dependence upon the Bondsman by devaluing and consuming the products of the Bondsman's labour. The Bondsman, though, was able to attain an authentic consciousness through labour. In this relationship the Lord, a rather lazy fellow, flees his dependence in the direction of what he is not, namely independent. The Bondsman, however, turns his attention to his essential character of dependency. Despite his seemingly lower status, Hegel viewed the Bondsman as having a more authentic existence because he does not deny his fear of death, dependence upon the other, and he gains these honest understandings through labor (Burston, 1997).

Nietzsche: self-destruction as collectivism. In sharp contrast to Hegel, Nietzsche insisted that collectivism of every kind undermines individual responsibility and fosters self-deception. He targeted organized religion, especially Christianity. Nietzsche's critiques of collectivism and Christianity were scathing:

> When we hear the ancient bells growling on a Sunday morning we ask ourselves: Is it really possible! This, for a Jew, crucified two thousand years ago, who said he was God's son? The proof for such a claim is lacking. Certainly the Christian religion is an antiquity projected into our times from remote prehistory; and the fact that the claim is believed—whereas one is otherwise so strict in examining pretensions—is perhaps the most ancient piece of this heritage. A god who begets children with a mortal woman; a sage who bids men work no more, have no more courts, but look for the signs of the impending end of the world; a justice that accepts the innocent as a vicarious sacrifice; someone who orders his disciples to drink his blood; prayers for miraculous interventions; sins perpetrated against a god, atoned for by a god; fear of a beyond to which death is the only portal; the form of the cross as a symbol in a time that no longer knows the function and ignominy of the cross—how ghoulishly all this touches us, as if from the tomb of a primeval past! Can one believe that such things are still believed? (Nietzsche, 1878, pp. 84–85)

Nietzsche contrasted two fundamental dimensions of human existence, the Dionysian and the Apollonian. The Greek god Dionysius represented the impulse to reverie, music, and intoxication. The Greek god Apollo represented the more restrained, thoughtful, and rational aspects of the self. Nietzsche asserted that self-knowledge arrived from the individual striving for power; specifically, in the individual willing the will to life. Further, self-knowledge arrived through understanding one's own Apollonian will and Dionysian drives; ignoring these constitutes self-deception. Self-knowledge sought the fusion of these two tendencies ultimately resulting in a life of controlled passion. Nietzsche noted that in a system such as Hegel's, reason becomes glorified and the passions completely ignored.

Nietzsche staunchly asserted that humans need to discover their own unique moral beliefs and that those beliefs should never be imposed from any collective. For Nietzsche individuation was motivated by the will to power, not collective or religious conviction. Self-knowledge as willing the will to power was the only knowledge that mattered to

Nietzsche: "The only reality is this: *The will of every centre of power to become stronger*—not self-preservation, but the desire to appropriate, to become master, to become more, to become stronger" (Nietzsche, 1886, p. 292). If taken to its limit, by going "beyond good and evil," an individual could reach his or her full potential and live a creative life (Nietzsche, 1886, p. 104).

In complete opposition to Hegel's theory of history as a slow, logical progression, Nietzsche believed that since the dawn of Christianity humankind began rapidly devolving. The reason for this retrogression was Christianity's perpetuation of *ressentiment*. But to understand ressentiment an understanding of Nietzsche's conception of Hegel's Independent and Dependent models of consciousness is necessary.

Though he never addressed Hegel specifically on this point, Nietzsche turned Hegel on his head by proposing that the Bondsman was more prone to self-deception and it was the Lord who was more genuine. Nietzsche believed that the Bondsman was deluding himself. In actuality his more 'authentic' way of being was just a way of coping with his existential impotence. Setting the Bondsman as authentic was to set the lowest standard possible; the Bondsman had no power, no will to power. The Bondsman could only level down and promote a bland humanity:

> We can see nothing today that wants to grow greater, we suspect that things will continue to go down, down, to become thinner, more good-natured, more prudent, more comfortable, more medio-cre, more indifferent ... there is no doubt that man is getting better all the time. (ibid., p. 44)

A greater threat than self-destructing humanity loomed with the Bondsman's way of being as a rule; ressentiment. The Bondsman twisted reality into a world where he possessed the true consciousness. This relatedness to the world, ressentiment, was a complex synthesis of feelings of envy and revenge, which are born of existential impotence and which get sublimated into compensatory fantasies of moral superiority. Nietzsche viewed collectives, especially Christianity, as exemplifying herd-consciousness, the apex of Bondsman consciousness, of ressentiment. Nietzsche said, "[I]t is contagious—on the utterly morbid soil of society it soon grows up luxuriously, now in the form of religion (Christianity) ... the vapours of such a poison-tree jungle out of putrefaction can poison *life* for years ahead" (ibid., p. 99).

Nietzsche's impact upon Freud. What was it that caused Freud to describe Nietzsche as the person who knew more about himself than anyone who ever had or would live? This is no small compliment considering that Freud was terribly suspicious of all philosophers. Freud said, "the degree of introspection achieved by Nietzsche had never been achieved by anyone, not is it likely to ever be reached again" (Kaufmann, 1992, pp. 911–912).

Thought Nietzsche carefully left his philosophy unnamed, he considered himself primarily a psychologist: "That a psychologist without equal speaks from my writing, is perhaps the first insight gained by a good reader" (Nietzsche, 1908, p. 266). Like Nietzsche, Freud sought to help the individual access and ultimately control his or her irrational drives in order to live a healthier, more balanced life; where there was id there ego shall be! Nietzsche actually preceded Freud by referring to the irrational drives, the Dionysian, as *das es* (*the id* or *the it*). Nietzsche also preceded Freud by developing the notion of sublimation as an explanation for art, cultural achievements, and dream content. For Dionysian impulses (what Freud called primary process) to be vented, they had to undergo modification (sublimation) vis-à-vis the Apollonian (what Freud called secondary process). It is also interesting to note that repression, a critical part of Freudian theory, also had its roots in Nietzsche, who said, "'I cannot have done this,' says my pride, remaining inexorable" (ibid., p. 89).

Despite their many similarities, one unbridgeable disparity was their views on determinism. Freud was an ardent determinist. Freud's deterministic notions may reflect his medical background, namely the influence of his University of Vienna professor, Theodore Meynert, who was a proponent of mechanistic determinism. Nietzsche said, "every man is a unique miracle"; "we are responsible to ourselves for our existence"; and "freedom makes us responsible for our characters just as artists are responsible for their creations" (Hergenhahn, 1997, p. 192). A second point of disagreement was their views on Darwin's theory in a chapter titled Anti-Darwin: "Species do not grow more perfect: the weaker dominate the stronger again and again the reason being they are the great majority" (Nietzsche, 1908, p. 87). Nietzsche's influence upon Freud's theory and therapy, though, greatly outweighs these differences.

Nietzsche's militant anti-religious perspective also echoed in the work of Freud. Freud when discussing religion said, "The whole thing is so patently infantile ... it is painful to think that the great majority of mortals will never be able to rise above this view of life" (Freud, 1930a, p. 9). Freudian theory and practice had no place for any deity of any kind since religious beliefs were considered to be nothing more than a projection; an infantile wish for a father. Religious beliefs were "the universal obsessional neurosis of humanity; like the obsessional neurosis of children" (ibid., p. 55). In passages Nietzsche could have written, Freud asserts:

> When a large number of people … try to obtain assurance of happiness and protection from suffering by a delusional transformation of reality, it acquires a special significance. The religions of humanity, too, must be classified as mass-delusions of this kind. Needless to say, no one who shares a delusion recognizes it as such. (ibid., p. 15)

Freud in *The Future of an Illusion* said that humankind created, rather reluctantly, society as a means of protecting themselves from nature and to more efficiently exploit nature's resources. There was a price to pay for the added advantages; with society came crime, conflicting needs and homicide. In a manner congruent with the "infantile prototype"; people developed the fantasy of a deity, a father figure that could control nature and protect themselves from themselves. Religious belief was a way for humans to contend with their impotence against their own destructive drives and nature's mighty fury. Freud further postulated that religious neurosis would be expected from the masses, since laziness and a lack of intelligence were also byproducts of civilization. Along with other factors, this process would provide the preconditions for widespread resentment. This sounds remarkably similar to Nietzsche's ressentiment: "It is to be expected that … underprivileged classes will envy the favoured ones their privileges and will do all they can to free themselves from their own surplus privation" (Freud, 1927c, p. 15).

Like Nietzsche, Freud was amazed with humankind's capacity for self-deception and self-destruction. Unlike Nietzsche, who emphasized the human will to self-destruction, Freud took self-destruction as innate to the psyche. The cornerstone of Freudian theory and therapy was the belief that humans possess irrational drives that can be sublimated through understanding them instead of using the all too common defense mechanisms of suppression and repression. Freud's defense mechanisms describe the ways in which the psyche deceives itself in order to maintain a positive sense of self. Suppression was a conscious self-censorship a person would use to avoid thoughts, fantasies, and memories that would cause him or herself to feel uncomfortable. Repression was similar to suppression but was an unconscious self-censorship, a double forgetting. Repression was especially important because it was found in almost all of the self-deceptive and self-damaging ways people would deal with their anxiety provoking drives.

Freud (1923b) referred to these animal-like drives in the same manner as Nietzsche before him by calling them *das es* (*the id* or *the it*). Freud said that countering the id was the moral *das uberich* (*the superego* or *the over-I*). The id and the superego, what Nietzsche would have called the Dionysian and Apollonian, were in conflict with each other. Unlike Nietzsche, Freud added a third component to the human psyche, *das ich* (*the ego* or *the I*); the conscious, rational decision-maker. Freud's therapy sought to bring to light with the patient the various ways drives would vent themselves by way of dreams and help the patient realize in what ways she or he was engaging in self-deceptive and maladaptive ways of being.

Freud: The vicissitudes of the death instinct. Freud did not conceive of the self-destructive impulse in purely societal-religious terms. Initially Freud understood the superego as that part of the psyche that represented one's introjected parental experience, both punitive and soothing. The essential relationship lay between the ego and the superego, which included the ego-ideal. Specifically, the superego (i.e. the unconscious conscious) consists of the ego-ideal and the daimonion. Freud used the term daimonion to denote the unconscious force within the human psyche, which aims at misery, unhappiness, and self-destruction (Bergler, 1955). Over time Freud revised this theory, since it could not account for the severity of self-destructiveness in the minds of his patients. The superego not only reflected the experience of parental castigation, but a transcending hostility in the mind.

In his work with melancholic patients Freud (1917e) discovered that their severe psychological self-attacks corresponded with ambivalent feelings towards a lost love-object. Over time, a division forms in the psyche of the melancholic: the ambivalence forms a centre, an ego that identifies with the idealized lost love-object. As this occurs, a second ego forms, one that reflects the primary hatred associated with the deserting object, introjected and thus bolstering the superego's malice against the self. The reprehension towards the abandoning object unconsciously and insidiously turns inward, attacking the ego, while another part of the mind identifies with the lost love. Freud astutely notes that this system though addictive and self-destructive, allows the melancholic to protect the love-object from hatred.

> The self-torments of melancholics, which are without doubt pleasurable, signify, just like the corresponding phenomenon in the obsessional neurosis, a gratification of sadistic tendencies and of hate, both of which relate to an object and in this way have both been turned round upon the self. In both disorders the sufferers usually succeed in the end in taking revenge, by the circuitous path of self-punishment, on the original objects and in tormenting them by means of the illness, having developed the latter so as to avoid the necessity of openly expressing their hostility against the loved ones. (Freud, 1917e, p. 172)

Freud revised even this theory, believing that it did not account for the profound sadism of superegos with some of his patients and their capacity to compulsively repeat self-destructive dynamics and behaviours.

In 1920 Freud presented the notion of a death drive (Thanatos) as a parallel to the life instinct (Eros) in the unconscious. The death drive worked in an aggressive fashion, destroying the labour of Eros. In addition to this, Freud proposed the existence of a primary mechanism in the ego, whose origins lie in that fragment of Thanatos that was not transformed by the life instinct into external aggression. With the failure of sadism being externalized, it continues to inhabit the internal world, leading to an alliance between a punishing superego and a masochistic ego. In this system, the masochistic ego both provokes and takes pleasure in the sadism of the superego, thereby establishing the repetition compulsion. In his later work, Freud described the compulsion to repeat as a force "defending itself by every possible means against recovery and which is absolutely resolved to hold on to illness and suffering" (Freud, 1937c, p. 242).

The repetition compulsion represents more than guilt and feelings of needing to be punished; its essence lies in the death-seeking element in all organic matter. Freud postulated *"an instinct is an urge inherent in organic life to restore an earlier state of things which the living entity has* been obligated to be abandon under the pressure of external disturbing forces ... *the aim of all life is death*" (italics in the original) (ibid., pp. 43–46). Freud describes the experience of the repetition compulsion as "being pursued by a malignant fate" and as being "possessed by some 'daemonic' power" (ibid., p. 23). In the same paragraph he uses the phrase "perpetual return of the same" synonymously with "repetition compulsion," which may suggest the influence of Nietzsche's seminal notion of Eternal Return. In any event, the repetition compulsion struck Freud so forcibly that he used it to differentiate primitive biological and evolutionary psychological processes from those operating under the influence of the pleasure-unpleasure principle (Fine & Moore, 1990). Clearly, for Freud the repetition compulsion represented the most extreme aim of the aggressive instinct, the degeneration of the psyche towards a zero point by attacking the life-principle of the psyche and destroying meaning. Freud was fascinated with the human capacity to destroy itself both psychologically as well as externally. Freud noted that while the impulses towards incest and cannibalism have been largely managed, the bloodlust of humans to kill other humans goes unabated. It is interesting to note that this insight was first published in 1927.

Klein: the destructive force within. Freud discovered the death instinct and gave it increasing importance over time. Klein took this a step further, making it the centrepiece of her psychology. Klein, a pioneer of child analysis, proffered the seminal notion of the paranoid–schizoid and depressive positions in psychological development. Kleinian psychology is heavily influenced by Freud, but differs in the emphasis it places on the death instinct and the belief in innate ambivalence within the psyche. For Klein, aggression is a projection of one's own inborn drive to self-destruction. A second difference with Freud can be found in Klein's belief that ego development is a function of ongoing projection and introjection of objects, not in stages of development. Third, Klein maintained that neuroses are rooted in developmental failures during the first year of life, specifically failures in passing through the depressive position. In Kleinian psychology, the depressive position takes the place of the Oedipus complex and her theory is one of object relations and is not founded upon instinct theory (Fine & Moore, 1990).

A fourth difference is found in Klein's (1946) insistence upon the importance of infantile ambivalence felt towards the mother and the breast. Much of the infant's difficulties lie in its fundamental ambivalence towards the breast, needing its sustenance, envying this need, and utilizing the breast for its own projections of the death instinct. The ambivalence Klein writes about is not a neutral ambivalence; it is inextricably tied to an innate force within the psyche to destroy itself. This internal impulse to self-destruction mobilizes primitive paranoid anxiety, which is managed through projective identification. By projective identification, Klein referred to the process whereby an object is identified with good or bad aspects of oneself. Klein asserted:

> Together with these harmful excrements, expelled in hatred, split-off parts of the ego are also projected onto the mother, or, as I would rather call it, into the mother. These excrements and bad parts of the self are not meant only to injure but also to control and take possession of the object. Insofar as the mother comes to contain the bad parts of the self, she is not felt to be a separate individual but is felt to be *the* bad self. Much of the hatred against parts of the self is not directed towards the mother. This leads to a particular form of identification, which establishes the prototype of an aggressive object relation. I suggest for these processes the term "projective identification". (Klein, 1946, p. 8)

The infant, born into the paranoid-schizoid position, must work through its fear and mistrust of the breast towards the discovery that what it both hates and loves is the same object. Along with fundamental ambivalence, Klein postulated that the infant's internal world is beset with phantasies of vivid violence and destruction. Phantasies are psychic representations of destructive, libidinal instincts and are the impetus for the formation of defenses. This was of such importance to Klein, that she considered the analyst's role to be that of interpreting unconscious phantasies, not defenses. For Kleinians, it is of paramount importance that the infant (patient) gradually internalize a primarily benevolent image of the mother (analyst), since this contributes to the patient's capacity for reparation, mourning, and loving. Although defined as self-destruction, the psychological mechanisms that activate suicidal and para-suicidal behaviors may be paradoxically attempts at creative and restorative acts (Cooper, 1990). Though thoroughly influenced by Freud, Klein differed in her placement of the self-destructive impulse, the death instinct, as the central focus of her psychology.

Bion: minus K (-K). The earliest and most primitive manifestation of K occurs in the relationship between mother and infant. According to Bion (1994), the domain to which he refers by the letter K is that of getting to know aspects of psychic and external reality. Like Klein before him, Bion believed that one's psyche contends with love and hate from infancy. He referred to L, H, and K as emotional links between the infant's developing mind and its primary object, the mother. The opposite of K, minus K (-K), is not tantamount to not having knowledge of something—it is an anti-knowing state of mind resulting primarily from a prevalence of envy. Envy, in this sense, is a result of a budding counter-adaptive set of processes, which evacuate meaning and replace thought with a primitive quasi-morality, a super-ego that pronounces an envious assertion of superiority lacking morality. The influence of envy in K results in an annulling kind of relationship (i.e. container-contained) wherein disconnection and morality replace meaning and valuation. Someone under the sway of –K functioning tends to experience the therapist's endeavour to understand him or her as depletion with the purpose of reducing the patient's own worth.

Minus K functioning occasionally denotes the onset of psychosis but more frequently results in defensive organization wherein the patient's real personality comes to be experienced as being little more than a husk or shell. What is signified by –K is an envious negative function, which operates in K as an agent of the death instinct, attacking links of thought and affect, substituting them with a false yet powerful command. When –K is active, the destructive narcissistic aspect of the psyche is experienced as though it were the central ego, but an ego which nonetheless pronounces stringently the efficacy of non-knowing.

The overall effect of the –K field can be seen as the combination of a destruction of meaning and a commitment to a thought-less morality. Bion's contributions differ from classical psychoanalysis, which views psychosis as id and its instinctual irruptions, driven by an excessive primary process that drowns the ego. Bion, rather, conceives of a defective or deficient alpha function that is less able to receive and digest the raw sensory data of emotional experiences (a.k.a. beta elements). This unsound alpha function allows for a vulnerability to psychosis by virtue of not being able to mitigate the impact of beta elements, the thoughts without a thinker, and the raw primary data of experience. In Bionian psychology, Freud's conceptions of the id impulses bespeak a failing alpha function that is increasingly incapable of digesting internal and external experience.

Odier: destructive magical thinking. Odier (1956) believed that all psychopathology could be traced back to early trauma. According to Odier, trauma at an early age causes anxiety in later life and results in one aspect of the ego remaining fixed at a regressed state. The regressed aspect of the ego lacks the capacity to relate to other aspects of the mind and is thus incapable of developing. Odier suggested that such trauma could be explained in terms of the helpless infant not receiving its mother's affection and protection. Such trauma leads the infant to experience transient episodes of extreme insecurity. Interestingly, Odier asserted that such traumatic experiences are somewhat dormant in the infant's psyche and are reawakened in later childhood when the person is faced with situations similar to the traumatic experiences. In such situations, the regressed aspect of the ego returns, bringing with it the unmanageable affect of the original trauma. The regressed ego also brings with it the terror and suspense of early infancy and the magical thinking characteristic of that age. Odier notes that anxiety begins to dominate as a vicious self-attacking dynamic emerges.

The thoughts, bodily sensation, and feelings associated with the infantile trauma are so horrible and ineffable that they themselves become traumatic experiences. Though the trauma lies in the past, the infantile magical thinking endures, carrying with it a sense of imminent death or catastrophe. The person becomes repeatedly traumatized, not due to external circumstances but due to the terrifying internal world.

> There is an irreducible opposition between affective prelogic and the logic of relationships; between the magic laws of the former and the implacable rational laws of the latter, laws which are too hard or painful for the abandonees to live by … . All compromises are faulty and give rise to a series of traumas and disappointments. Our patients constantly confront us with the harshness of this antithesis and betray their powerlessness to overcome it. (Odier, 1956, p. 301–302)

Odier (1956) astutely notes that the stress placed on the psyche causes it to oscillate between self-destruction and self-protection. Destructive magical thinking, the logical extension of infantile traumatic experience, and positive magical thinking, cast to protect and promote an idealized version of one's childhood. Associated with polarized magical thinking are its personifications, great beings, punishing or protecting, neglecting or nourishing. The victim of trauma thus becomes caught in a self-destructive cycle, haunted by fantasies of impending catastrophe, entrapped in positive and negative magical thinking, with an ego too wounded to contend with reality.

Contemporary psychoanalytic perspectives. Self-destructiveness is a popular topic amongst contemporary psychoanalytic theorists and therapists (e.g. Achte, 1983; Blumstein, 1959; Girard, 1977; Gronseth, 1998; Jacobs, 1965; Kernberg, 1983; Khantzian, 1989; Levinson, 1986; Orbach, 1996; Poeldinger, W. 1989; Quinodoz, 1989; Smith, 1996; Wainrib, 1996). Fairbairn (1941) describes mental development in terms of object-relationships and asserts that the various psychological illnesses do not differ in regressions to different stages of libidinal development, but in the use of different techniques during the second stage of development, the Stage of Transition or quasi-independence. During his first stage, the Stage of infantile dependence, the infant is totally dependent upon the mother (breast), and the relationship is initially characterized by non-ambivalence. Invariably, experiences of frustration and rejection by the mother lead to the schizoid position, during which the infant's ego splits into three aspects. Two aspects, the libidinal ego and anti-libidinal ego (the internal saboteur) become connected to two antithetical notions of breast, the accepting (exciting) object and the rejected (rejecting) object respectively. The third part of the infant's ego becomes the central ego to the super-ego. As the internal saboteur works against psychological growth, a corresponding false-self develops to contend with external reality. Schizophrenia and depression are in Fairbairn's view aetiologically related to disturbances during the Stage of Infantile Dependence. The goal of analysis then is to help the patient differentiate him or herself from internal bad objects, and to restore libidinal balance in the psyche.

Similar to Jung, Fairbairn uses religious metaphors when describing the personality's struggles with anti-growth forces in the mind. Fairbairn (1981) writes:

> It is to the realm of these bad objects ... rather than the realm of the super-ego that the ultimate origin of all psychopathological developments is to be traced; for it may be said of all psychoneurotic and psychotic patients that, if a True Mass is being celebrated in the chancel, a Black Mass is being celebrated in the crypt. It becomes evident, accordingly, that the psychotherapist is the true successor to

the exorcist, and that he is concerned, not only with "the forgiveness of sins', but also with 'the casting out of devils". (p. 70)

The notion of an internal saboteur is continued in the work of Guntrip (1969, 1971), who conceives of an anti-libidinal ego. This anti-libidinal ego reflects internalized bad parental objects, which are intolerant of the child's dependency needs. This ego is disgusted with its vulnerability and dependency upon rejecting parents and, over time, the personality becomes charged with internal hostility, hating to acknowledge the interpersonal needs we all share.

Golomb (1996) continues the theme of internalized negative parental objects, focusing specifically on the developmental life of a child with narcissistic parents. She notes that the hallmark characteristic of narcissistic parents is their unwavering belief that their needs and ways of being are of paramount importance. Children of narcissistic parents are left with the belief that they do not have the right to exist. Since the child is criticized, ignored, and manipulated from the earliest formative years, a negative introject forms in the mind, an inner reflection of the sadistic parent. This introject not only internally tortures the child, but sets the unreachable conditions that need to be met to earn parental approval. Aside from the other critical self-debasing qualities of the introject, there is rage at the child for not meeting the unattainably high demands of the parent. The result is that "the negative introject acts from within as a punishing enemy. It creates such severe anxiety that it paralyzes, produces such powerful guilt that the individual feels totally worthless. Depression, guilt, and inner conflict tear the person apart" (Golomb, 1996, p. 98). Golomb believes that this self-destructiveness of the psyche manifests in a number of ways: physical self-loathing, overeating, anorexia, bulimia, and addiction.

Eigen (1996) examines Freud's thought concerning the "force against recovery," Klein's idea of "a destructive force within," and Bion's notion of "a force that goes on working after it destroys existence, time and space" (Eigen, 1996, pp. xvii–xxi). He expands upon these contributions, offering the notion of psychic deadness. There are various kinds of psychic deadness, which pervade otherwise rich and meaningful lives. In other cases, people have "pockets of deadness that are relatively constant" and, in more severe cases, the "sense of deadness is pervasive. They describe themselves as zombies, the walking dead, empty and unable to feel" (ibid., p. 3). Focusing on the affective tone of the analytic relationship, Eigen works to discover what the psyche needs to open in order to let the deadness go. Eigen does not believe that the goal of therapy is necessarily aliveness:

> Aliveness ... can be a defense. There are individuals who play up their sense of aliveness at the expense of other people or other areas of experience. They may use an aspect of aliveness to ward off other aspects, or some grouping of alive feelings to ward off duller ones. (Eigen, 2001, p. 48)

Rather, Eigen sees therapy as a session-by-session experimental working of the aliveness-deadness between the analyst and patient. Eigen urges therapists to become aware of the aliveness-deadness capacity in themselves as well as their patients, so as to cultivate an analytic space for these capacities to develop together.

For Freud, motivation was a function of presumed drives and the force they could assert against the ego. In contrast, Grotstein seeks to introduce its dialectic, "the experience of the awesome force of powerlessness, of defect, of nothingness, of zero-ness ... an implosive centripetal pull into the void" (Grotstein, 1990). Moreover, Grotstein introduces the dialectic of nothingness and meaninglessness; in contrast to the traditional psychoanalytic tenet that drives are authoritative, biological forces, which impose themselves upon the psyche for satisfaction.

The experience of nothingness and meaninglessness can be distinguished from the more adaptive ability to experience nothingness and emptiness as a possibility of relating to future positive realizations. Secondly, the calamitous experience of nothingness and emptiness stands in disparity to no-thingness, the "non-substance or anti-matter, accumulated in the 'black hole' as entropy and whose seeming purpose is to fill the vacuum of 'nothingness' with its 'no-thingness', the latter designating the paradox of 'non-substantial substance'" (Grotstein, 1990, p. 269). Nothingness within a container tends to be healthier; the container affords a meaningful context. Nothingness without a container constellates the black hole and invokes the partnership of no-thingness in order to occupy it.

It is important to note that by unpacking the meaning of the psychic black hole in terms of meaninglessness and nothingness, Grotstein (1990) is not simply discussing one form of psychopathology amongst others. Rather, he understands the black hole phenomenon to designate (a) the most dreaded aspects of human experience and (b) primal fears of organismic anxiety and annihilation anxiety. Within this framework, maladaptive psychological behaviours are understood as defenses, varying in degree but not kind, against succumbing to the gravity of the black hole. The apparent bizarreness of psychotic behavior, for example, can be understood as an attempt, albeit extreme, to ward off experiencing the black hole. All neurotic and psychotic conditions bespeak the presence of the black hole and the underlying inherent and acquired phantasies, or mythemes, of predator-prey, persecutory anxiety.

Borrowing widely from Spitz, Sartre, Harlow, Winnicott, Balint, Tustin, and others, Grotstein developed his concept of psychological black holes. Grotstein (1990) believes that the black hole represents a more profound meaning of the death instinct; the death instinct foresees psychological collapse and moves in to arbitrate it. The encounter with the black hole is ostensibly hampered by defenses, which are released by traumatic events. These defenses and strategies of the personality reflect a spectrum of self-regulation, gap management, which seeks to nullify the extreme psychological catastrophe of toppling into the black hole. However, for Grotstein the black hole phenomenon denotes "not merely the psychotic catastrophe and the cataclysmic repression, implosion, and disorganization which heralds its onset, but it also represents the altered imploding, distorting, and perversely reconstructing laws of the new, perverse (and reverse) domain of madness" (Grotstein, 1990, p. 388).

Grotstein (1990) sees his conception of the black hole as being similar to Bion's (1994) notion of transformations in hallucinosis, where in the process of the alpha function is reversed. This means that the psychotic's world is a mirror image of the sane person's world. "In some ways one can picture psychosis, especially in its more sane forms, as sanity in reverse … a mock up of it, a sinister … bizarre imitation of it" (ibid., p. 387). Utilizing the metaphor of the black hole it is easy to see how the black quality of the black hole symbolizes the death of meaningfulness of the self and objects (i.e. decathexis). The hole stands for the awareness of a profound nothingness which, for the psychotic, now contains the disowned parts of his/her psyche, the "ghosts of abandoned meaning," the "beta prime elements," "bizarre objects," and "nameless dread" that Bion postulated (Bion, 1994, p. 257). Encountering the 'black hole' represents not only psychotic collapse, but also sanity gone awry and perverted into an alternate reality, the realm of madness. The black hole is bipartite in nature; it represents the ultimate psychological disaster as well as the experience of one having forfeited one's self of self-efficacy, a sense of being damned. Grotstein sees the development of the black hole to be largely due to early attachment and developmental failures, similar to Klein and Bion.

When writing about his work with less decompensated patients, Grotstein (1987) talks about a schism in the personality between an unmoving immature aspect of the self and a progressive self. He notes that the underdeveloped self often attacks the work of the progressive self to draw attention to itself. Grotstein also understands some psychological maladies in terms of addictive processes. "I have seen patients suffering from chronic depressive illness who seemed addicted to their depression and who … reveal that they were experiencing their depression as a split-off persona that was fighting for its own life" (Grotstein, 1987, p. 330). In such cases, Grotstein notes that there is a dependence upon the self-destructive processes at work. The metaphor he uses is an internal "Madonna of Sorrows" or an "autistic 'mothering self'" who soothes the underdeveloped self in the midst of disappointing childhood objects (ibid., p. 325).

Jung: trauma and the splintering of the psyche

Despite their numerous personal, professional, and theoretical differences, the self-attacking aspect of the psyche struck Jung, like it did Freud. Through analyzing the dreams of his patients Jung came to realize that through trauma, the psyche fragments, splintering into separate pieces. These fragments of consciousness coalesce around specific archaic, archetypal patterns that tend to be dyadic and can be understood as sub-personalities within the overall personality. Jung referred to these sub-personalities as complexes. A complex is a collection of images and ideas clustered around a common archetypal theme, and characterized by a common feeling-tone. When a complex becomes constellated, it contributes or even unconsciously dominates behaviour. Jung wrote, "complexes behave like independent beings" (Jung, 1934, p. 121) and noted that "there is no difference in principle between a fragmentary personality and a complex … complexes are splinter psyches" (ibid., p. 97). In trauma, typically one part of the psyche regresses while another part develops too quickly. The progressed ego, though well adapted to the everyday world, may take on a false quality and serves as a caretaker to the regressed ego.

Another way the psyche contends with trauma is with dissociation. The adaptive aspect of dissociation is that it allows the overall personality to continue functioning, while compartmentalizing the traumatic experience into different parts of the mind and body, especially the unconscious. Thoughts, affects, sensations, memories and mental imagery are not allowed to integrate, thus leading to an overall discontinuous sense of self. The progressed ego's everyday functionality comes at the price of internal strife. The fragmented and compartmentalized aspects of the mind do not disappear but haunt the internal world. Jung is clear that a traumatic complex causes dissociation in the psyche. Since the complex is not under control of the will, it is largely autonomous. Its autonomy lies in its power to reveal itself independently of the will and in its ability to force itself tyrannically upon the conscious mind. Jung describes the quality of affect as explosive and pouncing on the conscious mind like a wild animal.

Unbearable experience shocks the psyche and brings tension, which invariably leads to dissociation.

> The tension leads to conflict, the conflict leads to attempts at mutual repression, and if one of the opposing forces is successfully repressed a dissociation ensues, a splitting of the personality, a disunion with oneself. The stage is then set for neurosis. The acts that follow ... are based partly on the repressed opposite which, instead of working as an equilibrating force, has an obstructive effect, thus hindering the possibility of further progress. (ibid., p. 60)

Jung was struck by the fact that it mattered little if the trauma was real or imagined. He noted the aggression inherent in dissociation, noting that it involved one part of the psyche attacking another part. Specifically, Jung believed that trauma held the self-destructive potential to actually split an archetype at within the psyche.

As already stated, Jung believed that an archetype inhabited the centre of a complex. Jung differentiated archetypes-as-such from archetypal images, themes, affects and behaviours. Archetypes cannot be directly known or encountered and are impersonal, primordial structuring patterns of psychological life. For Jung, archetypes do not vary across time or culture, and they constitute the essential basis for instinctual behaviours and primordial images. For example, at the centre of a mother complex lies the mother archetype. The archetypes are bipolar in nature with one pole representing bodily instincts and affects and the other representing a spiritual factor, which are constituted by mental images. Psyche designates a third factor that works to combine both poles of the archetype—instinct,affect and spirit—and to produce unconscious fantasies as well as psychological meaningfulness. Optimally, the polarities are balanced and given symbolic meaning by the psyche, which in turn animates, heals, and ameliorates the ego.

The archetypes are bipolar in nature and as a whole they constitute the collective unconscious:

> [T]he archetypes are the unconscious images of the instincts themselves ... The hypothesis of the collective unconscious is, therefore, no more daring than to assume there are instincts ... The question is simply this: are there or are there not unconscious universal forms of this kind? If they exist, then there is a region of the psyche which one can call the collective unconscious. (ibid., pp. 91–92)

Stated briefly, complexes inhabit the personal unconscious and archetypes the collective unconscious. Corresponding to the ego of the personal psyche, Jung described the archetype of the Self. The Self represents the wholeness and the fullest potential and is the unifying principle of the psyche. Jung wrote that the Self does not only comprise the centre, but the circumference that embraces both the conscious and the unconscious. The Self seeks realization in the ego, but the ego cannot possibly accommodate the vastness of the Self in its entirety. As such, the relationship between the ego and the Self never ends, as the personality continues to individuate. With trauma, however, a destructive process begins in the psyche.

Trauma disrupts the balance within the psyche and in extreme cases the archetype itself may become split. In such cases, one polarity of the archetype attacks the other thereby (1) cutting off the ego's source of nourishment and flexibility, (2) evoking powerful affects, and (3) destroying the mind's capacity to translate such affects into symbolic meaning. The now traumatized mind loses much of its ability to contend with external and emotional reality and thus mobilizes counter-adaptive defenses, such as dissociation, which serves only to continue the vicious cycle of psychological self-attack. As already mentioned, the ego may become split in this process, with one part developing too quickly and the other remaining fixed at an early developmental stage. During this process, the individuating personality becomes replaced by a "survival Self," as psychological energy is mobilized to tend to the underdeveloped, fixed aspect of the ego (Kalshed, 1996, p. 97). Thus the victim of trauma is left with a dissociating ego that is less and less capable of symbolizing internal and external reality and is increasingly dependent upon primitive defenses. These defenses help the person to avoid unbearable affect, avoid re-experiencing the original trauma, and to maintain a survival ego. Over time, though, this system only furthers the depletion of psychological aliveness and insidiously consumes the mind. Jung likened this process to being possessed by a spirit or of losing one's own soul. Even instances of harming others are ultimately self-destructive acts. Discussing a patient who had murdered, Jung writes: "She was a murderess, but on top of that she had also murdered herself. For one who commits such a crime destroys his own soul. The murderer has already passed sentence on himself" (Jung, 1934, p. 123).

Contemporary Jungian perspectives

Stein (1967) saw self-destructiveness as a function of primitive defenses, what he called archetypal defenses. Such primitive defenses operate on a more primordial level than the ego and act similarly to the body's immune system. Specifically, Stein hypothesized that the primitive Self attacks aspects of the ego that it mistakes as psychic invaders. Like the immune system, the health of the psyche depends upon its ability to differentiate elements of the self from not-self and to eliminate anything designated as not-self. Interestingly, Stein does not delineate how the Self comes to mistakenly attack not-self elements, but he asserts that the health of the psyche depends largely upon the relationship between the infant's expectations and its experience of reality. In any event, Stein views self-destructiveness as occurring when archetypal defenses mistake elements of the psyche as not-self and then works to destroy those elements.

Fordham (1974) continued the metaphor of an immune system gone awry and placed great importance upon the earliest days of the infant's life. For Fordham, archetypal defenses are at work prior to ego development. Psychological stimuli experienced by the infant as being harmful, such as parental projections, are defended against through the autistic defense of withdrawal. Given enough traumatic experience, the archetypal defenses will facilitate complete withdrawal, cutting off the infant from reality. Now severed from reality, the infant experiences contact with reality as alien, potentially harmful, and thus attacks that experience. This evokes anti-life, anti-individuation forces in the psyche that work against change and growth in psychotherapy.

Neumann describes the infant's world as being utterly reliant upon the mother and being "helpless, empty and dependent, a defenseless part-existence; the mother is life, nourishment, shelter, security, and comfort in compensation for all negative experiences" (Neumann, 1990, p. 74). Neumann characterizes what happens when this relationship is disrupted:

> A reversal of the paradise situation is characterized by the partial or total reversal of the natural situation of the primal relationship. It is attended by hunger, pain, emptiness, cold helplessness, utter loneliness, loss of all security and shelteredness; it is headlong fall into the forsakenness and fear of the bottomless void. (ibid., p. 74)

Born in complete physical, psychological, and existential dependence, the psyche becomes increasingly vacuous and self-imploding without the necessary maternal care. Under such circumstances, the part aspect of the initial part-existence is exaggerated rather than the life-promoting element, leaving the psyche impoverished.

Woodman continues the theme of the empty psyche although she deals primarily with female eating disorders and addictive processes. She writes, "I think addictive personalities are unconsciously committed to self-destruction ... They have enormous energy, which they put blinders on, and just go for something. They deny their inner emptiness so they run as fast as they can to escape" (Woodman, 1993, p. 121). Woodman addressed the compulsivity used by some to deny their impulse to destruction.

Asper links self-destruction to emptiness, symptomatic of a narcissistically damaged personality. Asper understands the injured individual's inability to recognize and use symbols as well as stressing the importance of the mother-infant relationship. "Ultimately the emptiness signifies the inactive positive mother archetype, the absence of a good mother in the past and the lack of motherly caring for oneself in the present" (Asper, 1993, p. 219). Asper notes that the *modus operandi* of narcissistically wounded people is to avoid at all costs feelings associated with early trauma:

> Narcissistically damaged analysands prefer to cling for a long time to the negative transference. It protects them from the fear of plunging into emptiness and depression, guards against the repetition of traumatic events, and shields them from the fear both of loving and being loved. (ibid., pp. 206–207)

Narcissistically damaged, the mother archetype remains inactive, leaving the personality not only impoverished, but also clinging to maladaptive ways of being in interpersonal relationships, which are ultimately destructive to the psyche.

It is interesting to note that Estes does not view the self-destructive element of the mind as being associated with traumatic experience or developmental failures. For her, the "innate predator" simply "is what it is" (Estes, 1992, p. 46). Estes describes the innate predator as a "murderous antagonist born in each of us" that works to deaden experience and whose "sole assignment is to attempt to turn all crossroads into closed roads" (ibid., p. 40). She finds the drive to death to be an organic part of nature and archetypal reality: "The force called Death is one of the two magnetic forks of the wild. If one learns to name the dualities, one will eventually bump right up against the bald skull of ... Death" (ibid., p. 129).

Kalsched (1996) illuminated the way in which early trauma constellates in an extremely self-destructive cycle. Kalsched agreed with Jung that dissociation was the primary defense employed by the psyche of the traumatized individual. He also postulated that this dissociation involved a great amount of aggression. This aggression often involved an active attack by one part of the psyche on other parts. Kalsched noted that dreams involving a diabolic trickster figure often appeared in patients who had experienced early trauma. Kalsched offers his notion of the psyche's self-care system and likens this to the body's immune system. Like the body's immune system the self-care system works dynamically, identifying elements of me and not-me, differentiating healthy from pathological elements, and accepting those elements deemed life promoting. Strong affects or bodily sensations reaching the psyche must be digested symbolically, transformed into language and incorporated in the developing child's self. Not-me and affective elements recognized as negative are projected outwardly with a great deal of aggression and simultaneously (inwardly) repressed. With traumatic experience, the self-care system goes awry. Abused children tend to lack the ability to mobilize energy to expel pathological elements of experience. Unable to hate the loved parent, the child identifies with the aggressor, seeing the perpetrator as good and hating itself and its own needs.

Given enough traumatic experience, the psyche's self-care system can become like an autoimmune disease:

> [T]he self-care system carries out its functions by actively attacking what it takes to be "foreign" or "dangerous" elements. Vulnerable parts of the self's experience in reality are seen as just such "dangerous" elements and are attacked accordingly. These attacks serve to undermine the hope in real object-relations and to drive the patient more deeply into fantasy. And just as the immune system can be tricked into attacking the very life it is trying to protect ... so the self-care system can turn into a "self-destruct system" which turns the inner world into a nightmare of persecution and self-attack. (Kalshed, 1996, p. 24)

Though remarkably self-destructive, the traumatized self-care system works to save the personal spirit of the individual. It should be noted that Kalshed differentiates himself, in part, by integrating numerous and historically conflicting theoretical perspectives such as classical Jungian theory and classical psychoanalysis, as well as contemporary object relations.

Existential-phenomenological psychology on self-destruction

Existential-phenomenological psychology differs from the depth psychological approaches already discussed. "Existential-phenomenological psychology is an evolving approach to the treatment of mental disorder characterized by a close relationship to philosophical reflection on the human condition" (Burston, 1997). He goes on to write, "it is not easy to give a simple definition of what this approach is, because the major thinkers in this tradition tend to emphasize their differences, rather than their common ground" (ibid.). I would add to this that the existential-phenomenological approach is generally unknown in the United States, with its followers residing mostly in Europe. The result of these problems is that existential-phenomenological psychology remains either generally unknown, or seen as a "patchwork of contradictory philosophical opinions, rather than a diverse, dynamic but essentially unified field" (ibid., p. 1). Despite the great diversity in thought, existential-phenomenological therapists tend to agree on a few fundamental beliefs. One area of agreement is their belief that depth psychology relies too heavily upon supposed psychological drives and constructs rather than focusing on the patient's experience. Another area of agreement is the belief that analysts practicing depth psychology tend to leave their philosophical presuppositions unexamined. Despite differences, existential-phenomenological psychology shares depth psychology's interest in the psyche's capacity for self-destruction.

Binswanger: Self-Destruction as existential possibility. Perhaps the most vivid portrayal of existential self-destruction is Binswanger's (1958) *The Case of Ellen West.* Although controversial (e.g. Lester, 1972), what makes this an especially rich case is the availability of Ellen's poetry, diary entries, personal notes, historical records of two past psychoanalytic treatments, as well as the notes from the sanatorium where she was under Binswanger's care.

Ellen experienced little and infrequent relief from the anti-life aspect of herself. At nine months old Ellen refused milk, then her development is marked by "variability of mood" (Binswanger, 1958). By the age of 17, her poetry reflects the anti-existence element budding in her life:

> In one, entitled "Kiss Me Dead," the sun sinks into the ocean life a ball of fire, a dripping mist drops over sea and beach, and a pain comes over her: "Is there no rescue anymore?" She calls upon the cold, grim Sea-King to come to her, take her into his arms in ardent love-lust, and kiss her to death. (ibid., p. 239)

By the time she was 21 years old, she had developed a tremendous fear of getting fat. This marked the beginning of her life-long struggle with anorexia, although this diagnosis was not used during that time. Her poetry became continuously darker, reflecting corpse-like imagery and a profound sense of self-loathing. Ellen's condition continued to deteriorate. During a trip overseas when she was 25 years old, she was diagnosed with Baesedow syndrome, known today as Grave's disease. The doctor recommended bed rest and Ellen remained in bed for six weeks. She gained weight but lost it again shortly thereafter. In another poem, she referred to herself as a "cracked" and a "worthless husk" (ibid., p. 247). She married her cousin during her 26th year. By her 29th year, she continued to not eat, had a miscarriage, and was using large amounts of laxatives. Two psychoanalytic treatment episodes followed and there were multiple suicide attempts. Around this time she wrote, "In my innermost being nothing changes, the torment remains the same … I long to be violated—*and indeed I do violence to myself every hour.* Thus I have reached my goal" (italics in the original) (ibid., p. 255). At the advice of her internist, she discontinued her analysis and was admitted to Kreuzlingen Sanatorium, where she came under Binswanger's care.

After roughly two months, despite all efforts, Ellen's health did not improve at the sanatorium and she wrote, "I am perishing in the struggle against my nature" (ibid., p. 264). Ellen's level of suicidal ideation continued to increase. Binswanger consulted with Professor E. Bleuler and it was decided that, given Ellen's suicidal ideation, she was no longer appropriate for the general ward. The alternatives were that she leave with her husband and invariably kill herself or be placed in a more secure part of the facility. Consultations followed and eventually the doctors gave in to Ellen's demand to be discharged. Binswanger noted that her weight upon discharge was the same as when she entered the sanatorium, 104 pounds.

Ellen's condition worsened for two days and on her third day at home she experienced a radical transformation. On this morning she ate butter and sugar, and by lunch was satiated for the first time in 13 years. She took a walk with her husband, read poems and appeared to be in a great mood. She wrote many letters, the last one being to a patient to whom she grew attached. During the evening she took poison and was dead by the morning. "She looked as she had never looked in life—calm and happy and peaceful" (ibid., p. 267).

Ellen lived a divided existence, caught somewhere between the tomb world (degenerating body and society) and the ephemeral world (purity and goodness). Ellen attempted to ignore the tomb world, taking flight into the good and pure, and succeeding only in reducing her body to a skeleton. In giving thought to her death, Binswanger asserted, "We must neither tolerate nor disapprove of the suicide of Ellen West, nor trivialize it with medical or psychoanalytic explanations, nor dramatize it with ethical or religious judgments" (ibid., p. 292). Rather, from an existential analytic stance, the "suicide

of Ellen West was an 'arbitrary act' as well as a 'necessary event'"
(ibid., p. 295). Instead of utilizing psychological theory to explain
Ellen, Binswanger stuck closely to describing her existence, which
manifested itself so clearly in her poetry.

> I'd like to die just as the birdling does
> That splits his throat in highest jubilation;
> And not to live as the worm on earth lives on,
> Becoming old and ugly, dull and dumb!
> No, feel for once how forces kindle,
> And wildly be consumed in my own fire. (ibid., p. 246)

Perhaps what makes this case study especially thought provoking was
not Ellen's diagnoses, but her ability to so beautifully articulate her
existential condition and Binswanger's choice to listen to her profound
longing for non-being.

R. D. Laing: Understanding schizophrenic behaviour in a psychotic society.
Laing was a renegade phenomenologist, a highly original and controversial thinker, a spokesman for the marginalized. He was an aggressive
and indefatigable advocate for the mentally ill. His ideas and techniques
were, at times, highly unorthodox and this has added to the general
confusion that exists about him today. A. Laing (1996), Burston (1996b)
and Clay (1996) have attempted to clarify some of this confusion. Perhaps the most common and completely inaccurate criticisms leveled at
him are: (1) Laing dismissed biological factors in mental illness, (2) he
blamed everything on society, (3) he glamourized mental illness. Laing,
a well-trained medical doctor, certainly understood biology and did not
deny its presence in psychological illness. He critiqued the ubiquity of
psychiatry and its dispassionate nature, reifying relatedness with the
mentally ill. Laing accepted that biology was involved in psychopathology, yet did not feel that it was in every instance the solely causative
factor. Let us listen to Laing's own words on this score. Laing said that
schizophrenics do "need treatment" and was clear that he has

> never idealized mental suffering, or romanticized despair,
> dissolution, torture or terror. I have never said that parents or
> families or society "cause" mental illness, genetically or environ-
> mentally. I have never denied the existence of patterns of mind
> and conduct that are excruciating. I have never called myself an

anti-psychiatrist and have disclaimed the term from when first my friend and colleague, David Cooper, introduced it. (Clay, 1996, pp. 224–225)

More importantly, Laing understood people through relationship rather than through formal psychiatric diagnosis and treatment plans. In short, Laing saw his patients as unique, ineffable, and not problems to be corrected purely through medical management. The second and third misunderstandings can be simply dispelled by recalling Laing's assertion that insanity was often a maladaptive way of adapting to an impossible situation. So, it was important to examine the way the individual contends with reality as well as investigating the societal, familial, and medical elements that have contributed to the situation. The importance of examining the person's entire existential situatedness lies in the fact that one or more of these factors may not only trigger, but also facilitate the psyche's self-destruction.

Explicitly and implicitly the theme of self-destruction was found from his early work on how the mind disintegrates into madness, to his later work focusing on larger socio-cultural issues. In Laing's *The Divided Self* he strives to make 'insane' experience intelligible in terms of the patient's agency and societal context. Its purpose was "to make madness and the process of going mad comprehensible" (Laing, The Divided Self, p. 9). In contrast to the approaches of formal psychiatry and psychopathology, Laing sought an existential-phenomenological account of schizoid and schizophrenic people. Laing utilized the existential-phenomenological method to characterize the nature of the schizoid's and schizophrenic's experience of self and world. He wanted to describe the person's unique experience of being-in-the-world. Like others, (Szasz, 1970, 1974) Laing rejected the disease model of mental illness and expressed open hostility to exclusively genetic or organic explanations of mental disorder:

> It seems extraordinary that whereas the physical and biological sciences if it-processes have generally won the day … an authentic science of persons has hardly got started by reason of the inveterate tendency to depersonalize or reify persons. People who experience themselves as automata … are rightly regarded as crazy. Yet why do we not regard a theory that seeks to transmute persons into automata or animals as equally crazy? (Laing, 1990, p. 23)

Laing did not argue that schizoidness and schizophrenia were in no way biological. He disputed the assumed meaninglessness behind behaviors characteristic of these disorders. When examined phenomenologically, these apparent meaningless behaviours could be understood as the individual's attempts to contend with frightening existential conditions. These behaviours were not symptoms of a medical disease; they were defenses to ontological insecurity. Laing's and Esterson's work with people whom had been labeled schizophrenic led him to believe that their symptomatic behaviour may be understood as a defensive "strategy that a person invents in order to live in an unlivable situation" (Laing & Esterson, 1970, p. 186).

Laing (1990) asserted that the anxiety his patients defended against could be explained in terms of ontological insecurity; an insecurity about the individual's very being. Ontologically insecure individuals experience a split that extends into two relational dimensions: there is a disruption between self and world and within the personality itself. On one level, the individual experiences a split between self and others who become viewed as being potentially dangerous to self-autonomy. On another level, the split reflects a fragmentation such that a rent is experienced between aspects of the self, which have been accepted, and others that appear alien. Laing used the term schizoid to refer to an individual whose totality of experience is split in these two ways. The term schizoid was not restricted only to extreme forms of psychosis because most people experience some degree of schizoid splitness at times in their lives. The defensive behaviour of normal—that is ontologically secure—individuals differs only in degree but not kind, from that of ontologically insecure people.

The ontologically secure individual has temporal continuity and a sense of being with others who are real, continuous, and alive. The ontologically insecure individual is "pre-occupied with preserving rather than gratifying himself: the ordinary circumstances of living threaten his *low threshold* of security" (italics in the original) (Laing, 1990, p. 42). The ontologically insecure person feels dead, unreal, and is hardly able to differentiate self from the world. One's identity and autonomy are always in question. The schizoid/schizophrenic person also lacks temporal continuity, cohesiveness, and tends to have the experience of being partially divorced from the body. The ontologically insecure person becomes closed off from the world and begins to wither. This person "is developing a microcosmos within himself; but of course, this autistic, private, intra-individual 'world' is not a feasible substitute for the only world, the shared world" (Laing, 1990, pp. 74–75). Normal people dissociate from their bodies under extreme stress yet return once their crisis has passed. In contrast, the schizoid person experiences him or herself as unembodied and under the threat on a day-to-day basis thus never fully inhabiting his or her body (Burston, 1995).

The unembodied self becomes the onlooker to the actions of the body. Existing as separate from the shared world, the schizoid person "becomes more and more empty and volatized. The 'self' whose relatedness to reality is already tenuous becomes more and more engaged in phastastic relationships with its own phantom images" (ibid., p. 85). The ontologically insecure individual, having a fragmentary sense of self, questions being on three levels: existence (that one is), essence (what one is) and identity (who one is). With such insecurities, interpersonal and intrapersonal relations may be interpreted as threatening and to be avoided in order to preserve one's being (Spinelli, 1989).

The schizoid individual aims to divide private psychological life from what others can see. One can live in a seemingly normal way but may be schizoid. Laing (1990) presented the case of a man whose original complaint was that he could never have intercourse with his wife but only with his own image of her. This man's body had sexual relations with his wifes body but, during these acts, his mental self only served as an observer to what his body was doing. His wife was unaware that he was never fully present during these acts. A schizoid's actions may seem from another person's point of view normal while the schizoid feels he is not really participating. The schizoid's self, feeling disembodied, is free to engage in any fantasy she or he wishes yet this "freedom" becomes tortured by a sense of self-duplicity.

Laing presents three fears experienced by the ontologically insecure individual. These fears are not separate but ultimately linked in that they reflect anxieties about living. The fear, *engulfment*, is characterized by anxiety related to feelings of being taken over by some alien external force; engulfment is the "extreme duress of the person who finds himself under a compulsion to take on the characteristics of a personality ... alien to his own" (Laing, 1990, p. 58). The second fear, *implosion*, is similar to that of engulfment in that it too is a fear of being taken over. The difference is that one experiencing the fear of implosion feels the terror of emptiness. The ontologically insecure person experiences "the world as liable at any moment ... [to] crash in and obliterate all identity as a gas will rush in and obliterate a vacuum" (ibid., p. 45). People experiencing the third fear, *petrification*, are afraid of being depersonalized by others: "The people in focus here both feel themselves as depersonalized and tend to depersonalize others. By destroying, in his own eyes, the other person as a person, he robs the other of his power to crush him" (ibid., pp. 46–48). In the schizoid's attempts at self-defense we see the beginnings of what could evolve into schizophrenia. In defending against these fears, the schizoid may act in strange yet meaningful ways. Few mental health professionals who seek to help schizoids or schizophrenics view any of their actions as meaningful. Interpreting their behaviours as symptoms of illness, they succeed in further alienating the ontologically insecure person from his or her shared world.

Laing viewed his goal as one of discovering the hidden meanings behind the behaviour of the psychologically disturbed individual. He noted that the term therapist is derived from *theraps*, a Greek word meaning *attendant* (Evans, 1976, p. 80). "Rather than intervene, dispute the individual's claims or numb the fears with medication, Laing observed and provided … empathy so that he could eventually reconstruct the individual's situation and understand the fears being defended against" (ibid., p. 141). No matter how meaningless, odd, or self-destructive the schizophrenic's behaviours may be, they are attempts at self-survival.

What is the aetiology of the schizoid split? In a speech given at the Rochester International Conference on Schizophrenia, Laing (1967) said, "Everyone who has made a close study of the families of schizophrenics appears to agree that much, if not all, the apparent irrationality of the individual finds its rationality in the family context" (Kirsner, 1976, p. 120). In *The Divided Self*, Laing posits that the loss of the mother, at an early age, threatens the child with the loss of self. The mother is more than a person the child can see; she is also a person who sees the child. Thus, a necessary part in the development of the self is the experience of being viewed in the eyes of the mother. The emergence of the self, or a *being-for-itself*, is largely a function of the child's growing awareness of being an object for the mother's intentional activities—feeding, bathing, holding, and so forth. Laing implied that being-for-oneself and being-for-another are intertwined and if the two become confused, disturbance may result (Burston, 1997).

Laing emphasized early infancy as an important period for establishing later schizoid and schizophrenic personalities. Physical birth and existential birth do not necessarily occur at the same moment. For normal development, it is important that the child and mother recognize one another as individual persons at a relatively early stage. "It is out of the earliest loving bonds with the mother that the infant develops the beginnings of a being-for-itself" (Laing, 1990, p. 190). The mothers of schizophrenics often do not allow for this development and the baby comes to experience the world as not feasible to be in. Laing suggested that although the first years of life with the mother are important, the relationships with father and siblings should not be ignored with regard to schizophrenogenesis.

In a family the growing child learns what actions are acceptable and unacceptable based upon the reactions of family members. For Laing, the term good tends to be tantamount with compliance to the family's wishes and the term bad refers to acts that defy the family's code of conduct. The family reinforces good acts and punishes the child for bad acts. A problem arises when the family fails to distinguish between the child's actions and the child's being. Once a child's self is directly linked to actions, parents' attempts to punish or deny the child's actions become translated as threats to his or her being. Under the terms of this equation, schizoid fragmentation is almost always inevitable. In order to maintain the self, the child adopts a variety of fragmentary defenses. The child generalizes such experiences, believing that they will be repeated in the world. The family serves not only as the source of positive dimensions of the self but also serves to define 'bad' aspects of the self, which must not be allowed expression in thought or behaviour. To express them, the child believes, would threaten family relationships and his or her being.

Laing made use of Bateson's double-bind communications theory of the origins of schizophrenia (Kirsner, 1976). Bateson et al. (1956) described schizophrenia as a state of mind, the origins of which lie in impossible demands placed by parents, particularly the mother, on children. A double-bind communication sends two mutually incompatible messages despite how the child responds when she or he is wrong:

> A young man who had fairly well recovered from an acute schizo-phrenic episode was visited in the hospital by his mother. He was glad to see her and impulsively put his arm around her shoulder whereupon she stiffened. He withdrew his arm and she asked, "Don't you love me anymore?" He then blushed and she said,

"Dear, you must not be so easily embarrassed and afraid of your feelings." The patient was able to stay with her only a few minutes more and following her departure he assaulted an aide. (Bateson; Jackson; Haley & Weakland, 1956, p. 251)

In extremely schizogenic homes, anything the child does in accordance with the wished of one parent simultaneously displeases the other. The child becomes caught up in an impossible task in which there is no chance of success. The eleven families Laing and Esterson describe in *Sanity, Madness and the Family* (1970) fit this pattern. In each family, the parents viewed raising children as an insult, which challenged their opportunity to make demands upon the child that expressed the uneasy truce of their marriage. "These patterns ... become very complicated networks of slow and tormented human strangulation" (Friedenberg, 1977, p. 18).

Laing (1990) believed that the basis for severely schizoid individuals rested in their lack of any continuing development towards an autonomous identity. Schizoid people experience thwarted development due to their inability to incorporate the bad self into their identity. In childhood, the bad self comes to be perceived as an overwhelming threat to the self so they try to be good all the time in an attempt to seek approval from their families. The power to prescribe what is good lies entirely in the hands of family members and the family's love is removed when the child is bad. The child in this situation then draws the conclusion she or he must never behave badly; yet such a goal is impossible since the bad self cannot simply dissipate. The bad self may assert its presence verbally and behaviourally in outbursts that the good self can neither explain nor control. These outbursts tend to be interpreted by the family as symptoms of constitutional insanity. Laing's examination of the family structure of schizoid individuals revealed some common elements. One common feature of these families was a particular intolerance of 'bad' behaviour in their children. The families might act as if the individual simply did not exist when the 'bad' self emerged, as was the case with Peter in *The Divided Self*.

Laing's (1990) analysis of the schizoid split examines the existential conditions of the ontologically insecure individual. These dimensions tend to be ignored in psychiatric theories since they are mostly concerned with organic explanations of mental disorder. Laing did not summarily dismiss organic factors in insanity but was primarily concerned with utilizing the appropriate context to elucidate such phenomena. Laing writes:

> If I am disturbed, I may be disturbed spiritually, intellectually, emotional, and physically. Many neurologists, once they find something, as they say "organic," they think that's it ... Until chemists and geneticists see the focus within the *context*, and realize there is an interplay between chemistry and social interaction, we can't develop the theoretical speculation at a pure science level we must have. (Spinelli, 1989, p. 146)

An organic perspective is not the only appropriate context to examine schizoidness and schizophrenia due to the fact that who is deemed insane is socially determined. In *The Divided Self* reality is presented as a shared world of a common sense. Reality is what sane people take it to be and sanity is defined in terms of common consent. By common consent, the real world of sane individuals is taken as preferable to the private world of the schizoid. In cases where there is a radical scission between whom you think I am and who you think I am, one of us will be labeled as insane. This is a principle of interpersonal phenomenology, that insanity is a function of an "experiential disjuncture of some kind, of a rupture between one's being 'for oneself' and being 'for another'." Laing believed that one who attempts to construct an identity that is detached from communal meanings is truly, existentially mad and not merely the victim of collective fear (Burston, 1997, p. 69).

Laing argued that schizoids and schizophrenics need guidance and support to help them resolve, among other things, their split between being-for-oneself and being-for-another in order to encourage a more authentic identity. Laing believed that in exploring the created meanings of experience and exposing the existential anxieties that provide the context for the mental disorder, the apparent meaningless and self-destructive behaviour may be better understood, alleviated, and possibly even eliminated.

Where *The Divided Self* emphasizes how one self-destructs into psychological illness, *The Politics of Experience* (Laing, 1967) focuses on the socio-cultural dimensions of psychopathology. In this book Laing examines the alienation and technological objectification of humanity so prevalent in contemporary culture. He focuses on the reification of mentally ill persons not only by society, but also by the very mental health system purporting to help such patients. For Laing, socialization by family, education, religion, and so forth, creates a culture where people are either driven insane, adopt a quasi-sanity, or have human possibilities wrested from them. The result of such socialization is estrangement from ourselves internally as well as from others. What is worse, Laing says, is that this process is so commonplace it is forgotten about or complacently accepted as a part of life. Following Freud, he asserts that the alienating, reifying and leveling down of socialization leaves the ordinary person "a shriveled, desiccated fragment of what a person can be" (Laing, 1967, p. 26). Noting how often 'normal' humanity destroys its own kind, Laing notes that behaviour is a function of experience. Hence, if our experience is destroyed, our behaviour will become destructive. If this occurs, then we will invariably lose our ownmost identities and preclude the possibility of authentic relatedness.

Laing (1988) understands alienation in terms of humanity's capacity to destroy itself, although he abandons psychoanalytic concepts of self-destruction (e.g. death instinct), relying instead on a social phenomenological narrative. Despite this, he does acknowledge his indebtedness to Freud, Winnicott, and Bion. Repeatedly and passionately, Laing interrogates the question of whether something like mental health is even possible. Instead, he contrasts the normally alienated person from the schizoid or schizophrenic. What is normal about the normally alienated person is not psychological health as much as being just as much alienated as everyone else. Laing argues that such commonplace alienation, combined with complacency and forgetfulness, creates the illusion that the normal alienated person is sane. Commonness is not necessarily a testament to health; it may bespeak a person's ability to be like everyone else in average everydayness.

In contrast to the normal alienated person Laing presents schizophrenic alienation. He is clear that schizophrenia is a diagnosis given by some people to other people. This does not mean that the labeled patient is experiencing a pathological process of purely organic origins. He reiterates that schizophrenia is a way of adapting to an impossible situation. Moreover, adapting to a dysfunctional society is dangerous. Not denying the biological aspects of schizophrenia, Laing writes, "Our society may itself have become biologically dysfunctional, and some forms of schizophrenic alienation from the alienation of society may have a sociobiological function" (Laing, 1988, p. 120). In a vein similar to Bion, Laing asserts that the result of alienation is a self-destructive attack upon experience, which becomes generalized:

> We are born into a world where alienation awaits us. We are potentially men, but are in an alienated state, and this state is not simply a natural system. Alienation as our present destiny is achieved only by outrageous violence perpetrated by human beings on human beings ... our contemporary violation of ourselves. (Laing, 1967, p. 16)

Although Laing did not make this link, the etymology of the word alienation reveals the meanings, "Delirium: derangement of mental faculties; insanity." (Webster's, 1956, p. 43). Alienation is not simply being without the presence of others; it is the pathogenic attack upon relational-experiential reality.

What is worse, Laing says, is that such destructiveness is veiled as love: "We are effectively destroying ourselves by violence masquerading as love" (Laing, 1967, p. 58). The first socialization begins with the family in childhood. Laing writes:

> Long before a thermonuclear war can come about, we have to lay waste our own sanity. We begin with the children. It is imperative to catch them in time. Without the most thorough and rapid brainwashing their dirty minds would see through our dirty tricks. Children are not yet fools, but we shall turn them into imbeciles like ourselves, with high I.Q's if possible. (ibid., p. 58)

and

> The family's function is to repress Eros; to induce a false consciousness of security; to deny death by avoiding life; to cut off transcendence; to believe in God, not to experience the Void; to create ... one-dimensional man; to promote respect, conformity, obedience; to con children out of play; to induce a fear of failure; to promote a respect for work; to promote a respect for "respectability." (ibid., p. 65)

While the tone of *Politics of Experience* is sardonic, he offers a way to see through the hopelessness. He states that the psychopathology seen in patients stems from their own self-destructiveness, the tyrannical shadow of psychiatry, and the alienation of average everydayness.

Genuine sanity, according to Laing (1967), necessitates (1) the dissolution of the normal ego, that false self-adjusted to alienating social reality, (2) the openness to 'inner' archetypal mediators of divine power, (3) and eventually the birth of a new ego in the service of the divine. Laing was clear that psychopathology is not always biological condemnation to a terror-ridden existence. It may also represent a new emerging consciousness, a new way of knowing and being in the world. When this is the case, then it is a travesty to stall the death-rebirth process with medication, electroconvulsive therapy, and other such means. At worse, these interventions may actually preclude the possibility of the patient's recovery. The self-destructiveness of humanity fuelled Laing's animosity and disdain as well as his tireless need to liberate and warn others of societal truths. Laing concludes his book, "If I could turn you on, if I could drive you from your wretched mind, if I could tell you, I would let you know" (ibid., p. 190).

Summary. This chapter began by examining attitudes towards self-destruction in early Greco-Roman and Judaeo-Christian times. Greco-Roman attitudes varied greatly from the Platonic reproach to the Stoic belief in the individual's right to choose. Later Romans tended to view suicide as the right of those who could provide a rationale for such action. Judaism consistently held that suicide was always immoral since it is a violation of life's sanctity. While the community comforted the families with suicide victims, the deceased was shunned. Early Christians subjected themselves to ghastly violence, believing that they were following in Christ's footsteps and expediting their entry into heaven. Over time, the Church realized that it was losing some of its best and bravest members and quickly moved to demonize suicide. The early Christians went further than their Jewish counterparts on this score, asserting that suicide victims suffered eternal damnation. Suicide victims were denied proper Christian burial rites.

This chapter went on to explore the theme of self-destruction as it emerged specifically in depth and existential-phenomenological psychology. Nietzsche influenced much of Freud's metapsychology. Nietzsche's thought, in turn, can be viewed as a reaction to Hegel's rationalism and historicism. Both thinkers looked to the negative effects inherent in mass socialization and organized religion. Freud went further, offering the seminal notion of Thanatos, the death instinct. The notion of the death drive was amplified by many of Freud's followers, most notably Klein and Bion. This concept has undergone revisions over the years, yet remains a popular topic among psychoanalysts such as Eigen and Grotstein. Jungians focus less on the death drive and more on the effects trauma has upon the unfolding psyche. They also view this in terms of larger archetypal dynamics at work. Some classical Jungians such as Estes see self-destruction as simply a part of life while other more developmentally oriented Jungians, such as Kalshed, integrate numerous theoretical views. Existential-phenomenological therapists tend to view self-destruction as an essential possibility given to existence. Without it, we would not be truly free. With few exceptions (e.g. Menninger), they do not see suicide as being necessarily immoral. Rather, it may represent the first existentially responsible decision a person makes. Almost all the aforementioned theorists developed their ideas in praise of or in reaction to Freud's conception of Thanatos.

CHAPTER FOUR

Bion: the ghosts of abandoned meaning and formless destructiveness

B ion's investigations into the self-destructive capacity of the mind reveal that the very process of breaking-down can break down. He (1965) writes of a force that continues wreaking internal damage after destroying time, space, and existence. It is this phenomenon that caused Freud to comment, "For the moment we must bow to the superiority of the forces against which we see our efforts come to nothing" (Freud, 1937a, p. 243). The psychoanalytic way of 'seeing' phenomena contains a trace of self-destructiveness. In a letter written to Lou Andreas-Salomé, Freud (1972) writes, "I have to blind myself artificially in order to focus … on one dark spot" (ibid., p. 45). Oedipus blinded himself. Freud seems, at least implicitly, to understand that insight invariably is brought at the price of self-destruction. This is reminiscent of *harmartia*, the tragic flaw that has been used to explain Oedipus' actions ever since Aristotle's *Poetics*. Gaining self-knowledge at the price of self-destruction is tragedy and this is vindicated and universalized at the end of the Oedipus myth, where blindness becomes the porthole to ineffable, mysterious sight (Spitz, 1988).

When discussing O, the ultimate truth or reality, Bion said, "O is the spot that must be illuminated by blindness" (Bion, 1970, p. 88).

The opposite of the truth, obviously, is the lie, and the more the ego seeks to pathologically alter the unconscious, the more it becomes disingenuous. The lie (-K) is the truth working in reverse, a negative faith. An extreme demoralization occurs with a catastrophe that impedes movement from the paranoid-schizoid to the depressive position. Such a catastrophe reflects failures in the holding and containing environments. The catastrophe lunges the infant into the real, O, without having enough maternal digestion of its experience. Being orphaned from O, the personality aligns with the only alternative and unholy saviour, -K (Grotstein, 1997). Unable to develop ways of contending with internal and external reality, the infant withdraws, forfeiting future developmental growth. Before going further about the 'forces against which we see our efforts come to nothing' it is necessary to examine Bion's theory of thinking. Central to Bionian psychoanalysis is his notion of the internal thinking apparatus. First I will focus on Bion's understanding of how such an apparatus develops. Next I will focus on how the destruction of such an apparatus occurs as an active taking apart rather than a passive falling apart.

The development of the "Thinking apparatus"

Bion (1994) understands thoughts as existing prior to thinking and that thinking has to be developed as a method or apparatus for contending with thoughts. Given this, much emphasis is placed on whether the patient is evading, modifying, or being used to evade or manipulate something else. If thoughts are experienced as being "accretion of stimuli then they may be similar to or identical with beta-elements," and are subsequently evacuated from the personality via projective identification (Bion, 1994, p. 84). Communication, then, can be seen as serving the function of expressing one's emotional reality for the purposes of engaging in relationships. Conversely, communication can be used to evacuate unmanageable affects and un-integrated parts of the mind. This is will be expanded upon later.

The most basic element of the thinking apparatus is the alpha-function. The alpha-function refers to the mind's rudimentary ability to transform the raw data of sensory experience into digestible elements (alpha-elements) that can be dreamt, thought about, and integrated. The alpha-function is the gatekeeper that takes internal and external experiential data and controls its entrance into pre-consciousness.

I have suggested, the theory, namely, of a container-barrier owing its existence to the proliferation of alpha-elements by alpha-function and serving the function of a membrane which by the nature of its composition and permeability separates mental phenomena into two groups one of which performs the functions of consciousness and the other the functions of unconsciousness. (Bion, 1994, pp. 21–22)

Bion used the term beta-elements to describe experiential data that is not transformed by the alpha-function. By virtue of being undigested, beta-elements are not capable of being recollected or dreamt about. Beta-elements are experienced as things-in-themselves and tend to be evacuated through projective identification. They continue to be attached to the original stimuli and lack the symbolic structure that would facilitate their emergence into thoughts. Moreover, without the metabolization of the alpha-function, thoughts entering into consciousness lack internal mooring and cannot provide a correct account of internal experience.

The origins of the alpha-function are found in the infant's earliest experiences with its mother (or mothering parent). The infant projects much of its experience and unmanageable affects and the mother works to soften these affects by her expressions and attentiveness. The infant is thus able to re-introject the softened affects and experiences. With repeated interactions over time, the infant is capable of internalizing this, the alpha-function. The infant's ability to self-soothe corresponds to the alpha-function's linking of affect with symbols. The mother's capacity for reverie is critical to this entire process. If she is incapable of reverie and love for the infant, not only will she be unable to digest its experience, but also this fact will be communicated to the infant.

When functioning optimally, the alpha-function allows sensory data to enter pre-consciousness while repressing primitive impulses. When the alpha-function is in some way defective undigested beta-elements flood the conscious mind. In its worst condition, the alpha-function can actually be reversed. Rather than having sense perceptions being digested by the alpha-function, the contact barrier itself is destroyed. Working in reverse the alpha-function produces alpha-elements denuded of all qualities that separate them from beta-elements. These elements are then continuously projected, thus producing the beta-screen. In this self-destructing system, one encounters bizarre internal objects and beta-elements. Bion notes that the bizarre object and the beta-element are not separate entities. Rather, the bizarre object is beta-element plus fragmented bits of ego and superego. Moreover, the reversal of the alpha-function does damage to the structure associated with the alpha-function, the ego. From this perspective, all psychopathology is essentially disordered thought differing in degree but not kind.

Bion (1964) provides a way of understanding the development of affects, cognitions, and the multitude of ways they interact in health as well as illness. His theory of thinking maintains that thinking is fundamentally interpersonal. For a healthy alpha-function to develop in the infant there has to be another person to take in the infant's experience, soften it, and return it to the infant in a digestible form. The lack of such a person may produce a partially developed or damaged alpha-function. Without an operational alpha-function the psyche is subject to innate biological drives as well as an accumulation of beta-elements.

Bion (1964/went further to suggest that the infant has an aspect of its personality that is self-reflective. Prior to Kohut, Bion asserted that the process of self-empathy is a function of the empathy it receives from the environment. The importance and uniqueness of this idea can be found in the emphasis he placed on insight. Empathy, while extremely important, is not the only determining factor in Bion's system. With increased severity of mental illness, self-reflective consciousness decreases and vice versa. Corresponding to an increase in consciousness is one's ability to link together thoughts and emotions and thus be able to contend with reality, external and internal. The alpha-function is largely responsible for the barrier between consciousness and unconsciousness, and works to separate psychological phenomena such from images found in dreams and waking thoughts. Linked with such psychological phenomena is a sense of temporal continuity. In psychotics waking thoughts seem more like dream material and personality disordered persons have difficulty separating past from present experiences. What these experiences have in common are failures, in varying degrees, of the contact-barrier that is the basis for a healthy engagement with reality. When an excess of beta-elements are produced, a beta-screen forms, creating a deficient barrier between unconsciousness and consciousness. The beta-screen differs from the alpha-screen in that it lacks the healthy repressive function, leaving consciousness vulnerable to the psychotic part of the personality. The overall effect is a blurring between the distinctions of inner and outer, past and present, self and other, real and unreal. With the breakdown of the mind, the person is left with a decreasing capacity for symbolization and increasing confrontations with bizarre objects.

Thinking is born of the infant's earliest dialectical relationship with the mother. A critical dynamic of this relationship is the infant's projections and the digestion of these projections through maternal reverie. Under optimal circumstances the infant internalizes this function and is capable of self-soothing and relating to internal and external reality. Another crucial dynamic in this process is the personality's movements between the paranoid-schizoid and depressive positions. Klein postulated that the paranoid-schizoid position dominates in early psychological life and represents the infant's first attempts to contend with its own innate destructiveness (Fine & Moore, 1990). This position is characterized by the infant splitting its own ego, as well as its object-representations, into parts experienced as good and bad. The infant projects its destructiveness and rage upon the bad objects, which are experienced as persecutory. Of course, the more splitting and projecting into bad objects, the more they are experienced as persecutory. The more persecution there is, the more paranoid the infant is and will withdraw. The paranoid-schizoid position is the infant's first attempt to contend with the death drive. Failure to progress to the next position, the depressive position, explains most primitive mental disorders as well as obsessional neuroses. Failure to progress into the depressive position may also lead to the bad persecutory objects solidifying into a punitive superego.

The depressive position is attained when the infant realizes that what is hated and loved is the same object; the mother. This process tends to be repeated in analysis. With this realization the infant (or analysand) experiences ambivalence and concern to protect the object from his or her own hatred and works to make reparation. Klein believed this developmental process occurs with all infants, despite the quality of mothering. Further, the outcome of this process shapes all later development (Fine & Moore, 1990).

Confusion about this theory, fueled undoubtedly by Klein using the term depressive to demarcate health, arises: are depressed people in the depressive position? No, depressive illnesses bespeak a failure to leave the paranoid-schizoid position. What is depressive about the depressive position is the realization of one's splitting and projecting, and the healthy, not manic, wish to make reparation. Although I am not aware of Klein describing it in these terms, this seems to be like the process an addict goes through in recovery: recognizing one's responsibility in the problem, discarding rigid defenses such as denial, not blaming other bad people or situations, and making reparation where it is due. In the depressive position, one is able to tolerate frustration and anxiety, which facilitates symbolization and thinking (Fine & Moore, 1990).

This process in its entirety can only take place with the participation of maternal transformation. Under optimal circumstances the infant develops an alpha-function and the capacity for thinking emerges. Preconceptions become conceptions, which become concepts in the mind. For a thought to become a concept the infant must tolerate frustration and realize that conceptions differ little in quality. Discrepancies produce frustration that challenges the child to develop increasingly abstract ways to contend with reality. Failure to develop categories of understanding reality leaves one's ability to learn from experience damaged or non-existent. In this situation only information that fits rigid primitive categories is accepted, and concepts thatare more complex produce frustration and remain ignored. As already stated, thinking requires symbolization and a thinking apparatus, which is internalized from the mother. Over time, this capacity develops within the infant and it becomes capable of thinking thoughts charged with affect. If these capacities are not developed, psychopathology may ensue, as the infant mobilizes the primitive defenses of splitting and projection.

While Bion employs Klein's notion of the paranoid-schizoid and depressive positions, he differs from her in some important ways. Klein and her followers tend to understand the paranoid-schizoid position as being inherently pathological. It seems that the measure of health is the degree to which one abandons the paranoid-schizoid position and embraces the depressive position. Bion and his followers emphasize the importance of the interaction between these two positions as one goes through life. From a Bionain perspective these two positions are dialectical; the depressive position allows for the development of thoughts, but there would be nothing to become thoughts without the paranoid-schizoid position. A certain amount of paranoid-schizoid anxiety about the unknown enhances our capacity to experience a wider expanse of affective thinking. Moreover, the paranoid-schizoid position is the soil from which the depressive position emerges. Bion did not intend to place a higher position on the depressive position than on the paranoid-schizoid position. Bion's understanding of the relationship between the paranoid-schizoid and depressive positions is similar to Nietzsche's understanding of the relationship between the Dionysian and Apollonian aspects of life. The Dionysian may be an appropriate personification for the paranoid-schizoid position: the wild, creative will to reverie, the passions enflamed by contact with the unknown. A failure to move beyond the Dionysian may lead to madness and addiction. However, much of the literature about Dionysius suggests that it is essential to have the right kind of relationship with him, which means recognizing who he is and establishing an appropriate relatedness. For example in Euripides' *The Bacchae* (1997) Pentheus foolishly orders Dionyius to be taken into custody. Dionysius responds:

> I go,
> Though not to suffer, since that cannot be.
> But Dionysius whom you outrage by your acts,
> who you deny is god, will call you to account.
> When you set chains on me, you manacle the god.

> (Plecha et al., 1997)

On the other hand, the Apollonian, like the depressive position, represents the will to engage contentiously in reality, and fixation in this area leads to stagnation of thought and rigidness. The ability to integrate these two elements affords an ability to think about passions and, ultimately, to live a balanced life. In any event Bion believed that the splintering of rigid depressive qualities facilitates growth and openness to new symbolic and affective experience.

True, mature thinking, for Bion (1964), is not the rote memorization of facts and is not present in the individual cogitating mind. Thinking is essentially interpersonal. Further, this work attempts to more fully engage the person in the struggles of reality and serves the furtherance of life. The more damage there is to the development of this process, the less able one is to digest internal and external experience. In the most disturbed individuals the thinking apparatus is not simply absent; rather, a self-destructive process begins and continues its work even after time, space, and existence have been annihilated.

Primitive mental states and the damaged alpha-function

Bion (1964) postulated that every personality has neurotic and psychotic potentialities. Clearly, with a psychotic person, the psychotic part of the personality holds sway. In character and personality disordered individuals the healthy aspect of the ego is able to manage the psychotic part with some success. In relatively healthy individuals the psychotic part of the personality tends to be managed by the neurotic aspect or repressed. Repressed in this sense is healthy and does not reflect patho- logical splitting. Where disintegration of the self threatens borderline and psychotics, self-esteem is threatened in neurotic and narcissistic individuals. The difference being is that narcissistic and neurotic persons are better able to contain the psychotic parts of their minds. For Bion a failure in the containing function of the mind explains almost all psy- chopathology, since without this thinking, itself would be damaged.

The essential characteristic of the alpha-function is empathy and the failure of early maternal empathic attunement results in pathology of varying degrees. As already mentioned, it is the maternal contain- ment of the infant's unmanageable internal experience that affords the infant's ability to introject this relationship and develop the capacity for thought. The infant-mother dyad, the thinking couple, forms the basis for one's own ability to reflect on experience. Injury to this dynamic and the corresponding damage to thinking are expressed by Bion:

> If the patient cannot "think" with his thoughts, that is to say that he has thoughts but lacks the apparatus of "thinking" which enables him to use his thoughts, to think them as it were, the first result is an intensification of frustration because thought that should make it "possible for the mental apparatus to support increased tension during a delay in the process of discharge" is lacking. The steps taken by the patient to rid himself of the objects, the proto-thoughts or thought which to him are inseparable from frustration, have then led him to precisely the pass that he wished to avoid, namely to tension and frustration unalleviated by the capacity for thought. (Bion, 1994, pp. 84–85)

The damage is twofold. There is an absence of alpha-elements and the lack of a function to use alpha-elements. The personality is left with- out digested experience and with undigested facts. The accumulation of beta-elements leads to an insidious breakdown of the mind as the person struggles to find an object into which parts of the personality can be projected. Essentially, this is a breakdown in the internalized thinking couple. The primitively mentally disordered person cannot take in experience into an internal alpha-function for digestion. Rather, a vicious cycle ensues where one is increasingly unable to contend with internal and external reality. The increasing desperateness for a way to manage experience *itself* increases the need for what is lacking in the mind. Failure of containment, then, is the hallmark feature of mental illness. Without the maternal mind to process experience, the infant is left with its primitive terror of non-existence. Being left with such experience itself threatens the development of a thinking apparatus to assimilate experience. This developmental catastrophe haunts the personality, lingering near the surface of consciousness, to be awakened at any time by frustrating encounters.

When the alpha-function is working in reverse, beta-elements saturate the mind. In some instances, inanimate objects become the container for projected fragments of the mind and thus are experienced as being animate. With the destruction of affective thinking, the distinction between animate and inanimate becomes blurred. Autistic objects become mentalized or charged with the beta-elements of one's mind. Ogden understands this phenomenon in terms of the autistic-contiguous position, which is prior to the paranoid-schizoid position and represents the earliest stage of development. He writes, "The autistic-contiguous position is associated with the most primitive mode of attributing meaning to experience. It is a psychological organization in which the experience of self is based upon the ordering of sensory experience, particularly sensation at the skin surface" (Ogden, 1994, p. 14). Annihilation anxiety, for Ogden, represents the collapse of the sense of bounded sensory experience that is the foundation of the experience of a cohesive sense of self. In this primitive state the individual creates a secondary skin formation. The autistic-contiguous position is comprised primarily of autistic shapes and autistic objects. Autistic shapes are experienced as objects devoid of any sense of thingness as well as bodily substances such as saliva, faeces, and urine. Autistic objects, on the other hand, are experienced as hard, with an edginess that affords a sense of having a protective husk. One can imagine the experience of an autistic object as the sense of having a metal key pressed in the palm of one's hand (ibid., 1994). Autistic objects are associated with primitive fantasies and fears, and encompass pure sensory experience. Conversely, none of things seem linked consciously with the object, which implies a lack of an associative matrix. Such a lack bespeaks a callow, rigid, and fixed, yet exceedingly powerful meaning, which the object contains. In addition, autistic objects mediate a sense of safety and a bodily continuous sense of self. Autistic objects are devoid of the socially determined shared and evolving meanings that are present during healthy communication between infant and mother. Even words can be used as autistic objects. Operating in this way, autistic objects are not communicative in nature, but tend to be used defensively. Ogden describes a case where the patient, Ms. L., whose words were "not carriers of symbolic meaning; they were elements in the cotton wool insulation that she wove around herself" in the analysis (Ogden, 1994, p. 147). Autistic objects fail to have a communicative function, yet they mediate the earliest, most primitive actions. Grotstein (2002) disagrees with Ogden's notion of an autistic-contiguous position. The autistic-contiguous phenomena that Ogden discusses, in Grotstein's view, is characteristic of the early paranoid-schizoid position and does not need to be viewed as a distinct position. There seems to be little disagreement, however, about the existence of such phenomena and the destructive roles they play in later life.

The psychotic mind: the alpha-function in reverse

Under healthy conditions, the infant develops a gap or capacity for tolerating the no-thing during the early phases of paranoid-schizoid development. In psychosis this capacity does not develop. This mental space serves as the foundation for the capacity for thought. With the aforementioned maternal reverie and the corresponding ability to contain the infant's mind, the infant develops the concept of no breast, no object. This space is where the absent object can be recreated and repaired in fantasy. The infant's ability to represent or repair an object necessarily means that it has begun thinking. Having the space for representing an absent object also allows the infant to develop links between good and bad, self and other, inner and outer. The result is the ability to experience whole objects that reflect reality. This process, in reverse, is excessive splitting, projecting, and evacuating the mind to rid itself of having to contend with negative affects and conflicting aspects of reality.

Bion (1956) asserts that the difference between the non-psychotic and psychotic parts of the personality lies in the presence of massive projective identification, which destroys the capacity for thought. In this situation not only are fragments of the mind projected, but the function of the mind as well. The result is that inanimate objects take on the qualities of the sense organs. The inception of verbal thought characteristic of the depressive position becomes disturbed for the very reason that it organizes and articulates awareness of internal and external reality. It is the linking function of such thought that is repeatedly attacked, because it becomes increasingly painful for the psychotic to re-integrate projected parts of the personality. To re-introject these fragments of the personality would result in the depressive position, wherein one is able to experience conflicting aspects of the same object. The primary difficulty lies in the fact that the projected parts of the personality return with the same, if greater, affective charge they had upon departure. Haunted by these ghosts of abandoned meaning the psychotic continues to utilize the one defense he or she uses to contend with the situation; projective identification.

Throughout his career Bion retained these notions of projective identification and expanded upon them by suggesting that projection is the link the patient utilizes to connect with the analyst. He adds that the hallmark characteristics of primitive mental disorders are curiosity, stupidity, and arrogance. It is important to note that the curiosity he speaks of here is not the curiosity of K, of engaging and getting to know reality. Rather, this curiosity is in the service of knowing for the purpose of manipulation and avoiding contact with reality. In analysis the patient will occasionally ask personal questions of the analyst. Often, the analysand is not interested in the literal answer as much as knowing if the analyst is afraid of being known. This sort of questioning tends to represent healthy attempts to know and be engaged in the analytic process. This differs greatly from the personality disordered and psychotic's attempts at one-upmanship, which are in the service of distancing the other and reinforcing already mobilized primitive defenses.

Excessive projecting is a function of the infant's own innate destructiveness and envy, the failure of the environment to contain the infant's mind, or a combination of both. Bion writes:

> On the one hand there is the patient's inborn disposition to excessive destructiveness, hatred, and envy: on the other the environment which, at its worst, denies to the patient the use of the mechanisms of splitting and projective identification. On some occasions the destructive attacks on the link between patient and environment, or between different aspects of the patient's personality, have their origin in the patient; on others, in the mother, although in the latter instance and in psychotic patients, it can never be the mother alone. (Bion, 1959, p. 313)

Once these elements are present in the personality, a destructive developmental course begins. It is important to note that when developmental failures occur, he does not assert that the personality becomes developmentally frozen. An absence in Bion's psychoanalysis is an active rather than a passive phenomenon. Deficiences in the developmental process, especially when combined with the personality's own rage and destructiveness, begins a process of attacking links. The links attacked are those that serve to bring the mind into contact with external and emotional reality. Hatred is directed at other affects, including hatred itself, and external reality becomes hated because it evokes emotions. The thinking apparatus is damaged since healthy curiosity is attacked. The more this process continues, the more threatening reality becomes, the more the person relies on the self-destructive process. This process has an addictive quality, as the person becomes increasingly reliant upon the very thing that is the pathogenic agent. The very way in which one goes looking for his or her mind facilitates the illness. Co-occurring with this process is the solidification of an emotionless and opinionated super-ego that follows its own distorted logic. Fueling much of this process is an intolerance of frustrating experiences and feelings. The mind projects beta elements rather than processing thoughts. The arrogant quality of this lies in the belief that one cannot experience frustrating feelings by projecting them.

Learning from experience is impossible under this situation and so the person may employ the defenses of omniscience and omnipotence. These compensatory defenses serve as substitutes for learning but leave the mind increasingly impoverished, since these defenses distort reality. The person may begin writing an alternate script to reality, so to speak, in which he or she plays a powerful and important character. I remember a rather sad clinical example where a borderline mother was using her daughter as a psychological toilet, that is, using excessive projective identification to evacuate the psychotic parts of herself into her daughter. She took her eleven year old daughter to countless mental health facilities not to help her daughter get therapy, but to take copies of the intake evaluations. The mother would review them with her daughter as evidence of the daughter's badness and craziness. Over time, the daughter began withdrawing from reality and constructing her own universe. The increasing withdrawal from reality made her a laughing stock at school and was fodder for her mother's agenda. While I do not know what happened to this child—she was taken for another assessment—it serves as an example of how omniscience and omnipotence are protectively employed and the damage done to one's ability to have and maintain stable, healthy relationships and contact with reality.

Another phenomenon associated with -K is the attack upon language. Attacking language is an especially powerful and efficient way of attacking links since language itself serves the purpose of linking. The destruction of language and common understanding spreads confusion and makes cooperation impossible. Bion (1992) notes that patients often use language to defend against exploring a potentially menacing object. It is common for patients to present fruitful material and then quickly say something like, "That's all there is to it." The patient is therefore able to utilize language to defend against experiencing the haunting object and avoid affective awareness. With this patient, "A smile or a verbal statement must be interpreted as an evacuatory muscular movement and not as a communication of feeling" (Bion, 1994, p. 13). One or more of the sense organs can be used in reverse, a hallucinosis to project out, to force out reality. Another way to attack language is to render words meaningless. This is most evident with patients who use words charged with affect, without actually experiencing the affect. Bion believed that the ability to utilize language marks the difference between the psychotic and non-psychotic parts of the personality.

As already stated, the reversal of the alpha-function produces beta-elements. Beta- elements represent parts of the fragmenting personality that are violently projected and return with the same, if not greater, affective charge. Bizarre objects lead to an inaccurate experience of objects in internal and external reality. For neurotic persons, beta-elements tend to cause disruptive relationships and with psychotics beta-elements manifest as hallucinations. The counterpart of the healthy alpha-screen is the pathological beta-screen. The beta screen serves to keep the individual experientially isolated from others and from emotional reality. Clinically, the beta-screen manifests in the patient spewing forth disjointed, dreamlike, and confusing images and phrases. The purpose of this outpouring is to attack the link between the patient and the analyst by disrupting the analyst's ability to think. The patient does not take in the analyst's interpretations and the content of the patient's communication seems divorced from its original intent.

The beta-screen works against the interpersonal relationship between the analyst and patient. Paradoxically, the beta-screen represents the patient's best attempts at preserving a sense of self, and even psychosis can be seen as a tortured final attempt at organizing experience and fending off unmanageable emotions. The patient's experience of the analyst is characterized by profound ambiguousness. On the one hand, the healthy part of the patient's personality wants to engage in the analysis and heal. On the other hand, the self-destructive ways of contending with reality are the only ways the patient knows and thus he or she fears setting these aside. Moreover, the patient may spoil the analytic encounter with the envy and resentment of the analyst's ability to help.

The beta-screen facilitates anti-life, anti-hope forces in the psyche, damages object relationships, and leaves the patient with anxiety and dread. Underlying fears of fragmentation haunt the patient, who is inundated by ideas and images that are alien and intrusive. All the while, beta-elements saturate the mind, denuding experience of its affective character and proffering poor protection from external and internal reality. While this manifests itself as poor self-esteem in neurotic persons, the borderline experiences anxiety over the impending loss of self. Left with a discontinuous sense of self and with a failing alpha-function, the individual experiences criticism, however slight, as a part of the ongoing torment he or she has had to live with. This explains the hypersensitivity and acting-out that are characteristic of borderline and psychotic disorders.

No-thingness

Symbols can be used to represent emotional reality or to destroy it. They afford clear and free spaces for the unknown to manifest. The same symbols that facilitate growth may also be used to evacuate emotional reality. Bion (1962, 1963) utilizes signs in discussing two kinds of nothing. Bion's symbolic system evokes a sense of awe, when one discovers how thin the line can be between creation and utter self-destruction.

The grid's vertical axis (i.e. from top to bottom) marks the progression of raw affective data towards elements suitable for dreaming, thinking, and other creative ventures. It marks the increasingly sophisticated levels of thought. The horizontal axis (i.e. from left to right) represents the ways in which the mind works on emotions, thoughts, and ideas through consecutive stages of development. Bion (1962, 1963) used arrows to note movement on the chart. For example, an arrow pointing down marks the growth of raw affective data towards becoming elements increasingly usable for thinking and dreaming. However, the grid can work in reverse, which is symbolized by two arrows: an arrow pointing to the left and an arrow pointing down, respectively. The grid working in reverse reflects objects stripped of meaning, position, and therefore existence. Yet, as already stated, this does not bespeak a lack of movement, but an annihilating force that continues even after eliminating existence, time, and space. As Eigen notes, this means that the destructive force continues "off the grid after the grid has been annihilated ... or put out of play. The arrow points past the grid's origin, through zero, into a sub zero dimension" (Eigen, 1996, p. 63). This represents the movement of a psychic black hole, in Grotstein's terms, or the no-thing no-thinging.

Bion (1962, 1963) also used a point and a horizontal line to symbolize the breast and the phallus. The point can either stand for what remains after the breast is repeatedly attacked or it may stand for what is unknown about the breast. In the initial instance, the mind cannot withstand the experience of relationship and responds to its helplessness by reifying the breast to what can be manipulated or controlled. Bion is clear that the grid working in reverse differs from the point and line phenomena in that the latter represents the potential space of the object and the capacity to give thought to this potential space. The grid working in reverse means that a non-existent force continues its work towards an ever-vanishing zero-point after existence has been destroyed. An existing no-thing, like evil intentions, may be housed in a non-existent no-thing. Non-existent no-things do not have *substansia* (objective presence) as their kind of being and yet their impact cannot be denied.

This formless force is personified in mythological characters, such as Satan. "It is pure, formless destructiveness, where the term 'destructiveness' is a rigid and limiting naming of a domain for which we lack a language" (Eigen, 1996, p. 66). This is negation in its purest form, residing beyond the time and space it has destroyed. Bion (1994) describes -K clinically:

> In the first place its predominant characteristic I can only describe as "without-ness". It is an internal object without an exterior. It is an alimentary canal without a body. It is a super-ego that has hardly any of the characteristics of the super-ego as understood

in psychoanalysis: it is "super" ego. It is an envious assertion of
moral superiority without any morals. In short it is the resultant of
an envious stripping or denudation of all good is itself destined to
continue the process of stripping. (p. 97)

Some of Bion's thoughts about -K's effects upon the developing mind
are quite similar to the aforementioned Laingian ideas of petrification,
engulfment, and implosion. In both cases the individual's experiences
of space, psyche, and time are not felt as coexisting. The experience of
self is extremely tenuous and psychological development is arrested.
Often, one will hallucinate a psyche or develop the delusional belief in
a psyche that simply does not exist. Bion notes the ways that patients
develop imaginary psyches, false selves in Langian terms, to compensate for psychic gaps and developmental failures. In any event, this
force represents the breakdown of the breakdown, the lecherous will to
obliterate life rather than let it escape.

Pharmakon: poison-cure

Humans perpetually seek an 'other' to project themselves onto. Mostly
everyone wants to know that they make a difference to others and that
they have room for them in their minds. This helps form and solidify
a sense of self. The infant is a part of the thinking-pair. They essentially form a kind of relational unit. Seeking is an essential part of this
process:

> Seeking and projecting constitute a kind of drive to communicate
> self and touch reality. One reaches into outer space to find the inner
> space of another person. The image of sending signals into space
> in the hope that our messages will be met applies to what happens
> in fast motion between ourselves moment to moment. We try to
> communicate our capacity to communicate at the same time as we
> attempt to communicate ourselves. (Eigen, 2001, p. 66)

Optimally, the infant's communications are mediated and softened by
maternal reverie and returned to the infant in a more digestible form.
Over time, faith in the communicative process grows and the infant is
able to develop the capacity for thought. The thinking-pair can be damaged by the lack of a containing environment, an excess of the infant's

envy and rage, or a combination of both. Under these circumstances, the infant projects its unmanageable affects and they return either undigested or in ghastly half-recognizable partially digested forms. A pathological element forms in the personality that is hostile to communication. A minor form of this can be seen in the arguments and frustrating miscommunications that we all experience. The ramifications of this occurring during early development can be devastating. When projective identification runs into a non-receptive object during development, communication itself can be persecuting. The communicative capacity self-destructs and the personality seeks to cancel itself out. In projective identification one seeks the alpha-function of the other and the intolerance or unavailability of the other leads pathology. First, the seeker develops a sadistic superego that is hostile to communicative projective identification and to communication of any form. Second, partial reintrojection of the seeking projective identification is enclosed in the communication itself, whether it be sight, sound, or touch. Thus enclosed, the psychological hunger and its envelope are experienced as persecuted and persecuting.

Persecution saturates the personality as the self takes in the intolerance and unavailability. An ego-destructive superego forms and exacts damage to the object-seeking propensity of the psyche. Concordant to this is the personality's decreasing ability to communicate, and developmental milestones are forsaken. Communication, when employed, is in the service of the anti-hope, anti-life forces working in the personality. "This puts the personality in the untenable position of stimulating a force that destroys communication each time communication is attempted" (Eigen, 2001, p. 67). Bion eloquently tends to the phenomena of a self-destructiveness so profound that it escapes words. How does one represent a phenomenon that, by definition, obliterates representation? Such a searching requires the help of an other, but under the sway of this force the seeking capacity itself is attacked. The alpha-function of the other, which is so desperately needed, cannot be sought. Even if this meeting takes place, the patient may lack the psychological equipment to engage in such an alpha-function. Eigen describes this clinically:

> A person may come for help because elemental projective attempts turned to stone, became mutilated, encapsulated, partly murdered, or worn out. In many, partial annihilation of self is depicted in nightmares. These are individuals for whom having a nightmare

> is a step forward. A nightmare, at least, is able to image a bit of
> the terror that freezes psychic processing. It represents a portion
> of what cannot be represented before breaking apart (nightmares
> usually destroy themselves as dreams, awakening the dreamer).
> (Eigen, 2001, p. 68)

The patient's very fear of a sadistic superego is itself a communication of the fear that threatens the utilization of the alpha-function. The analyst's very presence can be experienced as persecutory, since it represents health, which, in the patient's mind, may facilitate the emergence of the tyrannical superego. The patient experiences the analysis as *pharmakon*, in a split form, without the ability to digest, to see it as an intermingling of the *remedy-poison* that, if ingested, holds the possibility of relatedness. Damaging the therapeutic relationship and one's own mind are kinds of relatedness and the only ways the patient knows. Openness to oneself and the analytic relationship equals vulnerability to (re-)traumatization by the intolerant, unavailable object that has since been solidified into the destructive superego. Putting oneself together is tantamount to putting together the odious superego.

Bion notes the places where fragments of projection survive yet depict damage, not just to the self but to the projective mechanism itself, and what makes utilizing this mechanism damaging. "Bion tips Klein over the edge by plunging the psyche into a field of continuous annihilation, so that to exercise the capacity to dream annihilation represents an enormous achievement" (Eigen, 2001, p. 69). A containing environment is necessary for dreaming. Does such an environment exist for this particular client? This brings into question the analyst's own availability to the patient. Is the analyst's alpha-function available for the patient or is it too damaged? Over time the remedy of the *pharmakon* does seep in if the analyst does not get pulled into the gravity of the damaging object and if the analyst's nourishment (alpha-function work) outweighs the anti-life forces of the patient's personality. Bion gave witness to the vicissitudes of the self-destructive forces of the patient's mind and their impact upon the ability to think in relation to others. As Bion tended to the most extreme forms of psychological self-destructiveness, tended to the destructiveness wrought upon Being and, ultimately, upon humanity.

CHAPTER FIVE

Heidegger: the eclipse of the sacred and the darkening of the world

Heidegger's phenomenological conception of dasein

Heidegger's *Being and Time* (1996) is an ontological study. Ontology seeks to answer the oldest and most basic question: what is the meaning of Being? What is its is-ness, the meaning of its is-ness, its structures? For Heidegger, such questioning has never accurately been asked because the question of the meaning of is-ness has never been properly formulated. The question of the meaning of Being was raised and Aristotle responded by giving priority to *substansia* and the categorization of substance things. But giving priority to that which is objectively present at hand covers over, if not blatantly ignores, the most primordial ground of Being; relatedness. But relatedness, and the meaning of relatedness, is the relatedness of a being towards that which is being related to (the world). What is this being that engaged itself in the questioning of its relatedness? It is that very being which raises the question about the meaning of its is-ness, Dasein, the human kind of being. It stands to reason, then, that methodological priority be given to this fundamental ontology, the human understanding of its own kind of being, and the meaning of its relatedness (the meaning of it as a being-in-the-world). Since the human kind of being's *is* lies in its is-ness in the world, empirical inquiries are not appropriate for explicating the meaning of its being. Dasein raises the question of the meaning of its being and is therefore the only appropriate starting point. Further, Dasein in raising the question of its own kind of being must already have an understanding, even if it is only a glimpse, of what it is interrogating. Dasein is the site, the ground, where the revealing of Being takes place, but it is not an instance of being as a representational abstraction of Being. Rather, it is the site for the disclosure of its own kind of being and other possible ontologies as well. This fundamental ontology, the analysis of Dasein, is in every way a philosophical anthropology. The Greek *anthropos* translates literally to 'man meaning'. Heidegger lays the ground for a philosophical anthropology, a human science of understanding the human kind of being.

Heidegger defines phenomenology etymologically: *phainomenon*, meaning what shows itself, the self-showing, or the manifest and *logos*, meaning letting something be seen (either truly or falsely) by indicating it. The combination of the two means, to let that which shows itself from itself, be seen as it shows itself from itself. Phenomenology is not an—ology like other—ologies (e.g. theology, biology) because it does not designate the object of its inquiry nor does it describe the content of its object. Rather, phenomenology is interested in precisely that which is not seen, the latent, and is therefore hermeneutic—it is necessarily interpretive. Being is not a thing and ontology asks the *meaning* of Being not *what* it is. Ontology is not pre-conceived, it is a pursuit. Fundamental ontology receives a methodological priority, since Dasein is the place for understanding its own kind of being. It is fundamental in that it has to understand its own essential character before understanding others. Ontology seeks the meaning of Being and fundamental ontology seeks the human understanding of its own kind of being. Heidegger believes that language has become saturated with the quantitative attitude. For Heidegger, etymology is of fundamental importance since it contains aspects of the first saying that have become covered over with time.

Heidegger (1927) asserts that there is a qualitative difference between humans and all other beings. The ontic distinction of Dasein is that it is ontological. Dasein is ontological in that is has a pre-ontological understanding of Being that is always already present. Heidegger utilizes a number of terms that are critical to his conception of Dasein:

1. Existence: The kind of being that Dasein is. Dasein has an understanding of its kind of being and other kinds of beings as

well. Dasein's kind of being is at issue and is radically contingent. Dasein is always engaged in mankind's sense of itself. Unlike substance-things Dasein possess relatedness and has the possibilities of different modes of relating. People can be as their ownmost selves (authentically) or as their 'they-self' (inauthentically).

2. Existentials: Existentials are arrived at via an existentiell (lived) understanding of existence and are possible ways of Dasein to be, are ontological structures, and are component dimensions of existence. Existentials are to Dasein as categories are to substance-things.

3. Existentiell: We come to terms with the questions of existence always only through existence itself. This ontic, lived, experiential, understanding of Dasein is existentiell and refers to Dasein's lived modification of being as everyone else.

4. World: As opposed to a world of things (the tool world), world refers to world as a totality of references; a weave of contexts where Dasein is the ultimate for-the-sake-of these references. Dasein is in no way opposed to the world but actually exists in it and is absorbed in it. World in an ontic sense refers to the totality of being objectively present. World in an ontological sense refers to a region that embraces a multiplicity of being. In a different ontic sense, world means world as a pre-ontologically present existentiell. World designates the ontological and existential concept of worldliness.

5. Worldliness of the world: Worldliness is an existential. It is the being of the ontic condition of the possibility of discovering inner worldly beings in general and in terms of their usefulness.

6. Circumspection: The catching sight of the world and the referential context that allows us to view readiness-to-hand. It is the pre-thematic looking around at the world and the sight of taking care.

7. Taking care: This is Dasein's everyday pre-thematic relatedness to the world and non-Dasein entities. It represents Dasein's relatedness to the handiness of the world.

8. Dasein: *Dasein* translates as *being there*. It is the human kind of being that pre-ontologically has an understanding of its own kind of being, its relatedness to the world. Dasein's ontic excellence is that it is ontological, and what is ontically closest is ontologically furthest away. Dasein's being is at issue and it is always already involved in an interpretive engagement with itself in an attempt to explicate the meaning of its being. Dasein always belongs to the individual pre-thematically. A person is always already Dasein and

in possession of the possibilities of authenticity and inauthenticity. Dasein is not an abstracted instance of Being but the site for the understanding of all possible ontologies. Dasein is the ultimate for-the-sake-of the world and is the ground for the disclosure of Being.

9. Thematic: This is the opposite of pre-thematic and comes into view when there is a disruption in the handiness of the world. When entities ready-to-hand change or break they become objects of reflection, and thus thematic. For this Heidegger says that knowledge is founded, not foundational. Said differently, ontology precedes etymology.

10. Pre-thematic: This is present when Dasein is in the inauthentic modality of relating to the world in terms of handiness. The pre-thematic relatedness to useful things ready—to—hand affords the smooth everyday functioning of Dasein.

11. The 'in' of Dasein's being-in-the-world: Dasein's being is grounded upon the constitution titled being-in-the-world. Dasein's being in is not the same as, for example, water's being in a glass. The 'in' in being-in-the-world refers to Dasein's absorption in the world (the totality of references) as encounter-ability. It is always already familiar with the world and it holds the world as something familiar. Being-in-the-world is being-in-a-world-with-others. Dasein has the human world as accessible to the human kind of being in the forms of distancing and de-distancing possibilities.

12. Handiness: Dasein's pre-thematic relatedness in average every-dayness to the world as a useful thing. Handiness is an existential.

13. Objective presence (presence-at-hand): When there is a disruption in Dasein's relatedness to handiness, that which was previously ready-to-hand becomes present-at-hand. Thus it becomes an object for thematic reflection. Objective presence is never the being of Dasein.

14. Ontic: The ontic question is, what are beings? The human-ontic is ontological in that a pre-ontological understanding of its own human-ness is always already present. It is existentiell in its way of understanding it's kind of being. What is ontically closest is ontologically farthest away.

15. Ontological: Dasein's existentials, its structures, of the meaning of its human kind of relatedness in a totality of references (the world). Existentials are to Dasein as categories are to substances. Dasein is ontological in its existentiell relationship with the tool world.

Through this existentiell relatedness to the tool world Dasein gains an understanding as to the meaning of its kind of being.

Ontological structures have ontic implications; for example, de-distancing levels down and bringing closer possibilities for being. It affords ways of being as a 'they' and publicness makes the everyday world go around. *The they*, or *das Man* as Heidegger (1927) calls it, also establishes what is real and unreal. Heidegger's conception of this is similar to Freud's notion of the reality principle. In one sense the ways of being as a they affords functional everydayness. In another sense, one's ownmost self can become mistaken for the they self. People catch sight of themselves always in terms of similarity to others and being as everybody is makes individual differences possible. Proximally and predominantly humans are in the world as everyone else is, in the mode of the they self.

Heidegger (1927) suggests that there are three existentials for Dasein's disclosedness: attunement, understanding, and discourse. Attunement refers to the fact that humans are effectively tuned-in to the 'there' of their being. There are three things disclosed through attune-ment. First, Dasein's throwness is disclosed. Throwness refers to the fact that Dasein is delivered over to existence without knowing why and having no control. Along with this is facticity, the fact that Dasein has little control over the cultural-historical situation in which it finds itself. Dasein is delivered to being the kind of being it is. The second thing disclosed is being-in-the-world as a whole. Things appear dif-ferently in different affective states. Things are disclosed differently in different attunements. Thirdly, the world is disclosed. The second exis-tential is projection, the structure of understanding, the throwing out of possibilities and disclosing of things in terms of possibilities. The third existential is discourse, the disclosure of that which can be meaning-fully articulated.

Dasein is immersed in the world and these three existentials are how people are in the world. Dasein is its disclosedness. Dasein is not an objective presence and does not illuminate itself outside of itself. It is there and the structures constitute that clearing. Another existential is fallenness, Dasein's entanglement in the they. We lose ourselves in our world as everybody is and in our ways of doing things as everyone does. A disclosure of the they self is found in idle chatter, the language of the they. Idle chatter makes information assessable to everyone. It does not afford a deep understanding, but functions to efficiently communicate data. It is this discourse that affords everyday functionality and can be understood as setting out circumscribed, prescribed meaningfulness. It limits the range of intelligibility. It conceals deeper intelligibility and is the they's version of discourse. Curiosity is the way things tend to be sighted and is the disposition of everydayness. The new becomes the familiar in idle chatter, as Dasein moves from one topic to the next. Ambiguity is the understanding of the they. Ambiguity does not conclude matters, but settles things enough so that Dasein can move on to the next order of business. Into this Heidegger adds alienation. Alienation is Dasein's being cut-off from being its ownmost self. This is similar to Freud's notion of the de-centred subject unknown to him or herself. Dasein gets entangled in its everyday functionality, its being as everybody is. One's being-in-the-world is set ahead, prescribed by the they in its moving from one thing to the next. Heidegger says that we 'fall prey to the they.' In falling into the world we fall away from our own possibilities for being. Caught in the whirlpool of everyday-ness we forget, lose track of even alienation itself. The they tells us that what we are doing is concrete and real. It gives us as ourselves in the they as living the correct life, that things are the way they are supposed to be. Descriptively, Heidegger notes that without such falling there is no humanness. It is a part of who we are as human beings.

Anxiety, for Heidegger, receives a methodological, not lived, priority, in catching sight of what is being covered over in falling into the they. Anxiety throws us back in the world so it is that which must be understood. Fear comes from things in the world so it cannot be applicable to Dasein, since Dasein is not a thing. Dasein turns toward the world in fear and away from it in anxiety. In angst Dasein cannot simply get on with it. Engagement with particular activities breaks down and Dasein is thrown back into its purest being possible. In angst, Dasein is disclosed to itself as being the kind of being that it is, a being-possible. Fallenness is a closed possibility, a freeing of letting Dasein be what it is. The sense of being at home afforded by the they collapses in angst. There is a sense of uncanniness that Dasein is not at home in its familiar world. What makes us feel uncanny is that we are not things; hence we can be terminated at any moment. As being-possible, Dasein has *not* being possible as a possibility. We are our possibilities and our own death, and this is what makes us uncanny and not things. The they has implic-itly promised immortality via the natural sciences' taking, equating the real with the quantifiable. We come to understand ourselves as things; things break, they do not die. Death is the mark of being human and it gives life its contours.

What is the meaning of death? Recalling the Stoic dictum;where death is I am not and where I am death is not; why should we be concerned? Death haunts us as our ownmost potentiality of our being-possible. Other things perish, but only Dasein dies. In anticipation death is free to be what it is, pure possibility, and not a literal event. It is the pure possibility of having no more possibilities. Angst is the anxiety about the possibility of death. Dasein is anxious about the possibility of having no more possibilities and subsequently flees into the disburdenment of the they. Uncanniness is the primordial ground of being at home with the they. As long as we are, we are dying. When death becomes demise, a literal event, it loses its bite. It is death as possibility that we are afraid of. Death is always impending and is something that happens to everyone sooner or later. Death is to be understood in terms of the human kind of being. In death Dasein can be grasped as a whole and it characterizes Dasein. To free death is to let death figure life and give it its contours. For death to be death (pure possibility) an authentic disclosure is necessary. This is not the same thing as expecting death. When this occurs, death is mistaken as a literal even, a thing. The idea is to let death individualize us as our ownmost selves, not in our they selves. In making human beings into things lies the natural scientific promise of immortality.

Heidegger (1927) notes that we need an existentiell attunement for understanding. This is the call of conscience. It is a call from Dasein's ownmost self from the they self and it pushes the they into non-significance. The call re-calls and claims Dasein as being the kind of being it is. The uncanny self re-calls the authentic self from the they.

> In its who, the caller is definable by *nothing* "worldly." It is Da-sein in its uncanniness, primordially thrown being-in-the-world, as not-at-home, the naked "that" in the nothingness of the world. The caller is unfamiliar to the everyday they-self, it is something like an *alien* voice. What could be more alien to the they, lost in the manifold "world" of its heedfulness, than the self, individualized to itself in uncanniness thrown into nothingness? "It" calls, and yet gives the heedfully curious ears nothing to hear that could be passed along and publicly spoken about ...

The call does not report any facts; it calls without uttering anything. The call speaks in the uncanny mode of *silence*. And it does this only because in calling the one summoned, it does not call him into the public idle chatter of the they, but *calls* him *back* from that *to the reticence of his existent potentiality-of-being*. When the caller reaches him who is summoned, it does so with a cold assurance that is uncanny and by no means obvious. (Heidegger, 1927, pp. 255–256)

We do not choose the call, but we can choose to hear or not to hear it. This is predicated in large by our desire to have a conscience, to be receptive to the call. Dasein can take up itself as itself, to be called forth, to stand reticent in the face of anxiety. Heidegger states that there is an unshakable joy that emerges if one stands reticent. These are orienting moments, not states, and Dasein invariably falls back into the they. There is a certain call, fall, call, fall cycle that takes place throughout one's existence.

Dasein is the null basis of a nullity. It is a null basis in that Dasein does not create itself, but finds itself delivered over to being what it is. It is a nullity in that it is a being-possible with non-being as its ultimate, not to be forsaken possibility. Dasein is also guilty in its refusing possibilities by taking up certain possibilities. Dasein cannot possibly take up all its possibilities. Death is defined by not and yet Being is disposed in the depths of our being. The evasion of death is an evasion of life. In understanding death we begin to live.

The unworld and the eclipse of time, being, and thought

For Heidegger (1954), the essence of technology is nothing technological. Moreover, technology is neither an instrument of humankind's construction or an enterprise under human control. Heidegger asserted that technology's essence is a revealing that challenges. In our age, the presencing of Being has persuaded humankind to interpret beings as a function of their usefulness to us. Heidegger dubbed this presencing the Enframing. In the Enframing all inner-worldly entities, as well as humans, become resources at our disposal (standing-reserve).

The Enframing is a destining of Being, a mode of revealing and in its sway nothing appears in its essential character. It veils its truth as a presencing of Being by appearing as though it is a product of human making. We become convinced that the only mode of disclosing the world is through quantitative calculation. We develop reserves of resources on call for technological purposes and amass supplies to be used at will. There is danger in the Enframing. Heidegger says:

> As soon as what is unconcealed no longer concerns man even as object, but exclusively as standing-reserve, and man in the midst of objectivelessness is nothing but the orderer of the standing-reserve, then he comes to the very brink of a precipitous fall; that is, he comes to the point where he himself will have to be taken as standing-reserve. (Heidegger, 1954, p. 27)

Dasein forgets that it is claimed and thus mistakes itself as lord and master over all things. Humanity's essence, our attending to the world as an open realm wherein Being presences, is covered over in the Enframing of technology. Heidegger asserts that once humankind is set upon this course of disclosure, the world becomes an unworld in which humanity engages in a "circularity of consumption for the sake of consumption" (Sipiora, 1991, p. 241). The essence of the human kind of being becomes homeless and alienated through our abandoning of Being and our disclosure of the world via quantitative technological rationality. Sipiora writes, "The very nature of human dwelling is being re-created in the alien image of technology. The result is the alienation of the everydayness of being-in-the-world" (Sipiora, 1991, p. 242).

In its homelessness, humanity seeks escape into the alien by becoming increasingly fascinated with the newest and most fantastic ready-made experience and devices. Heidegger also noted that along with our fascination with the fantastic comes grave boredom. This boredom (*das Unheimische*) is the uncanny grip of technology that prompts our flight into its unfamiliar and fascinating realms, thus alienating us from ourselves. This boredom is so profound that we become numb to our desires, interests, and concerns. Amidst this dullness we take further flight into the newest in hope of finding relief. Despite our attempts, this boredom cannot be shaken and so we continue further in our pursuit of stimulating experiences.

Caught in a whirlpool of production and consumption, everydayness becomes ever more tedious, boring, and meaningless. In boredom, phenomena appear to the individual only in so far as things and people are reveled as undifferentiated and equally meaningless. Nothing can engage a person ensnared in such world-weariness. This is not to say that nothing appears to the individual. Whatever does appear to the deeply bored person instantaneously withdraws, becoming yet another phenomenon that is of little concern. In this experience, one is not expectant of what is to come, has no sense of being supported by the past, and thus experiences the ennui of the present. Time itself is attacked and manically replaced with the ever-new products and topics of industry and technology. Heidegger calls this devastation "the high-velocity expulsion of Mnemosyne" (Heidegger, 1954, p. 30). This stands in contrast to understanding time as transitory, the past emerging into the present awaiting the future. Rather than letting time be time, it becomes replaced with the static yet ever-changing image of youthful *en vogue* trends. Not only does this image not let time be time, it is death evasive.

Heidegger turns to the ancient Greeks and he seeks a mytho-poetic imagining of the world. Myth, for the ancient Greeks, was the telling word:

> For the Greeks, to tell is to lay bare and let appear—both the appearance and what has its essence in the appearance, its epiphany. *Mythos* is what has its essence in its telling—what appears in the unconcealment of its appeal. The *mythos* is that appeal of foremost and radical concern to all human beings which lets man think of what appears, what unfolds. (ibid., p. 374)

Heidegger expresses concern that "Thought has scarcely touched upon the essence of the mythical" (Heidegger, 1975, p. 94). To understand how Heidegger approaches the mythic, it is important to understand his thinking concerning Dasein in our technological age.

Heidegger maintained that Dasein's entangled flight into being as everyone is represents a flight from its own uncanniness. Dasein's canniness lies in Dasein's throwness into being the kind of being that has death as its ownmost potentiality. Our self-forgetful lostness in the 'they', our normality in the Cartesian age, has led to the denial of the world, in the form of *injurious neglect*. Humanity's essence, tending to the world as humankind's open realm, is destroyed in the spirit of technology.

Hospitality towards the mystery of Being becomes latent when humankind takes itself as the master of technology. In the Enframing, the world becomes the world of Cartesianism, an un-world in which Dasein engages in a tautology of consumption for the sake of consumption. In the Enframing the world becomes a vast resource for our consumption. When we disclose beings as resources, we mistake ourselves as being in complete control. Absorbed in average everydayness, the call and claim of the other is drowned out.

In contrast to the un-world, which is driven by production and consumption, Heidegger offers the ontological, poetic image of the world as Fourfold. Heidegger frequently crossed out the word *Sein* (*Being*) to demonstrate that it is neither a metaphysical idea nor a physical thing. Moreover, Heidegger crossed out Sein not only to recognize its place in the neither-nor space, but to show that the four points indicate the quadrants of the Fourfold: heavens, divinities, earth, and mortals. The sky is the openness in which things may rise into unconcealment, the ineffable heavens wherein the divinities show their faces. The divinities are the physiognomies of the world and are encounterable in their claiming empowerment of humanity. They are messengers of the godhead, the wholly other. The earth is the mystery from which things emerge, and in its proffering of things to mortal, the earth withdraws into mystery. Humans dwell upon the earth as mortals not because they die but because they are capable of taking death as death that is, their not-to-be-surpassed possibility. The regions of the Fourfold are united in a simple oneness, a mirroring of each other's uniqueness. In the un-world the earth is exploited as a resource, the heaven are taken as a vast quantifiable expanse, mortals take themselves as lords and masters of the universe and, unwittingly, become resources themselves. Following the poet Holderlin, Heidegger noted that in the Enframing the divinities have departed and have left so long ago that they are not even remembered. Rather, the divinities are remembered by their absence. The gods are not dead; they simply have withdrawn and cannot be immediately encountered. Their presence can be described as self-withholding.

Boss says, "today, people [are] horribly depressed by the meaninglessness and tedium of their lives. Suffering as they do, these people often try to drown out their desperation through addiction to work, pleasure, or drugs" (Boss, 1971, pp. 222–223). Boss attributes the rise in crime and addiction to the growing damage of "the human soul by the apotheosized spirit of technology" (p. 283). All behaviour is grounded in humankind's fundamental nature, in its being-in-the-world and its being together with others in a shared world. Van den Berg (1983) suggests that the name neurosis is no longer an appropriate label to describe the disturbed human relations of our technological age. Van den Berg points out that whilst Freud took the neurotic symptom as psychological, he continued to believe that all neuroses could be traced back to physiological causes (van den Berg, 1983, p. 188). Placing neurosis in the realms of the individual and the anatomical ignores the fact that the underlying sociological character is illness. Moreover, Van den Berg states, "No one is neurotic unless made neurotic by society. In a neurosis is an individual's reaction to the conflicting and complicating demands made by society" (ibid., p. 187). In contemporary everyday-ness, all human relationships have been leveled down to the function and the pragmatic thus granting only one intelligibility. The result is that everything qualitative is taken as the same and all change is believed to be quantitative. For Van den Berg neurosis is worldly and society provides the possibility of producing psychologically ill people. Moreover, in today's society the individual does not know where the right path is and there is no guide. While the normal individual manages to stand on his own two feet, to 'have his shit together', the neurotic breaks down and suffers the illness of technological culture. Society has fallen into a state of norm-lessness and anomy brought about by secularization. We live scattered in the world and we can no longer recognize ourselves. "As a result of this condition, society fails to 'regulate' the individual, it does not keep him in his place; the groups to which he belongs are falling apart" (ibid., p. 161).

Today, we have a plurality of selves. We possess a self for every group we belong to. Though we all suffer from this, the neurotic is unable to maintain a unified identity in various contexts. Van den Berg suggests that pathogenic factors in mental illness are communicative rather than biological in nature. No one factor is solely concerned with the individual. It is only because society is ill that something like individual neurosis is possible. Van den Berg believes that it is more appropriate to speak of sociosis than neurosis (ibid., pp. 187–188). Our relationships are the pre-conditions of sociosis. Anomy results in our living in multiple-equal contexts that have little or no relation to one another. This multitude of functional contexts cannot be quantitatively ordered so we lead a divided existence in a complex society. With multiplicity the distance between others and ourselves increases, resulting in alienation, loneliness, and fear. Those who can cope with these factors suffer the least.

It is nonsensical to say that a person constructs individually the dynamics of his or her psychopathology *ex nihilio*. "A discerning conversation with any typical ... member of society shows that they all suffer—whether they consider themselves healthy or disturbed—the fate of the times" (Boss, 1971). He continues:

> It eats at them that this fate of theirs pressures them to regard everything in the world ... as nothing but interchangeable parts of a planetary machine. They know that components exist only to be meshed into production apparatuses which must yield more energy and more goods ... and that the particular kind and particular meaning of the product is a matter of diminishing significance. (ibid., p. 286)

The fate that emerges in taking up the world in this manner is one where humanity exacts ultimate control over all things as useful commodities, the human being included.

Romanyshyn (1989) describes the cultural vision in our modern technological society where the self is taken as a spectator, the world as a spectacle, and the body as a specimen. Congruent with Boss' discussion of the fate of our age, Romanyshyn asserts that in taking the body as specimen, we have come to believe that it is a machine whose parts are all interchangeable. Since all of our parts are replaceable, there will come a time when we will be immortal—machines do not die. The body is taken as incidental and not essential, to who we are as humans. Romanyshyn describes this body of replaceable and interchangeable components as the astronomic body: "It is a body turned inside out, re-dressed in terms of technical functions *on the way to being discarded*" (italics in the original) (Romanyshyn, 1989, p. 18). Romanyshyn further notes that the two hallmark characteristics of our age are the ability to leave earth and the ability to annihilate it with nuclear weapons. The flames of nuclear holocaust are the symptomatic aspects of the fires of departure. "Wedded in this fashion, departure takes on the character of psychological necessity. On an earth wired for destruction, space flight becomes a means of escape" (ibid., p. 23). The possibility of nuclear war was technically achieved and now this potentiality cannot easily be covered over. Caputo (1987) says that things are under threat "even if the bomb is not dropped, endangered in their essence ... namely, as the raw material of technical power. Things are put upon man because man is himself put upon by the way technology comes to presence … as Enframing" (Caputo, 1987, p. 232). We mistake ourselves as the creators of technology, forgetting that technology is a calling of Being.

What are some possible ways out of our self-destructive lostness in the contemporary technological world? Boss says that we must leap from our everyday technological stance towards the world into the letting-be worldview. He says that whoever succeeds in taking this leap will witness the scission between what most people accept as reality, and the rich meaning and significance phenomena hold, hidden though they may be. Those ruled by the spirit of technology mistake reality as that which is quantifiable. In the phenomenological view of the world we can remember that humanity is its world-spanning openness. It is because humanity is its world-openness that we can do justice to those things presencing in the light of our being. For Heidegger meditative thinking is the greatest action we can take to shelter our humanity from the shadow of technology. Releasement towards the things themselves and openness to the mystery of Being are the constituents of meditative thinking. Releasement towards things is recognition of the necessity of technology and an affirmation of our dependence upon it. The first step is admitting we have a problem. However, it is also a releasement of entities from our quantitative disclosure of them as resources and an acknowledgment of them as a clear realm wherein Being presences. To be open to the mystery of Being is to remember that technology conceals itself as a tool under human control. The mystery is "the meaning which lays claim to the world and our being in it and yet is withheld in the disclosure and use of beings as standing-reserve" (Sipiora, 1991, p. 244). Interestingly, Heidegger suggests that boredom may free us from the calculative disclosure of technology. In boredom lies the possibility of becoming indifferent to the ordering of technology and the opportunity of finding the meaning latent in the Enframing.

In addition to the boredom inherent in the alienation of everydayness (*das Unheimische*) Heidegger (1954) poses the uncanniness of Being, which manifests in our technological uncovering of the world, that he calls *das Unheimliche*. In this uncanniness lies the potency of Being that is both disguised and active in the Enframing. By cultivating openness to the mystery, we may recognize that the call of our homeland is addressed in our boredom *as* a summoning of Being. Boredom is a symptom of our self-destructive society but it is also a sheltering and a remembrance of the way back home. Perhaps one could even say that sociosis is homesickness. Romanyshyn (1989) says that a symptom as "a way of forgetting something is also a way of preserving or remembering it. Symptoms are a memory of ... this way home, this way back to what has been forgotten" (Romanyshyn, 1989, p. 13). Similar to Heidegger, Romanyshyn would like to re-collect the awe-ful power of technology: "*Technology is awe-ful*. And what fills us with awe, invites us to wonder and dream" (italics in the original) (ibid., p. 2). Another similarity to Heidegger can be found in Romanyshyn's insistence that technology is not a tool at humanity's disposal but "earth's call to become its agent and instrument of awakening" (ibid., p. 3).

Heidegger asserts that since the essence of technology is nothing technological, another revealing of beings into unconcealment is possible. Heidegger questions whether the mode of unconcealing that takes place in art can save humanity from the Enframing. The *saving power* (*poesis*), hidden in the Enframing, appears as that which can restore humankind to its appropriate role on earth namely, as the shepherd of Being. Reflection upon and confrontation with technology has to take place in a realm that is both akin to and different from it. Heidegger is clear that nothing will be possible without true thinking. Although placing less of an emphasis upon thinking, Romanyshyn too believes that art can be a way of remembering home. In our technological-cultural dream of departing earth and our bodies, art (especially impressionism) grants a manner of seeing free from the geometric, quantitative, vision. It is clear that this linear perspective vision (Romanyshyn, 1989), one-track thinking (Heidegger, 1954), and the objective look (Laing, 1982) are of paramount concern. In contrast, Romanyshyn describes an "eye ... in touch with the world, a vision that has been impressed and moved by the world" (p. 221). In discussing poetic thinking, the thinking attuned to what is most fitting to humanity's essence, Caputo says, "It achieves a relationship with the world which is more ... primordial than reason; it is in touch with things long before the demand for reason arises ... and is so deeply tuned to things that the need for reason never arises" (Caputo, 1987, p. 224).

Existential-phenomenological psychology's critique of our modern technological world does not call us to return to a pre-technological state of existence nor does it view technology as something evil. Rather, it seeks to reawaken our awareness of our participation with the world and to evoke responsibility in cultural reality. Perhaps we can cultivate an awareness of our shared world such that we can have both quantitative rationality and openness to the mystery of Being. In addition, maybe we can take the leap Boss speaks of, where things and others shine forth from their own meaningfulness.

It seems we continue to lose sight of ourselves as we are carried farther away in the undertow of the Enframing. We have become so convinced that we control technology itself that we find ourselves farther and farther adrift from any notion of what is most appropriate to our existence. Through cultivation of meditative thinking the repressed facets of human nature may be allowed a space wherein they can show themselves from themselves. Heidegger's Fourfold phenomenological seeing brings forth a specific quality of the image: its world disclosive character. This is demonstrated in a section of Heidegger's *The Origin of the Work of Art* (1936) where he describes a Greek temple.

> It simply stands there in the middle of the rock-cleft valley. The building encloses the figure of a god, and in this concealment lets it stand out into the hold precinct through the open portico. It is the temple-work that first fits together and at the same time gathers around itself the unity of those paths and relations in which birth and death, disaster and blessing ... acquire the shape of destiny for human being. (Heidegger, 1936, p. 168)

Such seeing affords humility and releases humanity from its addictive, self-destructive need to penetratingly understand, predict, and control all it encounters. This way of knowing and being in the world is so difficult, so alien. That nature can only be known through the language of mathematics (Galileo), that we should strive to be masters and possessors of nature (DeCartes), that the aim of science is to put Mother Nature on the rack and torture from her her secrets (Bacon); delimits our possibilities of relating to the natural world and to each other.

CHAPTER SIX

Contemporary manifestations of self-destructiveness

The disposable child

Perhaps no one feels the impact of human-to-human destructiveness more than children and it is difficult to imagine something more evil than harming a child. "We agree with Dostoevsky: a dying child is an evil that lacerates philosophical beauty. Goodness dies when a child dies" (Eigen, 2001a, p. 21). Destructiveness wrought upon children does not require a lengthy philosophical debate concerning the nature of evil; its evil is self-evident. It is appalling how millions of children and adolescents are treated both at home and abroad. America is the wealthiest democracy in the world, the last so-called super-power. Why is it then, that an American child is reported as being abused every eleven seconds? These are just the *reported* incidents. Considering that many children do not report experiences because they are threatened, fear the family will be broken up (and it would be his or her fault), and feel immense shame and guilt, it is impossible to tell how much abuse is occurring. There are 581,000 children in the foster care system with 127,000 awaiting adoptive families. As a side note, the foster care system itself has been the object of controversy for quite some time. There are some—certainly not all—foster parents who use the system as a way to gain access to children to use for labour or for their own sexual gratification. Returning to statistics, an American child is born into poverty every forty-three seconds. One in five children is poor during the first three years of life, a time that is critical for brain development. Every minute a child is born with no health insurance. An American child or teen is killed by gunfire every two hours and forty minutes every day. Guns have killed 87,000 children and teens since 1979. It is safer to be an on-duty police officer than a child under ten years of age in America. Millions of American children begin school not ready to learn and millions more do not have safe, affordable, child-care and early childhood education while their parents work (Children's Defense Fund, 2002).

In 1994, 1,271 child-abuse related fatalities were confirmed by CPS agencies. Since 1985 child abuse fatalities have increased by forty-eight per cent. This means that three children die from abuse daily. The states that track this statistic report that eighty-eight per cent of these children were under the age of five. Forty-six of these children were under one year of age. Forty-two per cent of these deaths were the result of neglect, fifty four per cent from physical abuse, and four per cent from a combination of physical abuse and neglect. Almost half (45%) of these children were known to Child Protective Services as past or active clients (Wiese & Daro, 1995).

Perpetrators of child abuse or neglect are defined as parents or other caretakers, such as a relative, baby-sitter, or foster parent, who have maltreated a child. For the year 2001, fifty-nine per cent of perpetrators were women and forty-one per cent were men. The median age of female perpetrators was thirty-one years and the median age of male perpetrators was thirty-four years. A parent or parents abused more than eighty per cent of victims (84%). Just their mother maltreated almost half of child victims (41%), and both their mother and father maltreated one-fifth of victims (19%) (United States Department of Health and Human Services, 2003). In other words, the ones doing the most damage are the ones upon whom the child is often most dependent. These statistics represent only American children.

The World Health Organization (1997) asserts that child abuse and neglect have been a societal phenomenon for centuries. The WHO admits that it is only now gaining a sense of the magnitude of the problem. Although it is difficult to achieve exact statistical figures, the WHO has drawn the following conclusions:

1. Child abuse is found in all societies and is almost always a highly guarded secret, wherever it takes place.
2. In countries with reliable mortality reporting, WHO estimates that as many as one in 5,000 to one in 10,000 children under the age of five die each year from physical violence, although much lower rates are also noted.
3. In the same countries, from one in 1,000 to one in 180,000? children are either brought to a health care facility or are reported to child welfare services as a consequence of abuse every year.
4. According to interviews of children or young adults in Finland, the Republic of Korea and the USA, from 5 to 10 per cent of all children experience physical violence during childhood.

The WHO sees the following as causal factors to abuse and neglect:

1. Physical violence often originates in the lack of parenting skills—particularly in the ability to respond to a young child's needs combined with unrealistic expectations for the stage of a child's development. This can be affected by the cultural acceptance of corporal punishment and violence within a society.
2. Other stresses contributing to child abuse and neglect may include: an unwanted child, an unsupported single parent household and the absence of other means of social support, financial pressures and/or unemployment.
3. Child abuse can be aggravated by substance abuse on the part of the child's parent or guardian. In substance abusing families there is a strong association between physical violence, sexual abuse and domestic violence directed at members of the family, particularly women and young children.
4. The perpetrators of violence or sexual abuse of children are often "trusted" individuals, usually males, often family members, in a position of authority.
5. Children who are victims of violence or sexual abuse have a high risk of becoming perpetrators of similar forms of abuse towards younger children. In later years, they may be physically violent to children in their care or to their own children.
6. Physical violence and sexual abuse in the home is a factor contributing to the phenomenon of "street children" in both developed and

developing countries. Further abuse on the street is an everyday reality.

The WHO concludes that the susceptibility of children to abuse and neglect is associated with the child's age. Simply put, the younger the child, the more damaging the impact of the abuse. The damage caused is both physical and emotional in nature. Specifically, those suffering from trauma are at risk of developing Post-traumatic Stress Disorder. (This is the same disorder discussed earlier in reference to the Vietnam veterans interviewed in Shay's (1995) *Achilles in Vietnam*.)

It is difficult to overestimate the psychological torment associated with this disorder. According to the American Psychiatric Association *Diagnostic and Statistical Manual of Mental Disorders* (1994) PTSD develops when one is exposed to one or more traumatic events. The person responds with intense fear, helplessness, or horror. The person then repeatedly re-experiences the traumatic event in one or more of the following ways: recurrent and intrusive recollections of the event, recurrent distressing dreams of the event, acting or feeling that the event is occurring (this can include hallucinations and dissociative flashback episodes), and intense distress at internal or external cues to the event. The developmental effects of abuse can be characterized in terms of loss of attachment, reduced self-esteem and fewer interpersonal relationships. There may also be problems of highly sexualized or highly aggressive behavior, substance use, self-injury, or other self-destructive ways of contending with stress and anxiety. None of this reflects larger health issues plaguing countless children.

Strapp (2003) published an article citing that nearly eleven million children do not live to see their fifth birthday each year due to malnutrition and disease, which are largely preventable. India, Nigeria, China, Pakistan, and the Democratic Republic of Congo and Ethiopia alone experience 5.5 million child deaths per year. Most of these children die from preventable or easily managed diseases such as measles, malaria, diarrhea, and pneumonia. Malnutrition is rampant in these areas and it makes children twelve times more likely to contract disease. According to Jean-Pierre Habicht, a professor of epidemiology and nutritional sciences at Cornell University, "Preventing deaths from these diseases costs only pennies per year" (Strapp, 2003). This article cites the WHO research indicating that there are 500 million new infections of malaria every year and, of the infected, one million die. In Africa, malaria accounts for one in five of all child deaths per year.

In the same article Dr. C. Gopalan, president of the Federation of Asian Nutrition Societies, says:

> Nearly 80 percent of pregnant women in this region are anaemic and, even more importantly, nearly one-third of infants are of low birth weight. The diets of pregnant women in poor communities in South Asia are as poor, if not poorer, than those of non-pregnant women. (Strapp, 2003)

A vaccine exists that can eliminate the problem. Measles, another virus that has a vaccine, kills one million children a year, half in Africa alone. Measles kills more African children than AIDS, tuberculosis, and malnutrition. Studies in Bangladesh, the Philippines, and Uganda yield that seventy-nine per cent of measles cases were complicated by pneumonia and diarrhea, which increased fatality rates. "We know how to prevent these deaths—we have the biological knowledge and tools to stop this public health travesty—but we're not doing it yet." (ibid.) Habicht concludes, "We know how to prevent the deaths of millions of children. Now we just have to do it." (ibid.)

More disturbing is a report by the United Nations International Children's Emergency Fund (2002) concerning the phenomenon of child trafficking. According to this document more than 1.2 million children are trafficked every year. These children are tricked, coerced, sold and/or kidnapped into living under horrid circumstances. They are exchanged and used for begging, gangs, domestic service, marriage, prostitution, pornography, as soldiers, for trade in human organs. Clearly these are the worst forms of child labour. Every country around the world—and no country is exempt on this score—is involved in child trafficking either as a receiving, sending, or as a transition location. This document reports that child trafficking is increasing and is the third most profitable form of global organized crime, after drugs and guns trafficking. Child trafficking generates three billion dollars annually. The present rate of trafficking in children is already ten times higher than the trans-Atlantic slave trade at its peak. Child trafficking is considered a contemporary form of slavery. The most vulnerable children in the world's poorest communities are most susceptible to trafficking. This population includes girls, ethnic minorities, homeless children, and orphans of HIV/AIDS. Children who are trafficked are denied their rights to family, education, protection from exploitation and abuse, and to develop in a healthy and peaceful environment with time for rest and leisure. In an interview given on 19 June 2001 a worker reported the conditions of children in her care:

> We have a whole range of abuse, from physical to sexual. We have rape cases in our centre. We have children really badly beaten. We have cases of domestic workers ironed by their employer ... the hot iron ... they put that in the back of the child, they put it sometimes in the legs. (United Nations, 2003)

These children are ripped away from their families and communities and deposited in a new place, alone and fearful. They are bound to their captors by threats, incarceration, debt bondage, fear and isolation. Many, perhaps most, lose their lives and at the very least suffer decimated childhoods.

There is (at least) a two-front war being waged against youth. There is the blatant emotional and physical damage being wrought upon children and adolescents and then there is the ravaging caused by, what Heidegger (1954) called, *injurious neglect*. The physical and emotional scarring is obvious. What is more latent is the idea that by not tending, by not acting, by not affording a maternal psychological space to hold children, they slip into the unconscious, into death or into madness (Peters, 1997).

The very system in place to protect children in America frequently damages children and families. In her book *Disposable Children: America's Welfare System* (1997) Golden examines the present system and questions whether or not the main goal of the child welfare system is to protect children. She points out that there is a hidden side to the system, one wherein children are removed from their homes only to be subjected to another experience of betrayal as damaging, if not more, than the abuse leading to the system's intervention. Although Golden does not do so, I think it is interesting to ponder the word *disposable*.

First of all there are few, if any, synonyms for this word. It seems to stand alone in its meaning. According to *Webster's New Twentieth Century Dictionary* (1956) *dis*—comes from Latin and refers to *two* in the sense of rendering asunder, having different directions, or referring to a negative or privative force. The second part of the word comes from the

Latin *ponere, to place*. So disposable, in its more essential meaning, refers to ordering in such a way as to have the power of disposal. I could not help but notice that immediately following *dis-* in my dictionary is *Dis*, a name given to Pluto in Roman mythology. Pluto, known as Hades in Greek mythology, was the god of the infernal regions. Another intuitive link can be made to the word dissed, which in teenage vernacular refers to being taken advantage of or being screwed over. In any event, the image inherent to the word disposable does not create a sensibility of care, especially when applied to vulnerable children. Moreover, it indicates a kind of comportment that reifies children to cases, which are things to be managed in the service of the interests of the professionals assuming power and direction.

Through a series of interviews with families refusing to be cases in the system, Golden shows how vulnerable children are introduced to a system where their frail sense of self-worth is reinforced. Lost in a sea of bureaucratic red tape, case-workers, probation officers, foster homes, therapists, psychiatrists, social workers, and treatment centres, the child becomes special to no-one. Under the circumstances, when the child acts out the system uses that as further evidence of deviancy. More often than not, the acting-out represents attempts to resume contact with the family from which he or she was removed. In my experience working with homeless and disturbed youth, the system literalizes the notion of family. For some of these children family does not necessarily refer biological relatives. Moreover, the system fails to appreciate that children often want to return to the abusive home. I am not advocating that children be allowed to return to such situations in all cases. I am saying that children often experience this need desperately. To fail to recognize this is to further invalidate the child and increase the risk of him or her lying or otherwise acting-out.

The State simply does not recognize the children's preferences and views them as property. Children are informed of changes moments or hours before they are to be implemented, leaving them lacking a sense of home. The notion of children as property varies qualitatively from the view that adults have a responsibility to discern the child's best interest. To view children as owned is to establish a power relationship whereby one person has no power and the other ultimate power. What is worse is that such a view detracts from the lack of job opportunity, decent housing, health care, and education that are at the root of the problem. Golden cites the U.S. Advisory Board on Child Abuse and Neglect:

> [T]he system the nation has devised to respond to child abuse and neglect is failing; there is chronic and multiple organ failure. Indeed, the system itself can at times be abusive to children ... Not only is child abuse wrong, but the nation's lack of an effective response to it is also wrong. Neither can be tolerated. Together they constitute a moral disaster. (Golden, 1997, pp. 46–47)

Golden asks how safe American children are when in a single twenty-four hour period three children die from abuse, nine are murdered, thirteen die from gun-inflicted wounds, thirty are wounded by guns, sixty three babies die before they are a month old, 101 before their first birthday, and 2,868 are born into poverty. The U.S. infant mortality rate ranks twenty-second worldwide. The black infant mortality rate ranks fortiethin the world, below poor nations such a Sri Lanka, Malaysia, Jamaica, and Portugal (ibid., p. 46).

To explain why so much harm is being done to children and families, Golden offers a story. One day villagers go to the river and are surprised to find a corpse floating by. They fish the body out, give it a proper burial, and offer a prayer. The next day the villagers discover two bodies floating by and, again, they retrieve the bodies, bury them, and offer prayers. The third day they discover three bodies. By the weekend there were so many bodies that the villagers organized themselves into three committees: one to retrieve the corpses, one to dig graves, and one to offer prayers. The villagers were so busy with their tasks that they neglected going up the river to see what or who was killing.

The American child welfare system is in crisis. The system limps from one emergency to the next, working in response to family crises and offering nothing preventative. Children become disposable in the system, seen often as cases to be managed, not as humans with potential. It forgets it is dealing with persons with problems and not problems themselves. The system's philosophical presupposition is often forced child removal, taking ownership, and forgoing the child's perspective. Also lost in this process is recognition of the underlying societal problems that are the preconditions for family chaos: lack of employment opportunities, education, affordable housing, childcare, health coverage, and substance abuse. When the traumatized child enters the system he or she is often subjected to more betrayal and chaos. When the child rails against the system and acts out, the behaviour is used as evidence that the child is disturbed. Such evidence is used to justify integrating the child deeper and deeper into the system. Children are subject to bureaucratic trauma and are not always safe in foster care. Children may experience foster care drift and may even be placed in homes with foster parents whose primary motive is exploitation. Golden is clear that the curative factor in working with such children is a loving relationship.

Case vignette

I work in a pressure cooker environment. I work with mentally ill and dually diagnosed children and teens at an inpatient unit. I understand that many well-qualified therapists applied for my position. I would not describe my job interviews with this facility as particularly good, but I think they liked the way I explained the nature of residential work: "You have to be comfortable with the 'air traffic controller' nature of the work." I am responsible for case management, individual psychotherapy, groups, lectures, case reviews, backing up the floor staff, crisis intervention, family counseling, assessments, and treatment planning. Every minute of every day is scheduled for the patients, who are beholden to a phase system. With each phase is a series of things that need completion before moving to the next phase. What I love most is working with the children and adolescents. It is amazing to see the relationships form, to see some trust, and relief from trauma and addiction.

I was in a particularly difficult group one day. The patients were arguing and I was basically setting down boundaries as quickly as I could speak. Out of the chaos, a voice emerged. I do not know how many times she said it, but a clear strong voice rose above the rest: "I'm sick of being sick and I'm sick of using. I've thought about it and it's time to change. I'm gonna be honest." Strangely, the group fell silent. We all looked at her. She sat slumped in her chair, hair down covering her face, arms crossed. Shannon was new to the group. I began meeting Shannon regularly. My rule with the patients was that I will meet with them for one one-hour session per week and they can request additional time.

Upon initial review of her chart I found that throughout her many foster care placements, she had numerous short-term superficial relationships with a multitude of social workers, probation officers, psychiatrists, and psychotherapists. Nothing worked. She was diagnosed with Bipolar Disorder, ADHD, Oppositional Defiant Disorder at different times in her life, and carried a host of chemical dependency diagnoses. She consistently refused medication management and generalized all healthcare professionals as counselors. In her estimation, "Counselors are all full of shit." Shannon was considered a problem case by the referring party and supervising professionals. She did not make connections with professionals charged with her care. No one understood why she would not get over her desire to return to her abusive family of origin. She was an addict and had multiple substance related arrests and charges. I was warned that she would likely be a danger to myself and others. No one understood why she would not get it together. Most did not understand why she would not give up calling her step-father father, especially considering how abusive he was.

"I'm going to get honest right now" and, for the most part, she did. I am not sure what helped Shannon engage in treatment. Maybe it was that she was forced to be there. I think that she genuinely was sick of street life. She was exposed to violence frequently and her drug use was making her ill. She would have friends inject her with meth as she looked away and then she would go to the bathroom and vomit. Shannon had wild tales of car chases, beatings, and other extreme sensation-seeking behaviours. A lot of it was over-stimulating and dangerous. She was also aware of what drugs did to her parents: their inability to be present in any meaningful way, finding them passed out and wondering if they were alive, wondering if she was going to find them dead. I think she knew that at fifteen years old she had a long road ahead of her and that her present life would likely end in death. It is a miracle that she is alive.

When she was a young child, her parents moved to a trailer "out in the middle of nowhere" to smoke and inject meth all day. Before continuing I would like to briefly note what a particularly dangerous and addictive substance meth is. Addicts I have worked with describe meth as "poor man's coke," since it is a synthetic, cheaper version of cocaine. Items seized by police from meth labs are lye, ether, iodine, Draino, ephedrine, brake fluid, lighter fluid, cold medicine, lithium metals, hydrachloride, hydriotic acid, red phosphorus, and anyhdrous ammonia. All of the meth addicts I have worked with describe meth labs as smelling like strong cat urine. Some of meth's side effects include hyperactivity, irritability, aggression, severe paranoia, bizarre and violent behaviour, vomiting, diarrhea, major depression, weight loss, malnutrition, anorexia, welts, uncontrollable body and facial twitching, delusions, hallucinations, and suicidal ideation. Meth, like other central nervous system (CNS) stimulants, simulates the reward center of the brain. There is no built in satiation point so people use it until they run out or die. In fact, in studies where animals self-administered CNS stimulants, the animals would self-administer until they died. Needless to say meth wreaks havoc on the body, causing brain damage and leaving the body susceptible to a host of diseases (Fisher, 2000). Without treatment, meth addicts invariably die.

Returning to Shannon's narrative, she described how her parents smoked and injected meth all day. Towards the end of the day, on a somewhat regular basis, her step-father would like to blast heavy metal music (the band Suicidal Tendencies) and "kick the shit out of my mom. She would be too out of it to do anything about it." Shannon described the horror of trying to soothe her younger brother on their bunk bed, while this was going on beneath them. This is when the running began. Shannon would run away from home frequently to get away from the violence. She said she wanted to "live with CPS." Shannon's father threatened to cut her throat if she continued talking that way. Father, it turns out, was not only beating mother but was sexually abusing Shannon. Shannon began trying to get CPS involved by telling everyone she knew what was going on at home.

Eventually, Shannon, her younger brother, and her mother moved; mother decided she could not take the beatings anymore and Shannon was raising concerns about her father molesting her. Shannon expected things to get better—they did not. In fact, mother began using more meth than before and began drinking heavily. Mother blamed Shannon for "breaking up the family by talking like that." Mother had to prostitute herself to get drugs, exposing the children to very dangerous people and situations. Shannon's mother became pregnant and Shannon had a younger brother. She struggled to connect with him, since she already had an infant brother die. The reasons for the death remain a mystery. Mother blamed father, father blamed mother. For some reason, no charges were filed against either parent. Shannon cannot (or will not let herself) remember many details. She simply woke up one morning and her brother was gone.

She recalled suffering much abuse at the hands of her mother. Mother on one occasion became inebriated, got in her car with the children and rammed it into telephone poles while screaming at them. She had multiple arrests and involuntary psychiatric hospitalizations.

Things continued to get worse as mother continued increasing her use. Dad was either in jail or out with warrants. In any event, he had little contact with them. Mother became increasingly paranoid and suicidal, often beating Shannon and telling her that everything was her fault. When she was not blaming Shannon, she blamed herself and would make suicide attempts in front of the children. Shannon would intervene and mother would lash out at her. Shannon took the beatings because if mother focused on her, then she would not try to kill herself or beat her younger brother.

One day state officials arrived at school to question Shannon. "They scared the shit out of me," Shannon said. To add to this, father told Shannon a long time ago what would happen if the state intervened. Not only would he harm her, but also he said they would not believe her. He said he was good at lying about things and could easily pass a polygraph. The officials left without taking action.

Father returned to the family and began molesting Shannon again. She recalled simply having to lie there and be as motionless as possible. She felt that if she moved, he would just get angry. Shannon pleaded to her mother for help and mother scolded her for "talking like that." The molestations were quite aggressive and, according to Shannon, would last about an hour and a half. Shannon continued running away and returning.

Mother went to jail on drug charges and Shannon recalled that this was when she started smoking cigarettes, marijuana, and drinking. At this time, she was eleven years old. Father was never around so Shannon, being the eldest, took care of her younger siblings. Eventually, they were not able to keep up on rent, lost their apartment, and moved in with relatives. The relatives, also addicts, were seldom around. Father went to jail and Shannon was responsible for the household. CPS intervened and removed the children from the home, placing them in separate homes. They are not allowed to have contact with each other. Shannon hated being in foster care and could not stand the lack of contact with her siblings. She desperately wanted to live with her father and siblings. Over the course of the next five years Shannon ran from every foster placement and group home given to her. She became increasingly involved with street life and was adopted by a street family. This street family (i.e. gang) convinced her to try meth. Shannon became addicted and continued using marijuana and alcohol. She hated herself for using meth because she saw what it did to her mother. Nonetheless, she was hooked.

Concerning this time she said, "I lost my soul. I lost all morality and self-respect." Her addiction reached a fevered pitch, as she began using meth and alcohol all day every day. Fortunately, she did not have to resort to prostitution because her boyfriend was supplying her, although he left her with a serious sexually transmitted disease. She was arrested for assault and court ordered to successfully complete treatment at my facility.

Shannon seemed open and honest about her past and her story seemed consistent with historical records. I felt an intense battle going on inside of her. Would the healthy part of her personality win or the destructive? I did not know, but I sensed a storm brewing on the horizon. Eventually, I suspected that she would want to know if I was serious about helping her, or if I was going to abandon her or hurt her like everyone else. Shannon trusted me with this information and it seemed that I was the first steady, healthy relationship she had.

At one point, though, I had to make a mandated CPS report when she disclosed abuse occurring with one sibling who, for whatever reason, still resided with father. Shannon raged at me for this. My nickname was now "asshole." In her mind, my actions were going to aid CPS' intent to separate her family and increase the likelihood that father will harm her. She refused to speak to me and caused problems on the floor.

My efforts to explain that CPS took it as an information-only call were useless. I had really damaged the relationship. Instead of attempting to draw her back in one-on-one therapy, I attempted to work with her and the other patients on the floor. I moved from a more psycho-analytic emphasis upon frame to a more phenomenological approach. I recalled Laing's dictum that people stop acting like they're insane when you stop treating them like they're insane. I thought about how Laing worked with patients and wondered if I could bring a similar sensibility to the milieu.

I noticed that every day I came to work the patients would crowd around me and yell my name, "I need … I need … I need!" Some of the more hysterical patients would actually throw themselves on the ground in front of me. "Why are they so needy?" I would think, "They get so much of my time." I began to reverse my perspective. Maybe the emphasis should not be on the frame of one-on-one therapy. Maybe I should just spend as much time with them on the floor as possible. I did not get rid of the one-on-one therapy, but I increased the time I spent with them.

At first they responded wildly; I felt completely drained. It felt like no amount of my time could satiate their need for attention. After time passed, the frequent contact with me worked so well that some of them would have nothing to talk about during the one-on-one sessions. Soon I came to work without being assailed. The less available I was, the more anxious they became. Simply being around them, being completely honest at all times, and being calm, helped them feel maternally held. The part of me that they experienced as mom had a schedule, did what she said she would do, would apologize for her mistakes, would arrive at a precise time, would leave at a certain time, and would genuinely advocate for their needs. They were, for the most part, content.

I knew I wrecked the relationship with Shannon. I decided I was just going to be a steady and kind presence with her on the floor. I was kind to her no matter what she did or said. She refused to eat food or drink water. I would quietly get her a bottle of water and place it in front of her. "I don't want your fucking water asshole." She would throw the water bottle and I would retrieve it, placing it again in front of her. I would then quietly leave. "I really care about you and your treatment" was my mantra with her. I meant it and I was unwavering in my belief that she was capable of completing treatment successfully.

I learned so much by being around the patients. One of the first things I noticed about Shannon was that she would pretend that she understood what people said. She had an extremely limited vernacular and would compensate by simply going along with the conversation. The more time I spent on the floor, the more Shannon was receptive to talking to me. I pointed out that I really did not think she understood a lot of what others and I said. She seemed to appreciate my attention. I noticed a dynamic emerging: front-line staff would give her directions, she would not understand them, they would get frustrated, she would escalate and then we had a crisis on our hands.

I adopted a practice of not using complex words with her and I encouraged other staff to do so as well. Most conversations ended with me saying, "Did you understand everything that I said?" I was shocked at how many words she did not understand. We would go through the conversation and discuss word-by-word what I meant. She felt more therapeutically held, incidents of her acting out decreased, and she was again willing to re-engage in one-on-one therapy. She was curious about why she did not know as many words as her peers. I was struck by the fact that whether she was being abused, doing drugs, or parenting her siblings, she was always simply surviving.

While Shannon's trust in me was growing, I knew that there would be a lot to weather before she was ready to leave. One day I followed a loud banging sound to find Shannon running and slamming her body against a locked door. She was hurting herself. I was surprised; I thought things were going well in the therapy. I noticed that I was shaking a little. I struggled to find the right approach. I figured I could either panic, call the police, attempt to find someone to help me restrain her, or come up with something to say. I said in a casual voice, "Hey, I was wondering if I could help you stop hurting yourself." She did not stop. I did not change my casual comportment. I was pretending to be calm. I thought that laying down firm boundaries would only cause her to escalate. I noticed that the door had been left unlocked. She was too hysterical to notice. Then I said the first thing that came to mind: "Shannon, I can't stand watching you hurt yourself." She dropped to the floor and curled up in the corner. I approached her and was simply silent. She began sobbing. Her voice deepened, the tears came, her nose ran, and her face was bright red.

What the hell was going on? Why was she so upset? In silence I just felt the power of her affect. It seemed like she was vomiting out all of the poison: the abuse, the unmet needs, the inability to have a healthy childhood, having to live in constant vigilance or distracted by mind-blowing drugs. I was very moved, but struggled with finding the words to help her digest her experience. The whole experience caught me off guard. I noticed some patients approaching. "Shannon, come to my office. I don't think you want the others seeing you this upset." She came to my office, sat down, and began writhing around in the chair. I was perplexed. She was groaning, tearful, and could not stop moving. I could not figure out what was going on. Were these post-acute withdrawal symptoms? Did she need medical attention? Who would I call? Would she experience my calling as an inability to contain her in the relationship? I needed to say something and say it quickly.

The words just flew out of my mouth: "You are going through withdrawals right now." "What? That's totally fucked up Brent. You know I haven't used in months." She continued writhing and groaning.

"No, you're a runaholic." She gave me a look of complete confusion. "You're not getting your runahol, so you're going through withdrawals." Now she was completely perplexed. "You've run from your own home countless times and from every treatment centre, foster home, and group home you've been in. You use running like you're using a drug." She still looked confused, but was calmer. I handed her some tissues. "This is the longest you've ever been in one place at one time, you don't know how to handle it, and overall your treatment is going well. These are all firsts to you. It's ridiculous to think that you should know how to handle these things, except to run. You're dependent on it whenever you feel stressed." She was now much calmer, wiped her eyes and I was surprised to hear her laugh. "I remember that all of my paperwork ends with 'she ran'." After a few more minutes of digesting this idea, she left my office and returned to normal programming. Of course, Shannon had to smile and mutter "asshole" right before she left.

Since that time Shannon became more motivated in her treatment. Over time the stress and drama of being in an inpatient unit ceased to bother her. I have noticed that patients turn a certain corner in their treatment when they begin focusing on themselves and care less about the concerns of others. I am not referring to disconnecting from others in a depressive or narcissistic way. I am referring to a certain focus, acceptance and peace of mind inherent in being motivated to improve oneself. Once this mindset is attained, more spontaneity, humour, and playfulness ensue. Generally speaking, I take playfulness and humour as signs of health. These are more mature and differentiated ways of digesting experience. Since I altered my language when speaking with Shannon, she took the opportunity to teach me some words she knew I probably did not know. Chillaxing, is a combination of the words chilling and relaxing. A grip refers to any large amount of something. It can refer to qualitative things like, "I haven't seen you in a grip," or it can refer to material objects as in, "He had a grip of magazines." I also learned about tweaking. Tweeking refers both to being high on meth (or any CNS stimulant) as well as becoming hyper-focused on one or more activities. Apparently, some meth addicts get high and then will, for example, take a computer apart and put it back together again or clean until their living space is spotless. In any event, I had connected with the healthy part of her personality and she was getting better. She graduated successfully and moved into an apartment subsidized by a local youth services agency.

Shannon continued making progress in treatment and was approaching graduating from the program. It was during this time that Shannon approached me, offering a penciled sketch of Dante Gabriel Rosetti's *Proserpine*. Some time ago I lent her a book, a pictorial guide to Greek mythology. I was quite surprised that of all my books in my office—and I had quite a few—she chose that particular book. Moreover, of the hundreds of paintings reprinted in the book, she chose that particular picture. When asked why she chose that particular picture she responded, "It just seemed like the right one to sketch and I wanted to give it to you." The myth is briefly delineated next to the picture, but she denied reading it. When I asked if she would like to know about the myth associated with the picture she politely declined: "That's like the school stuff you're interested in." I thanked her very much for the picture and told her I would keep it in my office. It must have taken her hours to complete such a finely detailed sketch. I was struck by the many elements of the myth that were reflected in Shannon's life. The myth is a beautiful and moving narrative of a young woman, a neglectful mother, and an unexpected yet fateful encounter with utter destructiveness.

The myth of persephone

Ceres is the Roman name for the Greek goddess Demeter. The introduction of the cult to Ceres in Rome dates back to 496 BC and seems to follow from the siege of the city of the Etruscans, while Rome was threatened with famine (Nilsson, 1972). Persephone, also known as Kore, is known both as the goddess of growth and as the goddess of the dead. The daughter of Demeter (earth goddess and goddess of grain) and Zeus (ruler of the Olympian gods), she has over time developed many aspects. Persephone and Kore were originally separate, distinct figures in the Greek pantheon. Kore (i.e. *girl* or *maiden*) is described as a young, beautiful girl, and Persephone (i.e. *she who destroys the light* or *bringer of destruction*) as a sinister, brooding woman of ghastly power, akin to the East Indian goddess, Kali. Late in the evolution of the Greek pantheon these two qualities were joined thus bringing to fruition the fair, sad character of a woman so well known in literature, art and poetry (Lefkowitz, 1990).

As the classical story goes, Persephone was out gathering flowers in a meadow when Hades, god of the underworld, caught sight of her.

Enamoured by her loveliness, he seizes her just as she is plucking a narcissus, and carries her off into the earth. Her mother, too busy tending to the earth, does not immediately notice her daughter's abduction. Later though, stricken by her loss, Demeter forgoes her divine obligations in order to search for her missing daughter, and the earth falls barren. Fruit withers on the branches, plants dry up and die and the animals either perish or slip into hibernation. Witnessing the havoc this was exacting on mortals, Zeus intervenes and demands the return of Persephone to Demeter unless she had, by some word or deed, consented to her capture. During her brief stay in Hade's realm, Persephone eats a pomegranate and, wittingly or not, commits herself. She is compelled to spend an equal number of months each year with her new mate in his dark realm according to how many pomegranate seeds she ate. The months of her absence from the earth mark the winter season as her mother falls into a grim, seasonal misery (Caldecott, 1993).

Although there are numerous stories retelling the Persephone myth, there are two versions that are considered the classics: the Orphic Persephone Myth and *The Rape of Proserpine* in Ovid's *Metamorphoses* (Hayes, 1994). Both of these versions proffer differing perspectives of the myth.

The Orphic version of the Persephone and Demeter tale is dispersed throughout a number of poems. In the Orphic telling, a poor man (Dysaules) and his wife Baubo entertained Demeter, who was searching the earth for her missing daughter. During her visit with the couple, Baubo made the grieving goddess laugh by dancing obscenely. Seeing Demeter in her grief, Baubo moved her hips in a manner that suggested sexual intercourse and shook her breasts as a part of her little jig. The couple's sons, Triptolemos and Eubeleus, told Demeter that they knew of her daughter's whereabouts. Specifically, they had inadvertently observed the seizure of Persephone when their herd of pigs fell down the fissure opened by Hades as he came from the underworld to take the youth. Demeter rewarded the sons by imparting to them her mysterious divine works, including how she made grain grow, and she made them responsible for teaching mankind these mysteries. Interestingly enough, the Orphic version never treats of Demeter's denial, in her grief over the loss of her daughter, to let anything grow on earth and the famine that resulted (Guthrie, 1966).

In Ovid's *The Rape of Proserpine*, a Roman telling, Venus saw Pluto, who was checking the foundations of Sicily for signs of damage to the roof of hell. Venus wanted to extend her empire to the underworld and at the same time desired to remove a potential maiden goddess from the class of the forever pure. Venus instructed Cupid to shoot his finest arrow deep into Pluto's heart. Cupid conceded and when the arrow met its mark, Pluto straightaway fell madly in love with Proserpine.

Proserpine was gathering flowers with her friends when Pluto found her. Mortified, she cried out for Ceres as Pluto carried her away in his chariot. Hearing her cries, the nymph Cyane tried to stop Pluto, but the Lord of the Dead hurled his sceptre at Cyane's pool. The sceptre hit the bottom of the pool and a gorge opened. The chariot plunged down to the underworld and Cyane, distraught over Proserpine's rape, shed tears until she vanished into her own pool.

Ceres, carrying torches, searched ceaselessly for her lost Proserpine. At one point she was given a sweet barley beverage by an old crone in a cottage and, during this time, a rude boy laughed at her—Demeter changed him into a newt. Later, Ceres came to Cyane's pool, where she found Proserpine's sash floating on the surface. Upon seeing this, she realized that her daughter had been kidnapped. Furious, Ceres caused the land to become infertile and thus blighted all of humanity with a terrible famine.

The nymph Arethusa informed Ceres about where Proserpine was located; she had seen Proserpine while in the underworld as the spouse of Pluto. Now even more outraged, Ceres sought out Jove with haste and demanded better treatment for their daughter. Jove tried to calm Ceres, reassuring her that Pluto was powerful and worthy. After all, he explained, her new son-in-law was Jove's brother. Moreover, Jove reminded Ceres that Proserpine could not leave the underworld if she had eaten there.

Sadly, Proserpine had eaten seven pomegranate seeds while wandering through an orchard in hell. Ascalaphus saw her eat the seeds and he vindictively reported the action. Angered, Proserpine changed him into a screeching owl. In the end, Jove decreed that Proserpine spend half the year with Ceres and the other half with Pluto. When her six months in Pluto's domain were over each year, Proserpine was filled with bliss as she went to join her mother in the upper world (Hayes, 1994).

Persephone's nightmarish abduction into the underworld was necessary for her ascension to being its queen. It is difficult to predict what would have happened if Persephone completely resisted her fate of becoming queen of the underworld. It is interesting that not only did she integrate the forces of the underworld, but actually gained in strength and wisdom by allying with them. The name Persephone means bringer of destruction. On the other hand, she did not completely identify with the underworld, spending roughly half of her life in the world of the living. The myth implies that it is not necessarily good to shun, pathologize, or repress destructiveness. It is important to recognize the role destructiveness plays in the larger unfolding of one's existence without identifying with it. I found the image Shannon penciled a thought-provoking and profoundly appropriate image of her life and struggle for health.

Vignette summary

Shannon's case is sadly not uncommon. There are elements of it that are common with many of the patients I have treated. The child is subject to one or more traumatic events. Trauma does not have to be a single event, like the sudden death of a family member. It can more subtle—the narcissistically unavailable parent, living in deprivation, having to endure parental conflicts. When trauma sets in, the part of the child psychologically freezes and becomes psychologically stunted at that age. Whilst that part is stunted, another part of the personality develops rapidly to take care of the younger self. This was very apparent with Shannon. When she first came to treatment and decided to try to be more honest and healthy, she would put her hair in ponytails and do cartwheels during recreation time. Other patients would criticize her and tease her for acting so childish. She would respond, "I'm liking being five." At other times I was struck by her mature care for others, undoubtedly linked to her having to care for her siblings. Qualitatively speaking, she was in some ways older than 15 years old. She had matured too rapidly not only in response to taking care of her younger self, but in learning how to survive on the streets. I have experienced this with many patients. They are part their chronological age, part traumatized child, and part adult caretaker. It is imperative that the therapist discovers and tends to all the parts of the psyche. Too often I have seen therapists assume that a child or adolescent is developmentally at his or her chronological age. This is a set up because the patient will invariably actout and others may use that as further evidence of a mental health disorder.

Outside of the obvious trauma, did Shannon have a mental health disorder? In my opinion, she did not have a mental health disorder. In my work with her there was no evidence of a mood disorder, attention deficit disorder, and I think anyone would be oppositional and defiant in her circumstances. Her drug use can be understood as a desperate response to survive in an unlivable situation. While I have never ingested a CNS stimulant, I have also been fortunate enough to not have to be raised under her circumstances. Quite honestly, I cannot say how I would respond when having to endure such a childhood. Shannon was not a 'problem case' and she was not mentally ill. If anything, her life circumstances and the welfare system were more ill than she was.

Placing her in homes where she did not want to be and moving her through a host of professionals established a serious barrier to my ability to serve her. Why should she listen to me? Shannon's acting-out at times was simply her attempt to see if I would be present to her in a genuine way when she was done. In a Bionian sense, I helped her metabolize and survive her destructiveness. As is typical, her perspective on things was not considered as she moved through the system. Shannon was shocked that I did not challenge her desire to return to her abusive family of origin or insist that she call father step-dad. Her biological father was completely absent so, qualitatively speaking, step-father was dad. To challenge that belief would only serve to further undermine her felt experience of family, and to increase the likelihood of her lying to me. This is not to say that I would recommend a return to the home. I simply let her have her belief and accepted that it in fact was of paramount importance to her. Why did she want to go back to that home? It perplexed me. It is counterintuitive to want to place oneself in a situation where harm has been done and is likely to continue. I was thinking about similar cases and it struck me: children and teens often want to be with whoever has been there the earliest and the longest. As strange as it might sound to us, mum and dad were there from the beginning and she spent the most time with them. Shannon also bore much unconscious guilt over the breakup of the family and compensated by maintaining an idealized image of what it would be like to live there now. Everything would be fine, nothing bad would happen, it would be great all the time. I would respond by attempting to awaken curiosity, not doubt: "I'm curious and I'm wondering if you're curious about having a great time all the time with them." She worked through that material. In the end she still wanted to return home but was able to afford a space where she could think about home in a less idealized fashion.

In therapy with Shannon and similar cases, I am always struggling to figure out what image they carry of me in their minds. Sometimes I felt like a dealer in the sense that I was the one responsible for giving (or restricting) privileges and other desirable things. At other times I felt maternal, both in the rule-enforcer sense as well as the nurturing, containing sense. Mum would make sure that all needs were met. Mum would not leave and simply not return. Mum did not need someone to be her mum. Mum would not harm anyone. Mum would be protective and was there when things were really rough. I experienced the father aspect more in the case management portion of the work. "Where is she going upon discharge? Is that the best place for her? How long does she need to be in the system?" and "These are my recommendations."

Shannon has a long tough road ahead of her. The severity of her substance abuse should not be taken lightly. The destructive-addicted element of her mind will always remain a part of her. Drugs and gangs are a part of the world and she will undoubtedly be tempted to relapse at some point. Also, she may discover that her past criminal history will limit future possibilities. The trauma she has endured will likely haunt her in various ways. It will take a lot more therapy to help her recover fully. I hope to have helped her understand that hope is possible, that trust is possible, and that relationships can help to heal.

CHAPTER SEVEN

Conclusion and discussion

Review

Self-destructiveness is an essential aspect of all psychopathology and human-to-human destructiveness. Freud rightly interpreted human-to-human destructiveness as the self-destructive impulse projected outward. As Donne so beautifully articulated:

> No man is an island, entire of itself; every man is a piece of the continent, a part of the main. If a clod be washed away by the sea, Europe is the less, as well as if a promontory were, as well as if a manor of thy friend's or of thine own were: any man's death diminishes me, because I am involved in mankind, and therefore never send to know for whom the bells tolls; it tolls for thee. Neither can we call this a begging of misery, or a borrowing of misery, as though we were not miserable enough of ourselves, but must fetch in more from the next house, in taking upon us the misery of our neighbours. Truly it were an excusable covetousness if we did, for affliction is a treasure, and scarce any man hath enough of it. (Donne, 2000)

Proximately and predominantly humanity seeks to further its own species and to preserve itself. Humanity is also inextricably socially interconnected. Knowing these things highlights the mysterious nature of self-destructiveness and the elusiveness as to why its manifestations are so prevalent, even epidemic, in the world today. Moreover, the measure and methods for self-harm and human-to-human violence are increasing and becoming more varied. There is no evidence suggesting that the rate of growth will decrease.

Every culture throughout history has had to contend with the phenomenon of self-destructiveness. It has been critically addressed in philosophy and in every school of psychology. For as long as humans have given thought to death, they have given thought to the fact that they can terminate their own existence. Plato understood suicide as ultimately a cowardly act, since self-harm was at variance with natural order. While rejecting much of Plato's metaphysics, Aristotle retained the belief that suicide was unnatural. The Stoics, on the other hand, considered suicide a reasonable solution to arduous life conditions. The Romans, following this logic, did not look disdainfully upon suicide but added that people wanting to commit the act had to make their case to the governing body. Ancient Hebrew society staunchly opposed suicide and, given their history of persecution, it is easy to understand why. Early Christians, on the other hand, believed that following in Christ's footsteps was of the utmost importance. Therefore, self-destruction was considered reasonable, since Christ sacrificed himself for man's sins. Early Christians often allowed others to murder them, often in horrific ways.

Christianity came to slowly reverse its stance on suicide out of fear that the Church would lose its most dedicated followers. The Church eventually renounced suicide and claimed it was something entirely inspired by evil. Shortly after this decree the Church went further to assert that those dying from suicide would be denied traditional mass and burial. Church doctrine eventually decreed that those completing suicide would be excommunicated and those surviving could be subject to material loss, institutionalization or, ironically, death. While clearly the practices have changed, suicide continues to be viewed negatively by Christianity and Judaism.

Around the nineteenth century European philosophers began giving thought to the phenomenon of self-destructiveness. Nietzsche attributed all forms of destructiveness to collectivism. Collectives, especially religious ones, were considered breeding grounds for *ressentiment*, a contagious and complex synthesis of moral superiority, envy, and revenge. Freud adopted many of Nietzsche's insights and expanded them in psychoanalysis. Early in his thinking, Freud believed that the unconscious comprised the vast majority of the psyche and asserted that it was a gurgling cauldron of instinctual drives. Later he offered the seminal notion of Thanatos, the psychological force operating in opposition to life. Most following in the psychoanalytic tradition gave thought to this and offered their own unique contributions. Klein made the destructive element of the mind of central importance in her psychology, but perhaps no one went as far in exploring this phenomenon as Bion. Bion gave thought to the part of the mind that sought health, but was too entangled with the destructive element of the mind. As Bion found, the compromised mind became increasingly dependent upon the very schizoid anti-life forces that would otherwise restore it to health. The result was a mind that relied upon attacking reality as a way of contending with reality. The mind became less able to adapt to internal and external reality as it became increasingly reliant upon attacking reality. When this happened the psychotic part of the personality took hold of the personality. Bion recognized the gravity of self-destructiveness and gave it an almost ontological gravity. On an archetypal level he recognized the existence of a destructiveness that persevered even after destroying existence, time, and space.

While psychoanalysis gave thought to the anti-life forces of the psyche, analytic psychology developed its theories concerning trauma, dissociation, and the underlying drama of the archetypes. For Jung trauma disrupted the psyche's natural tendency towards balanced wholeness. In extremis the psyche could experience an archetype as split. When this occurred, one polarity of the archetype was experienced as attacking its opposite pole. As the psyche became less centred, the ego received less archetypal nourishment, experienced powerful affects, and destroyed its ability for symbolic interpretation. Kalshed, following Jung, agreed that dissociation was a primary defense of the traumatized psyche. He added that the psyche has a self-care system that functions like the immune system of the body. This system identified psychological elements that were essentially, 'me or not-me' and differentiated between psychological nourishment and toxic elements. When this system became traumatized it turned into a self-destruct system that mobilized aggression and attacked aspects of the self, including the vulnerable parts. This system became especially pathological as the psyche continued to traumatize itself. Eventually, the psyche became caught in vicious cycle of self-traumatization and increasing vulnerability to raw archetypal forces.

Existential-phenomenological philosophy and psychology focused less on forces operating within the psyche and more on life experience. Binswanger published a controversial clinical account of a chronically depressed woman, whom he attempted to treat in an inpatient setting. Treatment did not work and Binswanger found himself faced with the decision of keeping her in a more restrictive setting or releasing her to her inevitable death by suicide. After much consideration and consultation, he decided to release her and she did, in fact, take her life. Rather than focusing on theoretical constructs to explain her suicidal ideation, he stuck closely to her life experience. Through his own clinical observations and interactions, he found that her longing for death constituted a certain existential necessity. Laing took a broader view of destructiveness, focusing not only on the self-destructive dynamics of the individual psyche, but on familial and cultural aspects as well. Laing's clinical findings suggested that the psyche fundamentally had two aspects, the true self and the false self. By false Laing was not referring to a fake or phony quality of the personality. Rather, it represented the aspect of the self that everyone possesses. It is the face that we all show to the world. The true self referred to our inner, private selves. Under favourable developmental conditions the two aspects do not conflict with each other. Under more pathological conditions, the two aspects do not develop normally and lead, to a greater or lesser degree, to a divided self. The true self becomes increasingly relied upon to defend against a true self, which is experienced as being under increasing threat. This dynamic explained much of the strange behaviour of persons diagnosed as schizoid and schizophrenic. In his later work, Laing focused on societal factors in psychological pathology. He asserted that persons diagnosed with mental disturbance are first and foremost *persons*, not the cluster of symptoms that constitute a formal psychiatric label. This was not at all to say that mental illness did not exist. In fact mental disturbance did exist and it varied in degrees, not kind, from the sense of alienation that most people experienced in our contemporary technological culture. Such commonplace alienation, combined with complacency and forgetfulness, created the illusion that the normally alienated person was sane.

Today the phenomenon of self-destructiveness holds sway over countless people. I have outlined many of these manifestations which include, and are certainly not limited to, eye enucleation, limb orgenital amputation, skin cutting, suicide, mental illness, and substance abuse. Many of these things have reached epidemic proportions in the United States and beyond. The fact that most of these things are preventable only highlights the thought provoking nature of this phenomenon. Perhaps no one feels the impact of human-to-human destructiveness more than the children of the world. I presented some striking statistics concerning child abuse, sexual and otherwise, and the further harm done by the very system set in place to care for such vulnerable children. Also, I outlined how unsafe the world can be for some children. Countless children are born with no health insurance, innumerable children and teens die from gunshot wounds, and millions of American children enter the school system unprepared. Child abuse fatalities have reached staggering levels and the majority of child abuse perpetrators are the very people—parents, caretakers, foster parents—charged with their care. The majority of these problems have reached epidemic proportions in the United States and beyond.

Of the many ways that children are being harmed, child trafficking is the most abhorrent. It is difficult to think of a more detestable crime than enslaving children for the purposes of labour, sexual acts, and organ harvesting. What is more disturbing is the realization that this is a widespread phenomenon involving numerous countries and generating three billion dollars annually.

Reflection

In our contemporary culture destructiveness is revealed with the technological disclosure of the world. This is not to say that what is named by the word technological and what is referred to as destructive are necessarily the same things. While their ontic manifestations often differ, they are close together ontologically. Also, I am not suggesting that in all instances the technological and destructive are evil. However, things like child trafficking are indeed reprehensible and I do not need to make an argument for this; it is self-evident. What I am suggesting is that the essence of what we have named by the word destructiveness and the essence of technology are in close ontological proximity. Considering child trafficking, for example, it is only possible to traffic children once children are disclosed as being the kind of things that can be taken and used to gain personal profit. It is only possible to traffic children once they are seen as ready-to-hand useful things. This is precisely the danger that Heidegger posed possible with the Enframing.

Recall that Heidegger did not consider the essence of technology to be anything technological. Technology is not a human invention and it is surely not something entirely under its control. Rather, Heidegger maintained that the essence of technology was an issuance from Being, a way of taking up the world in terms of its usefulness. The essential character of things becomes hidden in the Enframing. The essential character of things becomes increasingly covered over with humanity's increased reliance upon calculation as a way of knowing and being in the world. Given, such technological disclosure is often scientifically necessary and does yield knowledge that is quite useful. A mistake is made, however, when it is used as the only way of understanding the world. There is a considerable danger inherent in the technological disclosure of the world: as humanity goes about the world translating everything as standing-reserve it mistakes its own essence as the controller of the standing-reserve. Heidegger was concerned not only with this, but that it would be taken to its extreme and humanity would begin understanding and organizing itself as standing-reserve. Clearly, his fears have been realized in our contemporary technological culture. Taken to its vampiric heights, the world becomes an un-world in which humanity becomes entirely fascinated with consumption for the sake of consumption. While Heidegger did not specifically state it this way, this can be thought of as a profoundly self-destructive process. The more reliant humanity becomes on calculative disclosure, the most invested humanity is in its identification with itself as master controller of the world. This investment, in turn, is experienced as evidence of the success of the calculative disclosure of the world.

In this way the essence of technology and that of self-destructiveness lie close to each other. Once the possibility of utilizing human beings as substance-like things is disclosed, the possibility of covering it over becomes virtually impossible. The possibility of being near the essence of what it means to be human becomes ever more remote and the possibility of destructiveness grows ever closer. The destructiveness that draws evermore near is always and already self-destructive since it involves humanity in an essential way. This unconceals the ground wherein the various ontic possibilities of self-destructiveness can be taken up as well as the countless possibilities for human-to-human destructiveness. The unconcealment and presentation out of possibilities is sufficient but does not go far enough to explain the increasing variety and sheer power to metastasize that destructiveness has in our contemporary world.

Perhaps no one captured the dynamic and animated elements of destructiveness more articulately than Bion. Bion's characterizations of destructiveness take on an almost archetypal significance as he describes a force that wreaks damage even after existence, time, and space are annihilated. This is a force that eliminates even eliminating elements of the psyche such as depressive anxiety and emptiness. Bion found that even annihilating psychological states can be eliminated by such a force. On a psychological level this force could destroy the personality and, projected outward or experienced on a collective level, it is difficult to underestimate its injurious potential. This force is ultimately in the service of the lie yet occasionally is experienced if one prematurely encounters O. While Heidegger gives a gripping account of the shadow of technology in our contemporary culture, Bion tends to the depth and breadth of the psyche caught in a perpetual state of self-disintegration.

Heidegger imparts a sense of immanent crisis throughout the body of his work. For Heidegger the stakes could not be higher and he recognizes the growing destructiveness in the world:

> The darkening of the world, the flight of the gods, the destruction of the earth, the transformation of men into a mass, the hatred and suspicion of everything free and creative, have assumed such proportions throughout the earth that such childish categories as pessimism and optimism have long since become absurd. (Lemay & Pitts, 1994, p. 113)

The account Heidegger gives, for the most part, is a situation wherein Being and humanity are in a mutual reflective relationship. Being proffers itself to humanity and in its disclosure are possibilities for humanity to either take up or cover over. Humanity takes up some of these possibilities and pushes others away. I hasten to add that this is in no way a causal process. The relationship between humanity and Being is mutual and self-reflective. The disclosure of Being in our technological age delimits the range of possibilities that it can either take up or cover over. Overall Heidegger asserts that humanity, under the sway of the Enframing, is on a self-centred conquest towards dominating all that it encounters. Humanity, for Heidegger, is the only kind of being that believes that Being exists for its own purposes. As if that were not enough, Being is a concept largely forgotten about in philosophical discourse. His philosophy of Dasein represents a humble way of human being to be in relation to Being.

Making humanity the sole focus of philosophical discourse is itself responsible for the crises of the contemporary world. Rather than giving thought to the appropriate relatedness between humanity and Being, humanity asserts itself as the sole being for which Being exists. The result is a disclosure of the world as *bestand*, or *standing-reserve*. The end result is a narcissistic self-referencing whereby the world only appears in terms of usefulness for humanity's own purposes. Heidegger considers this a hangover from Descartes' dictum of *I think, therefore I am*. If we are the thinking beings, in this sense, then the world stands somewhere out there as something that is the object of thought or as delimited as being something that is caught sight of in terms of its usefulness. Once this assertion is posited then it becomes necessary to account for the link between the out there and the thinking subject.

Under the Cartesian worldview, the world is divided. Out there is the world of dead matter and animation only occurs within the psyche of the thinking subject. Of course the question arises concerning how the out there and the in here are connected. If the world out there is dead than the thinking subject must be projecting outward its own psychological activity. Heidegger, of course, completely disagreed with the Cartesian worldview and his work reflects the destructiveness inherent with this comportment. For Heidegger, destructiveness will become increasingly present as humanity mistakes itself as the measure of all things. This in combination with Bion's emphasis upon the dynamic, animated, and profound depths of destructiveness does much to account for its almost ubiquitous presence in our world. Moreover there is nothing in either of their work to suggest that such destructiveness will subside in the future. While their accounts do much to further our understanding of the phenomenon of destructiveness, perhaps more can be added.

The shadow of Being

The essence of technology is nothing technological, that is, it derives from an issuance of Being. The essence of self-destructiveness, as I have already asserted, is ontologically close to the essence of technology.

Since this is the case, then the essence of self-destructiveness too may not be self-destructive. In fact, like the essence of technology, the essence of self-destructiveness itself is an issuance from Being. Heidegger goes to great lengths to give thought to role humanity plays in the Enframing and its destructive vicissitudes. It is curious to me that he does not accent Being's role as being the source of the issuance. As I have already stated this is not at all to say that Being has a causal relationship with humanity. Rather Being proffers and then withdraws and humanity brings some possibilities close and pushes others away. The two are anything but mutually exclusive; they lie in an essential and reflective relationship. Nonetheless, Being does proffer Itself and if it did not, then humanity would not have the possibilities to either bring near or cover over. This includes the potentiality for self-destructiveness. To believe that humanity alone is responsible for the phenomenon of self-destructiveness is to further the same error in assuming that humanity is the creator and master of technology.

I am not raising the question of Being's role with destructiveness as a means of distracting or detracting in any way from the body of Heidegger's work. Contrarily, I think that this adds to the body of work considered thus far and may provide another avenue by which to give thought to the sway destructiveness has in the world. Heidegger clearly tends to the shadow of technology but he does not address the shadow of Being in any substantial or sustained fashion.

Throughout his work, Heidegger holds Being in a venerable and positive light. It is that which should be recalled, given thought to, and protected. The focus of what he considers problematic in our work largely is thought of in terms of humanity's comportment in the Enframing. Heidegger is not wrong in considering Being as something that is not just mysterious, but sacred as well. Also his veneration of Being makes sense in light of his early years as a devout Catholic. Catholicism maintains that God is ultimately a benevolent as well as a loving entity, and Heidegger's possible, perhaps unconscious, generalization to Being is understandable. However, Heidegger did not develop his thought concerning Being's role in destructiveness. He acknowledges that the Enframing is an issuance of Being but then spends the majority of his time explicating humanity's role in what he considers problematic in the world. Nonetheless it is Being that discloses and delimits the array of possibilities for human consideration and contemplation. These possibilities are not limited to only the life promoting; they include the destructive as well.

To say otherwise is to suggest that self-destructiveness emerged in history *ex nihilio*, out of nothing, or that it is solely of human design. Clearly it is not the case that humanity created the phenomenon of self-destructiveness and it is certainly not an object of human control. This is not to suggest that it is entirely out of the hands of humanity. To the contrary humanity is an active entity in the mutual reciprocal relationship between itself and Being. It is simply not the master of when, how and where Being proffers Itself. If Being did not proffer Its shadow, then giving thought to the destructive elements of the psyche could not be considered. Self-destructiveness has been thought about for as long as humans have been considering their mortality. Moreover, it has become a central theme in psychology. It is that which Freud was attuned to when he conceived of Thanatos, it is what called Bion to formulate his idea about an element of the mind that destroyed links between affect and image, flesh and mind, it is personified in Fairbairn's internal saboteur, it is what inspired Grotstein to posit the existence of psychic black holes, and it inspired Eigen's idea of a catastrophe machine that grinds bits of possible experiencing into ghastly nothingness. It is that which lays bare all possibilities for relating to each other and ourselves in ways counter to the promotion of life.

X

Eigen examines one of Bion's clinical cases. In this case X, Bion's patient, develops a fascination with spying on his mother's digestive-reproductive processes:

> Digestion-sex-reproduction amalgamate, and the patient becomes hypersensitive to a fusion of imaginary/amplified, at once physical and mental, the individual persecuted by his auditory capacity, engorged by fantasy.
>
> The result of this digestion-birth process is not to create a person, but a stool. X tries to spy on something degrading, a spoiling process, his own dehumanization. He is kind of a reverse alchemist, documenting the turning of gold to shit, birthing a familiar monster, the outcome of a sick or aborted digestive process. Mental digestion leads to birth through intercourse with life. X points to something going wrong, something *always* going wrong with life.

Life as digestion-birth doesn't work right. X gets banged and chewed to bits, a corrosive, fragmenting process, in which generativity seems turned against itself. He is looking for someone's insides to digest him. We take in what is good for us, things that taste good. We digest each other. But X no longer has faith in such a possibility, although he can't stop hoping altogether. In a malignant and persistent way, he spies on bad insides, hoping for something better, or at least to see things as they are.

He spies on someone's insides turning him to shit, as he is unable to generate a sound digestive process of his own. One partly does to others what was partly done to oneself. X is unable to digest another human being in a good way and persists in reliving, or rather, getting a view on (or control of?), a disaster that has befallen the capacity to be human. (Eigen, 2002, p. 117)

Eigen draws attention to the fact that such fantasies, as distorted as they are, are testimony to the interconnectedness of humans. Hatred, an affect often associated with destructiveness, is an empathic link. Like love, it seeks to bind one with the object. In hatred what binds one to the object is the desire to destroy it. What is interesting is that hatred is not the only affect associated with destructiveness. As Eigen notes there is a malicious quality associated with insanity, a certain malignant gleeful fascination with one's madness. All of these emotions intermingle with other affects like rage within digestive-sexual-birthing processes. Once digestive failure occurs, the mind becomes askew and grows evermore misshapen and freakish. There is a certain sinister voyeuristic delight one gains in witnessing this freakish process. One aspect of the ego is necessary to stay alive, to set the stage for future torture. Annihilation thus becomes time for rest for the next wave of tormenting acts to occur. One part of the psyche remains intact while gleefully watching the other parts atrophy and drift from normality.

As Eigen goes on to demonstrate, X's spying is demoralizing to the object and also leaves him demoralized. He is a kind of dehumanized-dehumanizing spy.

X's spying is parasitic. The promised land is mother-analyst's insides melded with paternal intercourse. X can neither truly enjoy what he sees, make use of digestive-generative capacities, not tear himself away. He is mesmerized by what he wishes he could be

and use, but remains in disdainful dread of. The land of plenty
is someone else. He can sneak a look and merely watch it all go
bad—a kind of reverse Midus, as if seeing spoils what is seen.
(ibid., p. 120)

Such vision requires that a fragmentary part of the ego somehow
become detached and view from afar. This is a terribly addictive process; as X becomes frustrated or confused he relies evermore on the very
dehumanizing-demoralizing vision that is problematic to begin with.
X is losing contract with his moral and existential center as he fixates
on the digestive-reproductive processes of the other. He is increasingly
reliant upon the internal processes of the other as he his own insides
dissipate.

The confusion expressed in the case of X as well as the reliance on
having destructive relationships are embodied in a song by the band
Tool on their recording *Undertow* (1993). This song, "Prison Sex,"
depicts such confused and confusing pathological processes inherent
in sexual abuse and other destructive relationships. In this song the
voice depicts a character that confuses self and other, love and hate. The
victim-perpetrator outlines an almost religious affinity, a depth of caring, that emerges in a perverted fashion. Many times such relationships
are relationships of depth, a kind of depth that is both parasitic and
destructive. It is like the depth inherent in a healthy, mutually loving
relationship but in reverse. Both kinds of relationships have the quality
of depth but vary in the degree that they either promote or destroy that
which affirms life and mutual potential. Such twisted voyeurism and
destructive processes, as in the case of X, represent attempts to understand how one is damaged and how it occurred. The problem is that the
methods used to understand damage are themselves destructive.

The delight in and voyeuristic compulsion to spy on such processes is
something that most people experience. It is a possibility delivered over
to all people. I am not at all suggesting that everyone experiences it to
the same degree that X does. It varies in degree, but not kind, between
those who are deemed normal and those considered disturbed. "Horror
fascinates us. It scares us into the realization that we can never fathom
the complexities of the forces we are enmeshed in. We can be wiped
out, warped, embalmed at any moment in any number of ways. Tragedy tries to channel what it can of complexities we can never master"
(Eigen, 2001a, pp. 94–95). It is this fascination that draws countless

people to horror films, to tragedy, to 'rubberneck' at traffic accidents, to images of war and destruction. It is the same allure that makes pornography such a lucrative business.

Pornography truly is a lucrative business and is testimony to the seduction of boundless invasive vision. For Romanyshyn (1989) such compulsive voyeuristic sight is a part of a larger cultural dream beginning in the fifteenth century and persisting into the present. According to him linear perspective vision has shaped the way we view the world and flesh. With the technological disclosure of the world the self is taken as a detached spectator, world as a spectacle, and flesh as a specimen. This vision is perhaps most concretely demonstrated in pornography.

> The split-off feminine fragment of the cultural-psychological life of humanity is not only murdered, it is also pushed beyond death. The discarded feminine is reduced to mere matter, which is the other side of the masculine spirit's flight from matter, a reduction achieved primarily through a *humiliation* of the woman's body, a term which literally indicates a coming back down to earth which in this context has nothing to do with return but rather with its opposite, escape. In humiliating the woman's flesh, the pornographic vision even deadens death ... Through the lens of the pornographic eye, we are invited to see that a cultural psychology which emphasizes only its masculine side is in pursuit of violence and death. (Romanyshyn, 1989, p. 211)

This way of knowing and being in the world represents and perpetuates a colossal failure of imagination, a literalism whose destructiveness is far-reaching. It even deadens death and at the same time is powerfully seductive. If this were not so then pornography would not be so prevalent in our culture.

Consider that for the year of 2003 pornography generated fifty-seven billion dollars in revenue. The United States generated twelve billion of this revenue and it is more than the combined revenues of all professional football, baseball and basketball franchises or the combined revenues of ABC, CBS, and NBC ($6.2 billion). Two-point-five of the twelve billion dollars is revenue generated from Internet porn. Once again, children are the ones who suffer the most from this compulsive vision. Roughly 100,000 websites offer illegal child pornography and it generates three billion dollars annually. Shockingly ninety per cent of eight to sixteen year-olds have viewed online pornography and the average age of first Internet exposure to it is eleven-years-old. The largest consumer of Internet pornography is the twelve to seventeen year-old age group (Bissette, 2004). It is interesting that this love of spying upon a freakish quasi-reality holds such a sway in our minds but is something rarely discussed. Demand for pornography is so strong that many large corporations participate in the market. General Motors, Mariott, and Time Warner are making millions from the pornography business. At present there are more than 800 million rentals available on VHS and DVD across America. If you think about it, it is probably not 800 people renting one million discs each. In California alone more than 12,000 people are employed by the pornography industry and it generates thirty-six million dollars in taxes for the state every year. In 2002 Comcast, America's largest cable company, made fifty million dollars from adult programming. Hilton, Marriot, Hyatt, Sheraton and Holiday Inn, all offer pay-per-view pornography for their guests. What is more surprising is that fifty per cent of all guests purchase in-room pornography and it accounts for seventy per cent of all their in-room profits. Moreover pornography has helped in the production of much of the latest media entertainment technology for the past twenty-five years and it continues to be a major driving force. This is due to the large success the pornography industry enjoyed with the invention of the VCR (Columbia Broadcasting System News, 2004).

This linear perspective vision, especially through the pornographic lens, deadens death and what deadens death deadens the psyche. Psyche and death are interrelated. "This relationship has also been put mythologically as the soul's connection with the night world, the realm of the dead, and the moon. We still catch our soul's most essential nature in death experiences, in dreams of the night, and in the images of 'Lunacy'" (Hillman, 1975, p. 68). It would be a literalism to assume that pornography alone somehow causes this deadening. What I am struck by is the fact *that* our culture is so devoted to this way of envisioning the world and I want to tend to it as a symptom. To orchestrate its annihilation, as if that were possible, would be to continue the literalism that itself is the problem and to suppress a symptom that would likely re-emerge in some compensatory fashion. Moreover the literalism of believing that pornography causes such vision would ignore that which calls for this particular vision, what makes it possible. What makes possible the pornographic imagination—what deadens death—is the same phenomenon that makes X's pathology possible.

At times destructiveness goes beyond trauma, leading to excruciating psychic freezing. This is the manifestation of psychological destructiveness *in extremis*.

> An attacking process gathers momentum, moves past the scream itself, silences screaming. The "I scream" becomes a "no-I scream": growth of negativism towards stupor, ever-increasing self-obliteration. The psyche freezes, falls silent, drops out of existence. From "No, I won't scream" to "I can't scream", as one is stricken with horror, especially horror of one's own destructiveness and destruction. (Eigen, 2001b, p. 30)

Under such circumstances the only thing that feels real and genuine is to attack all that one experiences as being real and genuine. Once this dynamic is established existential truth is experienced solely in terms of the annihilating force within and nothing else if felt as being real. The life-promoting elements of the psyche are crossed out and only destruction of these elements feels truly real. The fascination with others' internal processes, as in the case of X, gets x-ed out. The normal stream of varied and differentiated emotions get x-ed out as single raw emotions come to the fore. Such raw emotions may provide a sense of aliveness for a time, but ultimately they themselves get frozen. The personality deadens, becomes numb, and freezes. Even the processes of relieving such psychic tension—splitting, denial, and projection—are obliterated. What is left is not the dynamic animated pathology found in cases like X, but instead deadness. It is as if the psyche became a forsaken landscape, whose only inhabitants are the remnants of past meaning. Nothing and the continual disappearance of nothing comprise the internal world. One of the profound psychological aspects of the phenomenon of self-destructiveness is that it can make life seem unreal. It seems there is no measure for the depth and pervasiveness destructiveness holds.

The essence and depth of this phenomenon can be understood as an issuance from a not entirely benevolent Being. If these possibilities were not disclosed then humanity could not take them up. Admittedly, humanity can bring some possibilities close while pushing others away. Nonetheless not all possibilities disclosed are life promoting. Perhaps Bionian psychoanalysis can be furthered by examining the shadow elements of O. If O represents ultimate reality, then it necessarily contains the possibilities for destruction as well as creation. This is in no way to detract from the work of Bionian psychoanalysis or to suggest it is somehow deficient. Bionian psychoanalysis has perhaps gone further than any other branch of psychology in giving thought to the destructive elements of the mind. I am suggesting that, similar to Heideggerian philosophy, Bionian psychoanalysis emphasizes humanity's participation in destructiveness more than examining how these possibilities comes into being. Grotstein states:

> The options which are therefore available for the human being are as follows: (a) the experiencing of the experience (transformation in "O"); (b) the transformation of "O" into "K," in other words, facts about "O" in order to know enough about Truth so as to prepare for a future rendezvous with "O," yet necessitating a falsification of "O" by virtue of this detour through Knowledge because Knowledge cannot grasp Truth; and (c) the disavowal of Truth and transforming it into the lie which then absorbs the full use of thinking so as to maintain the Truth of the lie. The lie requires a thinker, as Bion cautions us. The Truth does not. All thinking begins as relative falsehood because it imperfects Truth and then, because of motivation (desire), can become the lie. Yet at the same time the thought-out lie is but the negation of the unthought and the unthinkable Truth which is now a hostage in a miscreant container, the lie. In other words, thinking is inadvertent falsifying because it is motivated by desire, whereas repressing is lying by intent, and the content of the repressed is designated a lie which really contains the Truth. However, one can also see from this vertex that the ego itself is a falsifier in the very act of thinking because of the motivation of desire implicit in it … Furthermore, "understanding" may be one of the more sophisticated ways of avoiding the Truth while believing at the same time that one has arrived at it. (Grotstein, 1981, pp. 27–28)

It is certainly the case that humanity is always already engaged in an interpretative relationship with all it encounters. Not all interpretations are correct but this fact does not negate the assertion that humanity is essentially an interpretive being. Grotstein's comments also seem consistent with Heidegger's notion that every translation is an interpretation. This means that the potential for misinterpretation varies as a function of the amount of interpreting being done. What I would add to Grotstein's summary is that destructive potential may be inherent in O itself. For humanity to have the option of interpreting away from Truth, this possibility would have to be disclosed *as* something possible. If it were not present as potential then humanity would not have the option of taking it up. Moreover, transitively, if it is the case that Being has a shadow then it is the case that O contains destructive potential. Giving thought to O necessarily means that it has the quality of being. Being, as the being of all beings, thus is a more essential being then O. Therefore since O has the quality of existence then it therefore has the qualities of Being. Also, O as the ultimate reality must contain some destructive potential since destructiveness is clearly a part of reality. To say otherwise would suggest that humanity itself is solely responsible for destructiveness and that it is something under human control. To assert these things would be to make the same mistake Heidegger noted concerning humanity's mistaking itself as the sole producer and master of technology. These misinterpretations not only cover over the essence of technology, or in this case O, but they conversely limit thought on humanity's essential relationship to it. I would also hasten to add that Bionian psychoanalysis is correct to think about things primarily in terms of the personal, since it is concerned primarily with psychology not ontology. What I am suggesting is that Bionian psychoanalysis, an already dynamic and insightful system, may benefit further from ontological considerations.

Thinking along these lines perhaps X can symbolize more than the man in Bion's case. Perhaps it can stand for the range of destructive potentials inherent in ultimate reality, O, and Being. X can stand for that which makes possible the pathology in the case of X and it can stand for all that gets x-ed out in the most extreme forms of deadening psychic collapse. It can stand for that which makes something like pornography (xxx) possible. It is that issuance and human response that makes all forms of destructiveness possible whether it is within the individual psyche or the collective. It can represent the shadow side of Being and the sobering realization that that which proffers to humanity is not entirely benevolent. X calls to be thought about not only because it is thought provoking but because when it is neglected or forgotten it becomes an autonomous force.

As depth psychology has demonstrated, when something in the psyche is denied or repressed it often becomes split off and projected.

When some element of the psyche becomes projected then it is seen as embodied out there and it assumes a moral value. The part of the self that has been ignored, neglected, and too painful to integrate is thus seen in the other. Thus the very aspect of the self that is unbearable, now seen in the other, must be extinguished. There is a moral charge to this relationship. That which is 'out there' is experienced as evil and, so deemed, the good assumes a moral obligation to eliminate it. What ensues is a parallel process of defining those who are out there as well as assessing who constitutes the sane group, us. Once the shadow is ignored or forgotten it assumes autonomy whereby and overarching ego achieves a super-ego status, believing that it needs to assimilate or eliminate that which is other. The most destructive acts, then, are those that are taken with X (ignored) and with a sense of moral superiority well intact. With moral superiority intact, the justification to act upon that which is deemed other is justified. Now justified, the morally charged ego proceeds with its own destructive purpose. The result is an ego alienated from its shadow, freed from constraints, liberated to act upon its own interests. This leaves the other a target of the ego, often vulnerable to the intents of its will. Of course, none of this would be possible unless Being disclosed Itself in such a way (X) that destructive potential could be considered at all. Moreover, if we do not consider the shadow of Being and ultimate reality, then we are in denial and the matter cannot be considered. Given the sway destructiveness has in the world today, it calls to be recognized, thought about, and related to in some way. If we fall out of relationship with it then it achieves autonomy and increases the likelihood of humanity acting out in destructive ways, thus pushing farther and farther away the possibility of relating to X. Consider the most heinous moments in human history: the dark ages, the crusades, the inquisition, manifest destiny and the genocide of the American native population, the witch hunts, slavery, the holocaust, humanity's alienation from nature, and the eclipse of the divine. They represent neglect of thought concerning that which I have represented by X and a mindless morality bent upon executing its own divine will. I offer here a few striking examples of these dynamics at work during a few of humanity's darkest moments in history. I could just as easily chosen other examples of these dynamics at work in individual pathology, such as the case of X, or these dynamics at work in other collective psyches.

Manifest destiny and the holocaust

In an article titled *The Great Nation of Futurity* (1839) published in The United States Democratic Review, O'Sullivan said:

> Yes, we are the nation of progress, of individual freedom, of universal enfranchisement. Equality of rights is the cynosure of our union of States, the grand exemplar of the correlative equality of individuals; and while truth sheds its effulgence, we cannot retrograde, without dissolving the one and subverting the other. We must onward to the fulfillment of our mission—to the entire development of the principle of our organization—freedom of conscience, freedom of person, freedom of trade and business pursuits, universality of freedom and equality. This is our high destiny, and in nature's eternal, inevitable decree of cause and effect we must accomplish it. All this will be our future history, to establish on earth the moral dignity and salvation of man—the immutable truth and beneficence of God. For this blessed mission to the nations of the world, which are shut out from the life-giving light of truth, has America been chosen … . (O'Sullivan, 1839)

Thus manifest destiny was solidified into a doctrine, a doctrine whose roots can be found in the 1600s. I am not at all suggesting that O'Sullivan brought manifest destiny or something like it into being. He articulated quite accurately the spirit of the times in which he lived.

In 1830, just one year after taking office, President Jackson pushed legislation called the Indian Removal Act through both houses of Congress. This legislation gave Jackson the power to negotiate removal treaties with native tribes living east of the Mississippi. Under these treaties, the natives were to give up their lands east of the Mississippi in exchange for lands to the west.

Jackson and countless others believed that Native Americans were like children, or savages, who needed the guidance of their superior way of life. From this perspective the removal of tribes was considered beneficial to the Native Americans. Most Americans thought that they would never extend beyond the Mississippi. Removal, then, would save Native Americans from the interests of whites and would resettle them in an area where they could govern themselves in peace. Some

Americans saw this as an excuse for a brutal and inhumane course of action and protested (to no avail). This began twenty-eight years of relocating southeastern nations. By 1837, the Jackson administration had removed 46,000 Native American people from their land east of the Mississippi, and had secured treaties which led to the removal of a slightly larger number. By this time twenty-five million acres of land was available to white settlement and to slavery. In 1838 federal troops evicted the Cherokees, who were resisting removal. Roughly 4,000 Cherokee persons died during the removal process, which included the tragic Trail of Tears. More than 100,000 Native Americans were moved under the Indian Removal Act.

Another tragic example of destructiveness reigning and a concordant mindless moralism is the Holocaust. It is, in fact, not the case that Hitler subscribed to atheism or polytheism. To the contrary, Hitler was a devout believer in the biblical God. Hitler was raised and educated in the Catholic tradition. At times he referred to his Catholic background but for the most part he referred to himself as a Christian. As twisted as his religious beliefs were, he consistently aligned himself with the Christian God: "Hence today I believe that I am acting in accordance with the will of the Almighty Creator: *by defending myself against the Jew, I am fighting for the work of the Lord*" (italics in the original). Hitler also stated:

> My feelings as a Christian point me to my Lord and Savior as a fighter. It points me to the man who once in loneliness, surrounded by a few followers, recognized these Jews for what they were and summoned men to fight against them and who, God's truth! was greatest not as a sufferer but as a fighter. In boundless love as a Christian and as a man I read through the passage which tells us how the Lord at last rose in His might and seized the scourge to drive out of the Temple the brood of vipers and adders. How terrific was His fight for the world against the Jewish poison. To-day, after two thousand years, with deepest emotion I recognize more profoundly than ever before the fact that it was for this that He had to shed His blood upon the Cross. As a Christian I have no duty to allow myself to be cheated, but I have the duty to be a fighter for truth and justice... And if there is anything which could demonstrate that we are acting rightly it is the distress that daily grows. For as a Christian I have also a duty to my own people. (as cited in Walker, 1996)

I am not at all suggesting that Hitler's interpretation of biblical text is valid or that he accurately represented the populace of the Christian body. I am accenting the anti-thinking moralism inherent in neglecting the phenomenon of destructiveness. The super-ego with its holy mission thus orders who constitutes us versus those who compose the projective receptacle of split-off destructiveness. The aforementioned quotes suggest that Hitler took himself as some kind of present day Christ or that he was identified with the archetype of the anointed one. Moreover, some Nazis went so far as to believe that Christ, the literal person, was not a Jew but of Aryan descent. Of course nothing could be farther from the truth. However, such borderline psychotic beliefs bespeak the depth and degree of commitment they had to their self-anointed cause and to the destructive potential inherent in maintaining such a belief system.

While Hitler did not represent the true values of Christianity, it is interesting to note that the Catholic Church adopted a stance of non-involvement during the Holocaust. Not only did the Church adopt this stance, but the Pope at the time helped the Nazis rise to unhindered power and thus helped seal the fate of the Jews and all others targeted by the Nazis. The papacy never actually deemed the Holocaust as an intrinsically evil presence on earth. While countless women, men, children and infants were being exterminated the Pope did little to assuage the damage. Under religious and political pressure to speak out against such events the Pope placidly responded during his 1942 Christmas broadcast homily to the world: "Humanity owes this vow to those hundreds of thousands who, without any fault of their own, sometimes only by reason of their nationality or race, are marked down for death or gradual extermination" (Cornwell, 2000, p. 292). This was the strongest protest against the atrocities being wrought against humanity that the Church uttered during the Holocaust.

Indeed such dynamics, both on the part of the Nazis and in Catholic complicacy, lead to one of the bloodiest moments in history. By the end of the war somewhere between 5,596,029 and 5,860,129 Jewish persons were murdered. This does not account for the countless murders of non-Jewish persons deemed inferior such as homosexuals, Gypsies, ethnic and religious minorities, as well as those accused of being mentally and/or physically deficient. Undoubtedly, countless people suffered and were murdered during the Holocaust and children were not excluded from the process. As has been demonstrated children have always suffered humanity's darkest moments.

Tragically, the precise number of children who were murdered during the Holocaust will never been known. Some estimates range as high as 1.5 million and this figure includes more than 1.2 million Jewish children, tens of thousands of Gypsy children and thousands of institutionalized and handicapped children. Nazi persecution, arrests, and deportations were directed against all members of Jewish families, without concern for age. Some children witnessed the murder of parents, siblings, and relatives, and incidents of children being executed in the presence of their parents were not uncommon. As if executions were not tragic enough, children experienced starvation, illness, and other forms of inhumane treatment. The chances of children surviving the Holocaust were less than their adult counterparts. In the latter part of 1942, 4,000 French children, forcibly separated from their parents, were taken to the Drancy detention camp in groups of 1,000. The children ranged in age between two and twelve years old and the older children were charged with the care of younger children.

> On arrival at the rooms where they were to be temporarily housed the children stood like frightened animals, afraid to advance. They hesitated for a long time, before they could bring themselves to lie down on the filthy mattresses. Most of them had lost their luggage. The women in the camp organized themselves into groups of volunteers to look after the children. The women washed little ones, dried them with handkerchiefs and stayed with them as long as they could. The small children could not get to the toilets and waited desperately for an adult or another child to help them. At night the continual crying of children, and the screams of those who had lost their minds, could be heard.
>
> On the night before they were to be deported to the Auschwitz death camp the children were searched. Rings and earrings were confiscated. A ten year-old girl, who had been too slow to respond to an order, had the earring ripped from her ear. Volunteers helped the children pack such belongings as they had been able to gather.
>
> On deportation day the children had to get up at 5:00 AM in the morning. They had to dress in half darkness. It was cold and they wore summer clothing. The smallest, walking half asleep, began to cry, and all the others started crying. The police forced the horrified,

screaming children, to the train. (Jewish Holocaust Museum and Research Center, 1990)

The selection of children by the Nazi regime was established all over the country. The selection process was duplicitous; parents were asked to sign authorization forms for severely disabled children to be transferred to specialized wards and parents were told that the children would benefit from being treated in such wards. The logic presented was that the disturbed children would have an opportunity to participate in state-of-the-art studies that may remedy their afflictions. It was under these conditions that Nazis obtained authorizing signatures from parents. Unlike adults children detained under these laws were kept for a period of four to eight weeks for clinical observation. None of these children were referred to foster/respite care or their homes of origin once taken to the Special Section. Most all of these children were murdered via injections of lethal substances and they were largely unaware of their fate (Sereny, 1974). These are two, amongst many, startling examples of what happens when destructiveness gains autonomy and that which I represent by X holds sway. The denial of destructiveness and the subsequent splitting and projection, a process of defining who constitutes the blessed majority and those who become the projective container for repressed destructive elements, have been involved in humanity's most destructive moments.

Concluding remarks

Clearly the phenomenon of self-destructiveness calls to be thought about. It calls to be thought about not only because it has been prevalent throughout history but because many of its contemporary manifestations are epidemic across the world. If we do not give thought to this we become vulnerable on a collective level to repeating the darkest moments in history and on an ontic level we neglect its psychological dynamics and depth. Giving thought to this phenomenon begins with facing bravely the grip it has on our contemporary world. The first step is acknowledging that many of its manifestations have reached epidemic proportions throughout the world and many tragically succumb to disease and death under its sway. Human destructiveness is difficult to comprehend, but if approached phenomenologically it proffers the many ways in which it exists. It wants to be known, it calls to be thought about, it exists and the more it is ignored the greater autonomy it gains. The greater autonomy it gains the more susceptible we are to unconsciously act it out and project it ontically and on a collective level. Giving thought to self-destructiveness is a challenging task; many of the topics inherent with this phenomenon are not popular. People in general do not like to hear about acts of self-destruction whether it is an individual's behaviour or moments of human-to-human destructiveness in history. However, not giving thought to self-destructiveness is far more dangerous.

To give thought to self-destructiveness is not to condone it. Rather, giving thought to it is precisely the way we can be more conscious of it and thus establish an appropriate relationship. This is a paradox of understanding self-destructiveness: We have to establish an appropriate relationship with it because the dangers of falling out of relationship are too great. We cannot contend with the pathological aspect of self-destructiveness unless we recognize its existence and the breadth of its purview. This is a difficult task because it means examining our own shadow and recognizing that the range of possibilities proffered from Being and ultimate reality are not altogether benevolent. None of this should be taken as detractions from the work of Heideggerian phenomenology and depth psychology. Rather such recognitions and thought clear a way for furthering and deepening their essential and necessary work.

The need to have an appropriate relationship to the phenomenon of destructiveness does not mean that humanity should engage in destructive acts or condone that which is destructive. By appropriate relationship I am referring to the kind of relationship that recognizes destructiveness but does not succumb to it. Concerning humanity's comportment with technology Heidegger suggests that we say yes and no to it. Perhaps we can apply the same kind of relationship to destructiveness. We can say yes in the sense of acknowledging its existence and powerful influence upon us. We can at the same time say no to being identified with it and to projecting it as much as possible. Another way to maintain an appropriate relationship is to differentiate the destructiveness that has healing potential and the destructiveness that is self-evidently evil. Following Jung I would like to emphasize that what constitutes the shadow is not necessarily evil. Evil is not the essence of destructiveness. What constitutes the shadow is simply that which on an individual and collective level lies in darkness. Darkness is not necessarily evil, it simply lacks light. Evil is in the neighbourhood, so to speak, of destructiveness, but it does not constitute its meaning and ground.

There are kinds of destructiveness that are not necessarily evil and are actually necessary for creative transformation. This creative-destructive element is vividly embodied in the mythology of Dionysius. Recall that Dionysius is the god of wine, agriculture, and fertility of nature. Interestingly, he was also the god of destruction, physical and spiritual inebriation and madness. There is no single myth on Dionysus, but they contain the same creative-destructive themes. According to one myth about Dionysius, the son of Zeus and Semele, Semele is destroyed by Zeus' lightning bolts while she pregnant with Dionysius. Dionysius is rescued and is birthed again after developing in Zeus' thigh.

Following his birth, Zeus gives Dionysius to some nymphs to be raised. According to a different myth Dionysius, son of Zeus and Persephone, Hera gets the Titans to lure the child Dionysius with toys. The Titans subsequently rip him to shreds and eat everything except for his heart, which is preserved by Athena, Rhea, or Demeter. Zeus recreates his son from the heart and embeds him in Semele who bears a renewed Dionysius. In the second myth it is interesting that Dionysus is the son of Persephone who, if you will recall, is Queen of the Underworld and whose name means Bringer of Destruction. As I have already stated, Persephone's abduction into the underworld was absolutely necessary for the fulfillment of her character. It is fitting, then, that she should be the mother of Dionysius who himself is born from destructiveness. This destructive-creative element is certainly not the kind of destructiveness that fosters evil. This is the *nigredo* of the alchemical process, the dark element of one that is the interim point whose fulfillment is found in the birth of the other. This is quite different from the kind of darkness that brings suffering and death. Clearly, it makes sense to align with the kind of destructiveness that is in the service of furthering life and to work against that which results in the mindless destruction of the other.

Such comportment with destructiveness necessarily means adjusting, affording room for the destructive elements inherent in human relatedness. If such mutual room is afforded then the need to literalize destructiveness may be diffused. By recognizing and giving thought to destructiveness, we can differentiate ourselves from it and thus diffuse its potential. By giving thought to destructiveness we can promote life.

It is necessary to make room for and give thought to destructiveness against the self. As I have already stated, such destructiveness exists whether we give thought to it or deny it. It is necessary to give thought and to accept the phenomenon of destructiveness in its essential manifestations as well as its literal (e.g. the desire to kill one's self). By denying this phenomenon we empower it. Psyche defines itself by its ability to destroy and renew itself and by denying this capacity we are in danger of acting it out against ourselves or others. An appropriate relatedness to destructiveness means accepting the self-destructive capacity of the psyche without killing ourselves and others. Attending to the soul, the essence of self-destructiveness, means tending to the ways in which it can be sublimated. Giving thought to its sublimation opens a clearing whereby we can give thought to how self-destructiveness may enhance our potentiality and thriving in the world.

CHAPTER EIGHT

Limitations and suggestions for future research

Certainly more thematic hermeneutic studies can be done comparing and contrasting different schools of thought about self-destructiveness. The essence and paradox of self-destructiveness remains a mystery. The mysterious and shrouded nature of this phenomenon calls to be thought about. In our time the number of suicides and self-destructive behaviors has sparked a growing concern among health professionals and researchers. Examining the cultural elements of self-destructiveness may provide informative about how to clinically assess and treat such populations. This study represents a regional ontology, that is, the thinkers outlined and examined were proximally and predominantly Western. On a societal level research should be conducted on how to offer better options than death and suffering to the difficulties of living. Cultures, for the most part, stigmatize self-destructive behaviors, which may exacerbate the problem.

Another fruitful area of exploration may be found in standardizing vocabulary and reporting techniques to gain a more salient understanding of the phenomenon in question. It stands to reason that a more differentiated and concrete approach to information gathering will yield more specific information of self-destructiveness.

The approach in this work has been largely hermeneutic and theoretical. It would be beneficial to research models of contending with self-destructiveness in terms of assessment, prevention, intervention, and aftercare. Traditionally reaction and crisis intervention, with little community support, has been the approach to handling behavioral problems. The factors of financial cuts to mental health services/ research and an increasing reliance upon troublesome psychiatric medication can only foster the already unabated growth of destructiveness. Further research should be done to document the extent and grip destructiveness has upon humanity. Hopefully such research will elicit funding to assess and attend to it. Funding for mental health services and research aids in keeping the symptoms of destructiveness close so that we can better understand, diagnose, and treat them.

Further research can be conducted examining destructiveness in different contexts. Destructiveness probably appears differently in different contexts. The manifestation of destructiveness in the workplace probably varies from that within the home. The appearance of destructiveness in the classroom is probably different from its appearance in the place of worship. It would be beneficial to examine how the phenomenon manifests in these and other contexts. It would also benefit us to examine the similarities and differences among these findings. Such research could not only help us differentiate the different kinds of destructiveness, but could provide us with the information necessary to help alleviate suffering and to determine the kind of relationship we should have with the phenomenon.

On a more ontological level we can follow Heidegger's and Bion's focus on the *approach* to the phenomenon. How we relate to destructiveness will determine what is shown and what is covered over. For both of them *thinking* is of paramount importance to their philosophies. I am not suggesting that they followed the same path when it came to thinking. I am suggesting that it is of central importance to both of them. They both identified the problematic areas inherent in calculative thinking. While Bion did not call it calculative thinking he clearly differentiated it from the nexus of linking emotions, ideas, and contact with reality. For Bion one of the highest regions an idea can achieve is action and faith. For Heidegger meditative thinking—openness to mystery and releasement to the things themselves—was the most essential thought and the greatest action to take. Concerning destructiveness perhaps our approach should reflect the elements of meditative thinking along with action.

We will continue benefiting from approaching destructiveness from a place of meditative thought and clearly action is necessary when evil presences. Meditative thinking is necessary to understand self-destructiveness but it is just as necessary to take action against it. As I said earlier, it would benefit us to differentiate those elements of destructiveness that serve life from those that are inherently evil. In the cases of child trafficking, rape, and other such atrocities, meditative thinking is simply not enough. If, for example, I come upon a person who has been stabbed and is in need of medical care, no amount of meditative thinking will save the person. It is a higher ethical obligation to take action and provide whatever assistance I can give. This does not discount in any way the necessity of meditative thinking. Where meditative thinking is necessary to comprehend the phenomenon of self-destructiveness, ontic action is necessary to combat its manifestations. There is considerable amount of work to be done in this area and this work will change as the phenomenon shows itself in different ways over time.

In conclusion there is a considerable amount of work to be done to understand the essence of destructiveness and our relationship to it. Some of the ontic areas of further work include conducting clinical, qualitative, and quantitative studies concerning the psychological vicissitudes of destructiveness. Further research is also necessary to understand its cultural and global manifestations. In every instance it would benefit us to differentiate between the different kinds of destructiveness, organizing them into the kinds that hold life potential and those that are evil. Clearly such things as child trafficking and rape are self-evidently reprehensible and should be eliminated. From a more ontological perspective more work can be done to further our understanding of self-destructiveness through phenomenology and meditative thinking as well as giving thought to the most appropriate kind of relationship humanity should have with it.

REFERENCES

Achte, K. (1983). Types of self-destruction. *Psychiatria Fennica*. (Suppl.), 41–44.

Alao, A., Yolles, J. & Huslander, W. (1999). Female genital mutilation. *Psychiatric Services, 50*(7), 971.

American Psychiatric Association. (1994). *Diagnostic and Statistical Manual of Mental Disorders* (4th ed.). Washington, DC: Author.

Asper, K. (1993). *The Abandoned Child Within*. New York: Fromm International.

Bateson, G., Jackson, D. D., Haley, J. & Weakland, J. (1956). Toward a theory of schizophrenia. *Behavioral Science, 1*, 251–264.

Bergler, E. (1955). A few examples of the superego's cruelty. *Samiksa, 9*, 63–70.

Binswanger, L. (1958). The case of Ellen West. In Angel, E., Ellenberger, H. & May, R. (Eds.), *Existence* (pp. 237–364). New York: Simon & Schuster.

Bion, W. R. (1956). Development of schizophrenic thought. *International Journal of Psychoanalysis, 37*, 344–346.

Bion, W. R. (1959). Attacks on linking. *International Journal of Psychoanalysis, 40*, 308–315.

Bion, W. R. (1963). *Elements of Psychoanalysis*. London: Karnac.

Bion, W. R. (1965). *Transformations*. London: Heinemann.

Bion, W. R. (1970). *Attention and Interpretation*. London: Tavistock.

Bion, W. R. (1992). *Cogitations*. F. Bion (Ed.). London: Karnac.

Bion, W. R. (1964). *Learning from Experience*. Northvale, NJ: Jason Aronson. [reprinted eg. London: Karnac, 1994.]

Bissette, D. (2004). *Internet pornography statistics: 2003* [On-line.] Available: http://healthymind.com/s-port-stats.html. Last accessed …

Blumstein, A. (1959). Masochism and fantasies of preparing to be incorporated. *Journal of the American Psychoanalytic Association, 7*, 292–298.

Boss, M. (1971). *Existential Foundations of Medicine and Psychology*. (S. Conway & A. Cleaves, Trans.). Northvale, NJ: Jason Aronson. [reprinted eg. London: Karnac, 1994.]

Burston, D. (1995). Laing's existentialism. *Journal of the society for existential analysis*. Chapter/pages?

Burston, D. (1996a). Conflict and sociability in Hegel, Freud, and their followers. *New Literary History, 27,* (1) [On-line.] Available: http://128.220.50.88/demo/nlh/27 lburston.html. Last accessed …

Burston, D. (1996b). *The Wing of Madness: The Life and Work of Laing*. Cambridge, MA: Harvard University Press.

Burston, D. (1997). *Foundations of existential-phenomenological psychology*. Cambridge, MA: Harvard University Press.

Caldecott, M. (1993). *Myths of the Sacred Tree*. Inner Traditions International: Country?

Caputo, J. (1987). *Radical hermeneutics: Repetition, deconstruction and the hermeneutic project*. Bloomington and Indianapolis, IN: Indiana University Press.

Children's Defense Fund. (2002). *The state of children in America's union: A 2002 action guide to leave no child behind* [On-line.] Available: www.childrensdefense.org/pdf/minigreenbook.pdf.

Clay, J. (1996). *Laing: A Divided Self*. London: Hodder & Stroughton.

Columbia Broadcasting System (2004). *Porn in the U.S.A* [On-line.] Available: www.cbsnews.com/stories/2003/11/21/60 minutes/main585049.shtml. Last accessed …

Cornwell, J. (2000). *Hitler's Pope: The Secret History of Pius XII*. New York: Penguin Books.

Cooper, V. (1990). The paradox of adolescent suicide: A Kleinian perspective. *Melanie Klein and object relations*. Jun. Vol. 8(1), 67–80.

Crowe, M. & Bunclark, J. (2000). Repeated self-injury and its management. *International review of psychiatry, 12,* (1), 48–53.

Delumeau, J. (1991). *Sin and Fear: The Emergence of a Western Guilt Culture, 13–18 centuries*. New York: Palgrave Macmillan.

Donne, J. (2000). *Meditation XVII* [On-line.] Available: www.online-literature/donne/409. Last accessed …

Eigen, M. (1996). *Psychic deadness*. London: Jason Aronson.

Eigen, M. (2001b). *Damaged bonds*. London: Karnac.

Eigen, M. (2001a). *Ecstasy*. Middletown, CT: Wesleyan University Press.

Eigen, M. (2002). *Rage*. Middletown, CT: Wesleyan University Press.

Estes, C. P. (1992). *Women who run with the Wolves: Myths and Stories of the Wild Woman Archetype*. New York: Ballantine Books.

Euripides (1997). The Bacchae. In J. Plecha, et al. (Eds.), *Order and chaos* (pp. 170–232). Chicago, IL: The Great Books Foundation.

Evans, R. (1976). *Dialogue with Laing*. New York: Praeger.

Fairbairn, R. (1941). *Revised Psychopathological of the Psychoses and Psychoneuroses*. London: Tavistock.

Fairbairn, R. (1981). *Psychoanalytic Studies of the Personality*. London: Tavistock.

Farber, M. (1968). *Theory of suicide*. New York: Funk & Wagnalls.

Farber, M. (1969). The phenomenology of suicide. In: E. Shneidman (Ed.), *On the Nature of Suicide*. (pp.). San Francisco: Jossey-Bass.

Favazza, A. (1989a). Self-mutilation and eating disorders. *Suicide and life-threatening Behavior, 19*, (4), 352–361.

Favazza, A. (1989b). Why patients mutilate themselves. *Hospital Community Psychiatry, 40*, 137–145.

Favazza, A. & Conterio, K. (1988a). Female habitual self-mutilators. *Acta psychiatry scan, 78*.

Favazza, A. & Conterio, K. (1988b). The plight of chronic self-mutilators. *Community Mental Health Journal, 24*, (1), 22–30

Favazza, A. & Rosenthal, R. (1993). Diagnostic issues in self-mutilation. *Hospital and Community Psychiatry, 44*, (2), 134–140.

Fine, B. & Moore, B. (Eds.) (1990). *Psychoanalytic Terms and Concepts*. New Haven, CT: The American Psychoanalytic Association and Yale University Press.

Fisher, G. (2000). *Substance abuse: Information for School counselors, Social workers, Therapists, and Counselors*. Needham Heights, MA: Allyn & Bacon.

Fordham, M. (1974). Defenses of the self. *Journal of Analytical Psychology, 19*, (2), 192–9.

Frankl, V. (1955). *The Doctor and the Soul*. R. Winston & C. Winston (Trans.). New York: Alfred Knopf.

Frankl, V. (1959). *From Death Camp to Existentialism*. Boston: Beacon.

Freud, S. (1917e). Mourning and melancholia. *S.E., 14*: 239–258. [reprinted eg. London: Karnac, 1963.]

Freud, S. (1920g). Beyond the pleasure principle. *S.E., 18*: 7–64. London: Hogarth. [reprinted eg. London: Karnac, 1961.]

Freud, S. (1923a). The ego and the id. *S.E., 19*: 3–66. London: Hogarth Press. [reprinted eg. London: Karnac, 1927.]

Freud, S. (1927c). The future of an illusion. *S.E., 21*: 3–56. London: Hogarth.

Freud, S. (1930a). Civilization and its discontents. *S.E., 21*: 59–145. [reprinted eg. London: Karnac, 1994.]

Freud, S. (1937c). *Analysis Terminable and Interminable. S.E., 23*: 211–253. London: Hogarth. [reprinted eg. London: Karnac, 1966.]

Freud, S. (1972). Letter to Andreas-Salomé, May 25, 1916. In: E. Pfeiffer (Ed.) and W. and E. Robson-Scott (Trans.) *Sigmund Freud and Lou Andreas-Salomé letters* (p. 45). New York: Harcourt, Brace, Jovanovich.

Friedenberg, E. (1977). *Laing*. New York: Viking Press.

Girard, R. (1972). *Violence and the Sacred*. (P. Gregory, Trans.). Baltimore and London: John Hopkins University Press. [reprinted eg. London: Karnac, 1972.]

Glick, A. (1974). *The Will to Live, the Will to Die: An Existential Analysis of Self-Destruction*. East Texas State University, Texas (Unpublished doctoral dissertation).

Golden, R. (1997). *Disposable Children: America's Welfare System*. New York: Wadsworth.

Golomb, E. (1996). *Trapped in the Mirror: Adult Children of Narcissists in their Struggle for Self*. New York: William Morrow.

Gronseth, R. (1998). On the question of the death instinct. *Nordisk psykologi, 50*, (1), 42–59.

Grotstein, J. (date). *Do I Dare Disturb the Universe? A Memorial to W. R. Bion*. London, England: Caesura Press.

Grotstein, J. (1987). An object—relations perspective on resistance in narcissistic patients. In J. Grotstein (Ed.) *Techniques on Working with Resistance* (pp. 317–329). New York: Jason Aronson.

Grotstein, J. (1990). Nothingness, meaninglessness, chaos and the "black hole": The importance of nothingness, meaninglessness, and chaos in psychoanalysis. *Contemporary psychoanalysis, 26*, 257–407.

Grotstein, J. (1997). *Bion's "transformation in 'O'" and the Concept of the "transcendent position"* [On-line.] Available: www.sicap.it/~merciai/papers/grots.htm.

Guntrip, H. (1969). *Schizoid Phenomena, Object Relations and the Self*. New York: International Universities Press.

Guntrip, H. (1971). *Psychoanalytic Theory, Therapy and the Self*. New York: Basic Books.

Guthrie, W. K. (1966). *Orpheus and Greek Religion*. New York: Norton.

Hayes, E. (1994). *Images of Persephone*. Florida: University Press of Florida.

Hegel, G. (1817). *The Encyclopedia of the Mind.* (W. Wallace, Trans.). Oxford: Oxford University Press. [reprinted eg. London: Karnac, 1973.]

Heidegger, M. (1954). *What is Called Thinking.* (J. Gray, Trans.). New York: Harper & Row. [reprinted eg. London: Karnac, 1968.]

Heidegger, M. (1975). *Early Greek Thinking.* (D. Farrell & F. Capuzzi, Trans.). San Francisco, CA: HarperSanFrancisco.

Heidegger, M. (1954). *The Question Concerning Technology and Other Essays* (W. Lovitt, Trans.). New York: Harper & Row. [reprinted eg. London: Karnac, 1977.]

Heidegger, M. (1936). The origin of the work of art. In D. Krell (Ed.), *Basic writings.* San Francisco, CA: HarperSanFrancisco. [reprinted eg. London: Karnac, 1993.]

Heidegger, M. (1927). *Being and Time.* (J. Macquarrie & E. Robinson, Trans.). San Francisco, CA: Harper & Row. [reprinted eg. London: Karnac, 1962.]

Heidegger, M. (1927). *Being and time.* (J. Stambaugh, Trans.). New York: State University of New York Press. [reprinted eg. London: Karnac, 1996.]

Hergenhahan, B. (1997). *An Introduction to the History of Psychology* (3rd ed.). Albany, NY: Brooks/Cole.

Herpertz, S. (1995). Self-injurous behavior: Psychopathological and nosological characteristics in subtypes of self-injurers. *Acta psychiatrica Scandinavica, 91*, (1), 57–68.

Hillman, J. (1975). *Re-visioning psychology.* New York: HarperCollins.

Hillman, J. (1996). *The Soul's Code: In Search of Character and Calling.* New York: Random House.

Hillman, J. (1998). *Suicide and the Soul.* Putnam, CT: Spring.

Hirsch, E. D. (1976). *The Aims of Interpretation.* Chicago, IL: University of Chicago Press.

Honerich, T. (1995). (Ed.). *The Oxford Companion to Philosophy.* New York: Oxford University Press.

Hoyert, D. L., Arias, E., Smith, B. L., Murphy, S. L. & Kochanek, K. D. (2001). Deaths: Final data for 1999. National Vital Statistics Report, 49(8). Hyattsville, MD: National Center for Health Statistics. DHHS Publication No. (PHS) 2001-1120.

Hutschnecker, A. (1951). *The Will to Live.* New York: Prentice-Hall.

Institute of Medicine: Committee on Patholophysiology & Prevention of Adolescent & Adult Suicide Board on Neuroscience and Behavioral Health. (2002). *Reducing Suicide: A National Imperative.* Washington, DC: National Academy Press.

Jacobs, L. (1965). The primal cure. *Psychoanalytic review. 52*, (4), 116–144.

Jewish Holocaust Museum and Research Centre. (1990). *Estimated Jewish deaths in the holocaust.* [On-line.] Available: www.arts.monash.edu.

au/affiliates/hlc/holocaust/statistics/losses.html   Last   accessed   ...
Holocaust Museum and Research Centre.

Jung, C. G. (1961). *Memories, Dreams, Reflections.* R. Winston & C. Winston
(Trans.). New York: Vintage Books. [reprinted eg. London: Karnac,
1965.]

Jung, C. G. (1928). The therapeutic value of abreaction. In: R. F. C. Hull
(Trans.) & H. Read, M. Fordham, G. Adler, W. McGuire (Eds.), *The Collected Works of C. G. Jung* (Vol. 16). (pp.) Princeton, NJ: Princeton University Press. [reprinted eg. London: Karnac, 1966.]

Jung, C. G. (1929). Phenomena of the way. In: R. F. C. Hull (Trans.) &
H. Read, M. Fordham, G. Adler, W. McGuire (Eds.), *The Collected Works
of C. G. Jung* (Vol. 13). (pp.) Princeton, NJ: Princeton University Press.
[reprinted eg. London: Karnac, 1967.]

Jung, C. G. (1944). The prima materia. In: R. F. C. Hull (Trans.) & H. Read,
M. Fordham, G. Adler, W. McGuire (Eds.), *The Collected Works of C. G.
Jung* (Vol. 12). (pp.) Princeton, NJ: Princeton University Press. [reprinted
eg. London: Karnac, 1968.]

Jung, C. G. (1954). The archetypes and the collective unconscious. In: R. F.
C. Hull (Trans.) & H. Read, M. Fordham, G. Adler, W. McGuire (Eds.),
The Collected Works of C. G. Jung (Vol. 9). (pp.) Princeton, NJ: Princeton
University Press. [reprinted eg. London: Karnac, 1969.]

Jung, C. G. (1934). A review of complex theory. In: R. F. C. Hull (Trans.) &
H. Read, M. Fordham, G. Adler, W. McGuire (Eds.), *The Collected Works
of C. G. Jung* (Vol. 8). (pp.) Princeton, NJ: Princeton University Press.
[reprinted eg. London: Karnac, 1969.]

Jung, C. G. (1937). Psychological factors determining human behavior. In:
R. F. C. Hull (Trans.) & H. Read, M. Fordham, G. Adler, W. McGuire
(Eds.), *The Collected Works of C. G. Jung* (Vol. 8). (pp.) Princeton, NJ: Prin-
ceton University Press. [reprinted eg. London: Karnac, 1969.]

Jung, C. G. (1928). On psychic energy. In: R. F. C. Hull (Trans.) & H. Read,
M. Fordham, G. Adler, W. McGuire (Eds.), *The Collected Works of C. G.
Jung* (Vol. 8). (pp.) Princeton, NJ: Princeton University Press. [reprinted
eg. London: Karnac, 1969.]

Kalshed, D. (1996). *The Inner World of Trauma: Archetypal Defenses of the
Personal Spirit.* New York: Routledge.

Kaufmann, W. (1992). Nietzsche as the first great (depth) psychologist. In S. Koch & D. Leary (Eds.), *A Century of Psychology as a Science*
(pp. 911–920). DC: McGraw-Hill.

Kernberg, O. (1983). Paranoid regression, sadistic control, and dishonesty
in transference. *Revista de psicoanalisis, 40,* (2), 323–328.

Khantzian, E. (1989). Addiction: Self-destruction or self—repair? *Journal of
substance abuse treatment, 6,* 75.

Kirsner, D. (1976). *The Schizoid World of Jean-Paul Sartre and Laing.* Queensland, St. Lucia: University of Queensland Press.

Klein, M. (1946). Notes on some schizoid mechanisms. In M. Klein, S. Isaacs & J. Riviere (Eds.). *Developments in psychoanalysis* (pp. 292–320). London: Hogarth Press.

Kunnap, A. (2000). *The Landscape of the Inner Critic: A Fairytale Synthesis of Classical Theories of Personality.* Pacifica Graduate Institute, Pacifica Graduate Institute, Carpinteria, CA (Unpublshed master's thesis).

Laing, A. (1996). *Laing: A Biography.* New York: Thunder's Mouth Press.

Laing, A. (1967). *The Politics of Experience.* New York: Ballentine Books.

Laing, A. (1982). *The Voice of Experience.* New York: Pantheon Books.

Laing, A. (1988). *Is Humanity Preparing for Species Suicide?* [On-Line.] Available: www.globalvision.org. Last accessed …

Laing, A. (1990). *The Divided Self.* New York: Penguin Books.

Laing, A. & Esterson, A. (1970). *Sanity, Madness and the Family.* New York: Penguin Books.

Lefkowitz, M. R. (1990). *Women's Life in Greece and Rome.* Johns Hopkins.

Lemay, E. & Pitts, J. (1994). *Heidegger for Beginners.* New York: Writers and Readers.

Lester, D. (1972). Ellen West's suicide as a case of psychic homicide. *Psychoanalytic Review, 58,* (2), 251–263.

Levenkron, S. (1999). *Cutting: Understanding and Overcoming Self-Mutilation.* New York: W. W. Norton.

Levinson, V. (1986). The alcoholic's self destructiveness and the therapist's role in mobilizing survival energies. *Alcohol treatment quarterly, 3,* (3), 23–35.

May, R. (1961). *Existential Psychology.* New York: Random House.

McWilliams, N. (1994). *Psychoanalytic Diagnosis: Understanding Personality Structure in the Clinical Process.* New York: The Guilford Press.

Meerloo, J. (1968). Hidden suicide. In: H. Resnik (Ed.), *Suicidal Behavior: Diagnosis and Management* (pp. 82–89). Boston, MA: Little Brown.

Meerloo, J. (1962). *Suicide and Mass Suicide.* New York: Grune & Stratton.

Menninger, K. (1938). *Man Against Himself.* New York: Harcourt, Brace.

Menninger, K. (1969). Expression and punishment. In: E. S. Shneidman (Ed.). *On the Nature of Suicide* (pp. 68–73). San Francisco: Jossey-Bass.

Neumann, E. (1990). *The Child.* Boston: Shambala.

Nietzsche, F. (1908). *Ecce Homo.* (W. Kaufman, Trans.). New York: Random House. [reprinted eg. London: Karnac, 1967.]

Nietzsche, F. (1886). *The Gay Science.* (W. Kaufman, Ed & Trans.). New York: Randon House. [reprinted eg. London: Karnac, 1974.]

Nietzsche, F. (1886). *Beyond Good and Evil.* (H. Zimmern, Ed. & Trans.). New York: Random House. [reprinted eg. London: Karnac, 1989.]

Nietzsche, F. (1887). *On the Genealogy of Morals.* (W. Kaufmann, Ed. & Trans.). New York: Vintage Books. [reprinted eg. London: Karnac, 1989.]

Nietzsche, F. (1878). *Human, all too Human: A Book for Free Spirits.* (M. Faber & S. Lehmann, Trans.). Lincoln, NE: University of Nebraska Press. [reprinted eg. London: Karnac, 1996.]

Nilsson, M. (1972). *A History of Greek Religion.* Greenwood.

Odier, C. *Anxiety and Magic Thinking.* (M. -L. Schoelly & M. Sherfey, Trans.). New York: International Universities Press.

Ogden, T. H. (1994). *Subjects of Analysis.* Northwale, NJ: Jason Aronson.

Orbach, I. (1996). The role of the body experience in self-destruction. *Clinical and child psychology and psychiatry, 1,* (4), 607–619.

O'Sullivan, J. (1839). *The great nation of futurity. The United States Democratic Review* [On-line.] Available: www.mtholyoke.edu/acad/intrel/osulliva. htm Last accessed …

Peters, R. (1997). *She in the marketplace: An exploration of feminine agency in the world of business.*, Pacifica Graduate Institute, Carpinteria, CA (Unpublished master's thesis).

Pies, R. & Popli, A. (1995). Self-injurious behavior: Patholophysiology and implications for treatment. *Journal of Clinical Psychiatry, 56,* 580–588.

Poeldinger, W. (1989). The psychopathology and psychodynamics of self-destruction. *Crisis, 10,* (2), 113–122.

Quinodoz, J. -M. (1989). Clinical implications of the psychoanalytic concept of the death drive. *Revue Française de Psychanalyse, 53,* (2), 737–749.

Rank, O. (1936). *Will Therapy.* (J. Taft, Trans.). New York: New York: W. W. Norton. [Reprinted eg. London: Karnac, 1978.]

Romans, S., Martin, J., Anderson, J. & Herbison, G. (1995). Sexual abuse in childhood and deliberate self-harm. *American Journal of Psychiatry.* Sep. Vol. 152(9): 1336–1342.

Romanyshyn, R. (1989). *Technology as Symptom and Dream.* New York, NY: Routledge.

Rycroft, C. (1995). *A Dictionary of Psychoanalysis.* New York: Penguin Books.

Schneider Institute for Health Policy. (2001). *Substance Abuse: The Nation's Number One Health Problem.* Princeton, NJ: Brandeis University.

Sereny, G. (1974). *Into that Darkness: From Mercy Killing to Mass Murder.* New York: McGraw-Hill Book Company.

Shay, J. (1995). *Achilles in Vietnam: Combat Trauma and the undoing of Character.* New York: Simon & Schuster.

Shields, T. B. (2002). *Reverie and the Phenomenology of Pantomime: Inhabiting Countertransference.* Pacifica Graduate Institute, Carpinteria (Unpublished doctoral dissertation).

Sipiora, M. (1991). Heidegger and epideictic discourse: The rhetorical performance of meditative thinking. *Philosophy Today*, Fall Issue. 239–253.

Sipiora, M. (1997). *Phenomenology and Critical Social Constructivism: A Dialogue with Sampson*. Lecture presented at Duquesne University.

Smith, J. (1996). Original evil and the time of the image. *Journal for the Psychoanalysis of Culture and Society, 1*, (2), 35–46.

Spinelli, E. (1989). *The Interpreted World*. New York: Sage.

Spitz, E. (1988). The inescapability of tragedy. *Bulletin of the Menninger Clinic, 52*, (2), 377–382.

Stapp, K. (2003). *Preventable diseases claim 11 million children each year* [On-line.] Available: www.cyberdyaryo.com/features/f2003_0708_02.html. Last accessed ...

Stein, L. (1967). Introducing not-self. *Journal of Analytical Psychology, 12*, (2), 97–113.

Substance Abuse and Mental Health Services Administration. (2001). *Summary of findings from the 2000 national household survey on drug abuse.* (NHSDA Series: H-13, DHHS Publication No. SMA 01-3549). Rockville, MD: Author.

Suyemoto, K. (1998). The functions of self-mutilation. *Clinical psychology review, 18*, (5), 531–554.

Szasz, T. (1970). *Ideology and Insanity*. Harmondsworth: Penguin Books.

Szasz, T. (1974). *The Myth of Mental Illness*. New York: Harper & Row.

Tool (1993). Prison sex. (Recorded by S. Massy). On *Undertow* [CD.] New York: BMG Music.

Turell, S. & Armsworth, M. (2000). Differentiating incest survivors who self-mutilate. *Child Abuse and Neglect, 24*, (2), 237–249.

United Nations. (2003). *Women's watch: Women's issues on UN radio* [On-line.] Available: www.un.org/womenwatch/news/unradio/progs/2003Jun18.html. Last accessed ...

United Nations Children's Emergency Fund (UNICEF). (2002). *Edunotes* [On-line.] Available: www.unicef.ca/eng/unicef/edunote/edu3-vol3.html. Last accessed ...

United States Department of Health and Human Services. (2003). *2001 National statistics on child abuse and neglect* [On-line.] Available: http://nccanch.acf.hhs.gov/pubs/factsheets/canstats.cfm. Last accessed ...

Van den Berg, J. H. (1983). *The Changing Nature of Man: Introduction to a Historical Psychology*. New York: Norton.

Wainrib, S. (1996). Anxiety of annihilation, fascinations of self-destruction. *Revue Francaise de Psychanalyse 60*, (1), 65–76.

Walker, J. (1996). *Hitler's religious beliefs and fanaticism: Selected quote from Mein Kampf* [On-line.] Available: www.nobeliefs.com/hitler.htm. Last accessed ...

Walters, G. (1999). Survival and the self-destruction paradox: An integrated theoretical model. *Journal of Mind and Behavior, 20*, (1), 57–78.

Webster's New Twentieth Century Dictionary of the English Language. (1956). New York: Standard Reference Works.

Wiese, D. & Daro, D. (1995). *Current Trends in Child Abuse Reporting and Fatalities: The Results of the 1994 Annual Fifty State Survey.* Chicago, IL: NCPCA.

World Health Organization. (1997). *Children: Abuse and neglect* [On-line.] Available: www.who.int/mediacentre/factsheets/fs150/en/index. html. Last accessed ...

Woodman, M. (1993). *Conscious Femininity.* Toronto: Inner City Books.

INDEX

addictive processes 61, 65
AIDS 5, 121–122
alcoholism 16
aliveness-deadness 59
American Psychiatric Association 120
analyst's alpha-function 100
Andreas-Salomé, Lou 83
annihilation anxiety 7, 60, 91
anti-libidinal ego 57–58
anti-thinking moralism 159
Apollonian 24, 47, 49, 89, 51
archetypal defenses 64–65
Aristotle's *Poetics* 83
attention deficit disorder 137
autistic-contiguous position 91

Baesedow syndrome 68
Bateson's double-bind
    communications theory 75
Berg, Van den 26, 111
    neurosis 112
Binswanger, L. 12–13, 20, 142

care 68–69
existential-phenomenological
    psychology 12
self-destruction as existential
    possibility 68–71
The Case of Ellen West 68
Bion, W. R. 19, 58, 141
alpha-function 84–86, 95, 99
alpha-screen 95
beginnings of psychopathology 8
beta-elements 95
borderline and psychotic
    disorders 96
catastrophe and traumatic impact
    18
characterizations of
    destructiveness 145
damaged alpha-function 89–92
destructiveness 93
Klein's notion of paranoid-
    schizoid and depressive
    positions 88

179

minus K 54–55
non-psychotic and psychotic
    parts of personality 92
no-thingness 96–98
notion of transformations in
    hallucinosis 60
paranoid-schizoid and depressive
    positions 87–88
pathological beta-screen 95
Pharmakon, poison-cure 98–100
primitive mental states and
    damaged alpha-function
    89–92
psychoanalysis 94
psychoanalytic tenets 8
psychology 26
self-destructive capacity 83
symbolic system 96
thinking apparatus development
    84–89
thoughts about-K's effects 98
Bionian psychoanalysis 27, 40, 84,
    153–155
    existential-phenomenology 40
Bionian sense 137
bipolar disorder 125
Bondsman 46
    consciousness 48
    labour 24
borderline and psychotics 90
    disorders 96
borderline psychotic beliefs 159
Burston, D. 70

central nervous system (CNS)
    stimulants 127
child abuse 118–119, 123–124, 143
    fatalities 143
    perpetrators of 118
child protective services 118
child trafficking 121, 143, 167
chillaxing 132

chronic depressive illness 61
Clay, J. 70
collective unconscious 63
collectivism 24–25, 46–47, 140
conscious death wish 16
contemporary culture
    destructiveness 143
contemporary technological culture
    1, 142, 144
counteradaptive defenses 63
creative-destructive themes 163
criminal justice system 5
cultural-historical index 34
cultural-psychological life 151

daimon 10, 20, 51
Darwin's theory 49
Dasein 26, 35–37, 101–111, 146
    alienation 106
    disclosedness 105
    ownmost self 107
    throwness 105
death-rebirth process 80
delusional transformation of reality
    50
Demeter's denial 134
depth psychology and
    phenomenology 18
desperateness 91
destructive-creative element 163
*Diagnostic and Statistical Manual of
    Mental Disorders* 120
digestion-birth process 148
digestion-sex-reproduction
    amalgamate 148
digestive-generative capacities 149
digestive-reproductive processes
    148–150
digestive-sexual-birthing processes
    149
Dilthey 22, 34–35
    influence 35

methodological hermeneutic
     circle 37
ontological hermeneutic circle 37
Dionysian 24–25, 47, 49, 51, 88–89
     impulses 49
     paranoid-schizoid position 89
Dionysius 24, 47, 89, 163
disposable child 27, 117
dream annihilation 100

ego-destructive superego 8, 99
ego-ideal 51
egoism 46
Eigen, M. 58–59, 81, 97, 99, 148–149
     alpha-function 99
     force against recovery 58
Ellen's 68–69, 103
     demand 69
     diagnoses 70
     level of suicidal ideation 69
emotional life 9
emotional reality 8, 63, 84, 94–96
empirical psychology 2, 20
erotic gratification 6
erotogenic masochism 6
Euripides' *The Bacchae* 89
existential-phenomenological
     account of schizoid and
          schizophrenic people 71
     account of self-destructiveness 17
     method 71
     of Heidegger 40
     philosophy and psychology 142
     psychology 2, 12–19, 41, 67–81,
          115
     therapists 15, 17
     thinkers 18

Fairbairn, R. 57, 148
Farber, M. 13, 15, 20
Federation of Asian Nutrition
     Societies 121

feminine masochism 6
feminine sexual relationship 6
Fordham, M. 64
fragmentary personality 61
Freudian theory and practice 50
Frankl, V. 13, 17
Freud, S. 7, 83
     animal-like drives 51
     Beyond the Pleasure Principle 5
     collectivism to explain
          self-destructiveness 25
     defense mechanisms 50
     dictum 25
     erotic gratification 6
     existence of primary mechanism
          52
     force against recovery 58
     The Future of an Illusion 50
     Kleinian psychology 53
     notion of reality principle 105
     notion of Thanatos 15
     pleasure-unpleasure principle
          53
     psychological illnesses 19
     seminal notion 5
     seminal notion of death instinct
          20
     theory 25
frustration 57, 88, 90, 94

Gabriel, Dante 133
Gadamer, fusion of horizons 40
genuine sanity 80
Glick, A. 41
Golomb, E. 58
Gopalan, C. 121
Grave's disease 68
Greco-Roman views of
     self-destruction 41–43
Grotstein, J. 59–61, 81, 92, 97, 148,
     154–155
Guntrip, H. 58

Habicht, Jean-Pierre 120–121
hallucinations 95, 120, 127
    notion of transformations 60
Hegel, G. 24, 46–47, 80
    independent consciousness 24
    rationalism and historicism 24,
        45, 80
    theory of history 48
Heidegger, M. 2, 19, 21–22, 26–27,
    35–37, 39–40, 122, 144–147,
    154–155, 162, 166
    Being and Time 101
    conception of Dasein 102
    essence of technology 108
    Existential-phenomenological
        psychology 115
    existentiell attunement 107
    Fourfold phenomenology 116
    injurious neglect 122
    ongoing emphasis 37
    The Origin of the Work of Art 116
    phenomenological conception of
        Dasein 26, 101–116
    qualitative difference 102
    The they, or *das Man* 105
    uncanniness of Being 114
Heideggerian
    depth psychology 162
    existential-phenomnology 40
    hermeneutics 22
    phenomenology 27, 162
herd-consciousness 25, 48
hermeneutic engagement 29–30
hermeneutics ontological importance
    36
hermeneutic theory 21, 29–30
    origins of 30
Hillman, J. 13, 16, 20
    Jungian analyst 9
    suicidal fantasies 11
    suicidal impulse 10
Hirsch, E. D. 30, 32

perspectivism 22, 31
    positivism 31
homicide 3, 50
homoeroticism 6
Honderich 34–35
    hermeneutics into modernity 32
Humanity's essence 109–110, 115
human-to-human destructiveness 15,
    20, 27, 39, 117, 139, 143, 145, 162
Hutschnecker, A. 13

Indian removal act 157–158
infantile dependence, stage of 57
infant-mother dyad 8, 90
infant's ability 90, 92
    to self-soothe 85
infant's communications 98
infant's dialectical relationship 87
infant's ego 57
intuitionism 30–31
intuitivism 21–22, 31

Jungian psychology 2

Kalshed, D. 9, 66–67, 81, 141
Kantian philosophy to social sciences
    22
Kant's ideas to social sciences 34
Klein, M. 7–8, 20, 25, 53–54, 61, 80,
    87–88, 100, 141
    idea of "a destructive force
        within" 58
    infantile ambivalence 53
    notion of paranoid-schizoid and
        depressive positions 88
    paranoid-schizoid position 87
    psychosis 8
Kleinian psychology 7, 53
Kunnap, A. 20
    self-destructive behaviour 11
    self-destructive feelings 12
    self-discovery 11

Laing, R. D.
  clinical findings 142
  The Divided Self 71, 74, 77
  destructiveness 79
  dictum 129
  existential-phenomenological
    account 71
  humanity's capacity 78
  The Politics of Experience 77, 79
  psychoanalytic concepts of self-
    destruction 78
  Sanity, Madness and the Family 76
  schizoid analysis 76
  schizoidness and schizophrenia 77
  schizophrenic alienation 78
  schizophrenic behaviour 70–80
Laingian ideas of petrification 98
libidinal ego 57–58
linguistic hermeneutics 33
lucrative business 151
Lunacy 152

maladaptive cognitive distortions
  and addiction 12
malnutrition 120–121, 126
manifest destiny and holocaust
  157–161
masochism 5–6
masochistic ego 25, 52
May, R. 12–13
Meerloo, J. 12
Menninger, K. 13, 81
  conscious death wish 16
  unconscious suicide wish 16
mental digestion 148
mental disorder 67, 71, 76–77, 87, 93,
  120, 136
mental illness 19–20, 26, 70–71, 86,
  91, 112, 142–143
methodological hermeneutic circle 37
Meynert, Theodore 49
mother-infant relationship 65

narcissistic parents 58
negative parental objects 58
Neumann, E. 65
neurosis 5, 27, 50, 52, 62, 112
neurotic and psychotic potentialities
  89
Nietzsche, F. 47–51, 53, 80, 88
  anti-religious attitude 25
  Christianity humanity 24–25
  collectivism and Christianity 47
  conception of humanity 25
  contention 24
  insights 141
  response 45
nothingness and meaninglessness
  59, 97

obsessional neurosis 52, 87
  of humanity 50
O'Sullivan, J., *The Great Nation of
  Futurity* 157
Oedipal development 6
Oedipus
  complex 53
  actions 83
  myth 83
ontological anxiety 12, 17
ontological hermeneutic circle 37
oppositional defiant disorder 125
Ovid's *The Rape of Proserpine* 134

paranoid–schizoid
  and depressive positions 53–54,
    87–88
  development 92
  position 54, 87–89, 91
parental castigation 51
parental fallacy 9
pathological splitting 90
Persephone's nightmarish abduction
  135
personalism 9

personality disordered individuals
   89
perspectivism 22, 32
Peter, R.
   The Divided Self 76
phantasies 25, 54, 60
Pharmakon, poison-cure 98–100
phenomenological hermeneutics 36
pleasure-unpleasure principle 5, 53
Pluto in Roman mythology 123
pornographic imagination 152
pornography 121, 151, 155
   demand for 152
   internet 152
positivism 22, 31–32
   presupposition of 31
post-traumatic stress disorder
   (PTSD) 13, 120
power relationship 123
praxis of method 38–40
premature deaths 4–5
projective identification 7–8, 25–26,
   54, 84–85, 92–94, 99
psyche's
   defense mechanisms 25
   propensity 15
   self-care system 66–67
   self-destruction 71
psychiatric hospitalizations 127
psychic
   freezing 153
   processing 100
   reality 11
psychoanalytic thinkers 18, 20
psychological
   aliveness 64
   destructiveness in extremis 153
   disaster 61
   illnesses 19, 57
   maladies 61
   necessity 113
   self-attack 51, 63

psychosis 3, 8, 18, 55, 60, 72, 92, 96
psychosomatic illnesses 16
psychotic behavior, bizarreness of 60
psychotic collapse 60
psychotic mind, alpha-function in
   reverse 92

Rank, O. 13
repetition compulsion 5, 19, 25, 52–53
Romanyshyn, R. 27, 113, 115, 151

sadistic parent 58
schizoidness and schizophrenia 72,
   77
schizoid and schizophrenic
   personalities 74
schizoid fragmentation 75
schizoid's and schizophrenic's
   experience 71
schizoid/schizophrenic person 72
schizoid splitness 72
schizophrenia and depression 57
schizophrenic alienation 78
Schneider Institute for Health Policy
   4
secularism 9
self-attacking dissociative process 9
self-care system 66–67, 141
self-destructing humanity 48
self-destructing psychotic mind 8
Schleiermacher, Friedrich 22, 32–34
   conception of hermeneutics 32
   hermeneutics 34
   psychological commonality 34
self-consciousness 24, 46
   authentic 24
   dependent 46
   independent 46
self-destruction 16, 18, 20, 39, 41, 43,
   51, 79, 83, 99, 140, 143–144, 148,
   153, 161–167
   as existential possibility 68–70

behaviours 12–13, 20–21, 42, 165
Bion minus K 54–55
Bion's investigations 39
case vignette 125–133
conclusion and discussion 139
consciousness of 41
contemporary Jungian
    perspectives 64–81
contemporary manifestations
    117
contemporary psychoanalytic
    perspectives 57–61
cycle 3
definition 1
destructive magical thinking
    56–57
destructive potential 159
Dionysian impulses 47, 49
elements 39–40
elusiveness 140
empirical psychology 20
existential-phenomenological
    psychology 12–18, 67–81
forces 26, 100
Freud's collectivism 25
Freud's seminal notion 5
gravity of 141
Greco-Roman views of 41–43
Hegel's rationalism and
    historicism 45
Hegelian tradition 45
Heidegger's ontology 39
historical attitudes 41
historical depth psychological
    views 45–61
human 20
humanity's participation 154
human-to-human destructiveness
    20, 39, 117, 139, 143
Judaeo-Christian views of 43–45
Jungian perspectives 9
Kunnap understandings 20

Laing, R. D., schizophrenic
    behaviour 70–80
limitations and suggestions
    165–168
lostness 114
myth of persephone 133–136
Nietzsche's thinking 45
Odier, destructive magical
    thinking 56
of humanity 80
organization of text 19–28
paranoid anxiety 54
patients 19
personal account 39
phenomenon of 2, 23
post-Jungian perspective 20
potential 62, 147
process 61, 89, 94, 144
psyche's capacity for 2, 68
psychoanalytic concepts 78
psychoanalytic perspectives 5–9
psychological mechanisms 54
psychological views 24
Romans views 43
severity of 51
shadow of being 146–148
situations 5
societal views 41
society 114
split-off destructiveness 159
statement of problem 19
Stein, L. 64
thematic hermeneutic disclosure
    of 21
theme of 39, 71
to emptiness 65
trends 16
understanding of 18
vignette summary 136–138
work of Bion and Heidegger 19
self-duplicity sense 73
self-injurious behaviour 3

self-mutilation
  eye enucleation 2
  genital amputation 3
  psychological disorder of 2
self-sameness 24
self-trauma system 13
semantic holism 32–33
sensation-seeking behaviours 126
sexual abuse 119, 159
sexualization 6
Shay, J. 13–15, 120
  *Achilles in Vietnam: Combat
    Trauma and the Undoing of
    Character* 13
  Vietnam War 14
Sipiora, M. 109
sociosis 27, 112
  homesickness 115
splinter psyches 61
Stein, L., self-destructiveness 64
suicidal and para-suicidal
    behaviours 18
suicidal fantasies 11
suicide 15, 41–42
  Aristotle belief 42
  Augustus era 44
  Christianity's stance on 44
  early Christian societies 23, 44,
    140
  existential-phenomenological
    stance on 16
  Hebrew societies 23, 43–44, 140
  Judaeo-Christian views 45
  necessary-voluntary consequence
    12
  ontological anxiety 17
  phenomenological perspective 16
  Plato's metaphysics 42

Plato understandings 42
Pythagoras philosophy 42
Romans system 23
sadistic superego 6, 8, 99–100
self-destructive capacity 20, 39, 83,
    164
self-destructive dynamics and
    behaviours 20, 39, 52, 83, 164
self-destructive impulse 20, 51, 54,
    139
superego 51–52, 55, 57, 97–98, 156
  destructive 100
  ego-destructive 8, 99
  malice 51
  opinionated 94
  punitive 87
  sadism of 52
  sadistic 6, 100
  sadistic aspect of 25
  tyrannical 8, 100

thematic hermeneutics 21, 29, 165
  method 38
trans-Atlantic slave trade 121

uncanniness 106–107, 110, 114
unconscious
  conscious 51
  self-censorship 51
  suicide wish 16
United Nations International
    Children's Emergency Fund 121
U.S. infant mortality rate 124

Walters, G. 1
Winnicott, Donald 18, 60, 78
World Health Organization 118